Hazrat Ayesha Siddiqa

Hazrat Ayesha Siddiqa

Her Year of Marriage and Personality

Atika Sadeeqa

First published in 2017 by Createspace.com
EAN-13: 9781546749189 (CreateSpace-Assigned)
ISBN-10: 1546749187

"Your knowledge of the Arabic language is subpar, but you have also proven to be unfamiliar with things of simple association with faith such as nature and healing. About the mention you have made about Hazrat Ayesha Sadeeqa (ra)'s marriage ceremony at the age of nine, firstly, there is no mention of it by the Holy Prophet (SAW) himself anywhere, nor is there any revelation to this effect, nor it is reported in any parallel narrations proving the age to be nine years. It is derived only from one narrator. Arabs were generally not known to keep written memorandums because they were illiterate."

[1]

---

1   Hazrat Mirza Gulam Ahmad, Ruhani Khaza'in Vol. 9, p. 377, Qadian, India, published 1895.

Table of Contents

Preface

THE FIRST INCENTIVE for me to write this book came to me when Hazrat Mirza Masroor Ahmad, the supreme head of the worldwide Ahmadiyya community, encouraged my efforts to respond to Shirley Jones' book *The Jewel of Medina*, a book I felt was a mischief in disguise. She had ridiculed Hazrat Ayesha Siddiqa (ra), the Prophet's wife, for being a baby bride of 9 years of age. When Hazrat Mirza Masroor Ahamd visited Los Angles in 2013, he encouraged and advised me to read certain books before writing about Hazrat Ayesha.

After the *Hijrah*, the Prophet's migration from Medina, when it was necessary to render service to religion, Ayesha distinguished herself in the Prophet's house. God Almighty had bestowed her with extraordinary brilliance. She had an inquisitive nature, and she did not blindly accept whatever she heard. She would analyze according to the criteria of the Qur'an and the *Sunna* (meaning "practice of the Prophet"). Ayesha became a bridge between the time of the Prophet and the future of Islam.

Ayesha represented the vitality of revelation during the half century after the death of the Holy Prophet. When controversies arose, Ayesha was a kind arbitrator. For mistakes on religious issues that emerged, she was a dignified corrector, and a decisive and patient example of the straight path of Islam. It is recorded by Muslim historians that there was no one who came to her with a question and was unable to get an answer for it from her. She concluded nearly every matter in light of the revelation, and found solutions to other problems directly from the Qur'an and the Sunna. In other matters, she evaluated, compared and interpreted based on her own vast knowledge of the religion.

Ayesha was the mother of all believers. Among the things that passed onto us from her, there was certain information that would normally remain private between spouses. Out of necessity, she appeared to convey details of the religion. Many matters would have remained unknown to us if she had not existed. Behind closed doors, she passed the most intimate questions to the Holy Prophet, so she could respond to women's questions. Ayesha is inviting people of conscience to the straight path of Islam.

I want to thank several people who assisted me and gave me advice while compiling this work:

Dr. Karimullah Zirvi: I must express my heart-felt gratitude for all advice I received from Dr. Sahib.

I wish to gratefully acknowledge the help given by Imran Jattala in many areas.

Atayya Choudhry: I thank you for the time you spend reading thoroughly even with your busy schedule.

I appreciate Lali Chudhry; you have been a friendly and loyal sister for over many decades. I thank you for your help and support.

I would like to also thank Mike Valentino for review and corrections he proposed to the menuscript of this book.

In the end, I thank my husband Amir-ud Din for taking care of all my needs. Without his help and co-operation it would have been impossible to complete this manuscript.

HAZRAT Ayesha Siddiqa and Her Parents.

HAZRAT AYESHA'S FATHER was Hazrat Abu Bakr (ra). Hazrat Abu Bakr's first name was Abdullah[2], based on his son's name, Bakr. He was known as Abu Bakr. It was his patriotic appellation (*kunniyat*), a nickname, which is usually derived from the name of the first son or daughter of the first adult man according to the Muslim traditions. Abu Bakr translates as, "One who does things the earliest". Because he was a believer in Islam without hesitation, his nickname is more familiar than his first name.

The Holy Prophet [SAW] changed his name to Abdullah. He was the son of Utham bin Aamir whose *kunyat* was Abu Quhafa (c. 573-August 23, 634/13 A.H.). He is the first Caliph of the four rightly guided Caliphs and holds a unique position in the history of Islam. He was called Al-Siddiq (The Truthful) and was known by this title by later generations of Muslims. He married four times, two before the advent of Islam and two afterward. His wives before Islam were Qutaila, also known as Fatila, daughter of Abdu 'Uzza (Divorced), and Ummi Rooman, daughter of 'Amir bin 'Uwymir.'His wives after Islam were Asmaa, daughter of 'Amees (also spelled as Umays) and Habeeba, daughter of Kharijah.

From these wives, he had three sons and three daughters. His sons were Abdur Rahman, son of Ummi Ruman, Abdullah, son of Qutaila, and Muhammad, son of Asma.

---

2 Bukhari, vol. 1, page 551.

His daughters were binti Qutaila, Asma binti Abu Bakr 'Binti Ummi Ruman was Ayesha binti Abu Bakr Binti Habibah was Umm Khultum[3]. Binti Abu Bakr.

The famous classical historian of Islam, Ibn Jareer Tabari, writes on page 50 of volume 4 of his *Book of History*:

"In the time before Islam, Abu Bakr married two women. The first was Fateela, daughter of Abdul Uzza, from whom Abdullah and Asma were born. Ummi Rooman was the second, from whom Abdur -Rahman and 'Ayesha were born. These four children of Abu Bakr were born in the pre-Islamic days."

It is a well-known fact of history that Abu Bakr's son, Abdur-Rahman, fought against Muslims in the battle of Badr. His age at the time was around 21-22 years, and although he was older than 'Ayesha, there is no evidence that shows that the difference between their ages was more than three or four years. This fact supports the view that Hazrat 'Ayesha was born four or five years before the advent of Islam. Abdur-Rahman became a Muslim after the Treaty of *Hudaybia* was signed, six years after the *Hijrah*. He was careful not to encounter his father at the Battle of Badr in the second year after the *Hijrah*, and at the time Abdur-Rahman was 20 years old.[4]

Hazrat Ayesha (ra) was 19 years old, not 9, at the time of her marriage with Mohammad (SAW). Accusations are answered in the following pages.

When covering the life of the Prophet (SAW), one of the most debatable topics is that of the age of his wife Ayesha (ra) at the time of their marriage. Her alleged young age has been used in smear campaigns against the Holy Prophet (SAW).

---

3 *Tartib wa Tahthib Kitab al-Bidayah wan-Nihayah* by ibn Kathir, published by Dar al-Wathan Publications, Riyadh Kingdom of Saudi Arabia, 1422 Anno hegirae (2002). Compiled by Dr. Muhammad ibn Shamil as-Sulami, page 16, ISBN 979-3407-19-6.
4 Ibn Athir, Usdu'l Ghaba, 3:467.

Many anti-Islamic sites accuse our beloved Prophet (SAW), God forbid, of marrying a minor. We present here several historical proofs to clear this blasphemous charge. Most narrations carry misstatements about the age of Hazrat Ayesha (ra) at the time of her marriage to the Holy Prophet. They place this marriage in the tenth year of the Call and state that she was 6 years old at that time. Upon searching the historical data, we found facts and it becomes evident that she, in fact, was about 19 or 20 years of age when she arrived in the house of the Holy Prophet (SAW) as his wife in 2 A.H.

It will be proper to quote from the writings of two well-known Muslim scholars of the present century who are the main exponents of the view that Hazrat Ayesha was 6 years old at her *Nikah* and 9 years old at the time of the consummation of her marriage. Both Maulana Syed Sulaiman Nadvi and Maulana Syed Abul Ala Maududi are well known authors of Seerat (biography).

Nadvi and Shibli's Views

———— ⌘ ————

Maulana Syed Sulaiman Nadvi writes on page 21 of his book *Seerat-i-Ayesha'*:

"Books of history and biography are generally silent about the birth date of Hazrat Ayesha. The historian Ibn Sa'd, whom many later biographers have followed, has written that Hazrat Ayesha was born in the fourth year of the Call, and was married at the age of 6 years in the tenth year of the Call. But, that works out to 7 and not 6. The fact remains that some matters related to the age of Hazrat Ayesha are admitted to be correct by most historians and biographers, such as that she was married three years before *Hijrah* at the age of six years old. That the marriage was consummated in the month of Shawal, in the year 1 A.H., when she was 9 years old. And that she became a widow in *Rabi-al-Awwal* in 11 A.H., at the age of 18 years. According to this account, the correct date of her birth works out to be the end of the fifth year of the Call, or 514 A.D. of the Christian calendar. For a proper comprehension of the event of history, one should bear in mind that out of a total period of 23 years of the Call, the first 13 years were passed in Mecca and the last 10 years in Medina. Thus, the fourth year of the Call had already been out before her birth and the fifth year was running."[5]

———————

5 Maulana Syed Sulman Nadvi Seerat (biography) Ayesha, page 21.

4

Nadvi was the loyal disciple of Shibli Nomani, who was working with him as his literary assistant on the project of *Sirat-Nabi* (Life of the Prophet). Nomani had only managed to complete the first two volumes before he died in 1914. It is strange and surprising that Shibli Nomani did not describe the name of any member from the Abu Bakr's family in the list of the first and foremost believers in his book *The 'Seerat-un-Nabi, Vol. 1*. He did not even mention the names of the daughters of the Holy Prophet, but remembered to write Hazrat Ali. Other historians have written an answer to Shibli's '*Seerat-un-Nabi*, and in their lists of the First and Foremost in Islam, the name of Hazrat Asma on the 16th order and the name of Hazrat Ayesha on the 17th place appear. Nadvi had copied Shibli and quoted the same years of [Nikah] and wedding being the loyal disciple of Shibli.

Maududi's View

———— ❧ ————

I<small>N THE ARTICLE</small>, "The *Nikah* Date of Ayesha", published in the *'Tarjuman al-Quran'* of September 1976, *Maulana* Abul Ala Maududi wrote:

"It is apparent from the detailed reports of Imam Ahmad Tibrani, Ibn Jareer and Baihaqi that the *Nikah* of Sayedah 'Ayesha was solemnized before the *Nikah* of Sayedah Sawda. It is also evident that her *Nikah* with the Holy Prophet (SAW) was solemnized in the month of *Shawwal* of the tenth year of the Call, three years before *Hijrah*, when she was 6 years old. Here a question arises. If Sayedah Ayesha was 6 years of age in the *Shawwal* of the tenth year of the Call, then shouldn't she have been 9 years of age at the time of *Hijrah* and 11 years old in 2 A.H. at the time of consummation? But all narrators agree that her *Nikah* was solemnized when she was 6 years old and the marriage was consummated when she was 9 years old. Some *Ulema* have tried to meet this discrepancy by saying that the marriage was consummated seven months after *Hijrah*. Hafiz ibn *Hajar* has preferred this view. On the other hand, *Imam* Nauvi, in his *'Tahzeeb al-Asma 'a al-Lughat'*, Hafiz ibn Katheer in his 'Al-Badaya' and Allama Qustalani in his 'Mawahib al-Deeniah', all report consummation in 2 A.H. Hafiz Badr-ud-Din Aini has written in his *Umdat l-Qari* that the marriage of Ayesha Siddiqa was consummated in Shawal 2 A.H., after the return of the Holy Prophet (SAW) from the battle of Badr. Imam Nauvi and Allama Aini consider the above–quoted reports of consummation of marriage seven months after *Hijrah* as irresponsible and untrustworthy. Thus, we are faced with the question that if the marriage was consummated at the age of 9 years in *Shawwal* 2 A.H., then what should be the date of *Nikah* which should tally with her age of 6 years? An answer to this question is found in Bukhari, wherein it is reported from Urwah ibn Zubair that "Sayedah Khadijah died three years before *Hijrah*; the Holy Prophet solemnized one year before *Hijrah*, when she was 6 years old and consummation took place in 2 A.H., when she was 9 years old."[6]

The quotations above prove that both *Maulana* Nadvi and *Maulana* Maududi agree that Ayesha was 6 years old on the occasion of her *Nikah* and 9 years old when the marriage was consummated. There mistake seems to be the calculation of the correct year of the Call and the *Hijrah*. Both of them start with a preconception that the age of 6 years old at the time of *Nikah* and 9 years old at consummation are correct and true, and set out in search of the correct year of the Call and *Hijrah* in which these preconceived ages will fit in. This hardly can be called a scientific method of finding her correct age. Rather, this can be called an effort to find a correct date for a given age. From the year of 1924 to 1938, there was a controversial debate between *Maulana* Muhammad Ali and Sulaiman Nadvi on the age of Hazrat Ayesha. The debate was published in the third edition of '*Seerat-i-Ayesha*' by Sulaiman Nadvi. Part of it is shown below:

"Some irresponsible people, who think that the Holy Prophet's (SAW's) marriage with a girl of tender age was not befitting, have tried to prove that the age of Hazrat Ayesha Siddiqa at her marriage was 16 years instead of 6 years. All such efforts are useless and all such claims are illogical. Not a single word from the Hadith or history can be found in their support."

---

6   Maulana Abul Ala Maududi. The Nikah Date of Sayedah Ayesha, Tarjuman al-Quran of Sep. 1976.

Followers of such historians are convinced that Ayesha was a 9-year-old bride. Some of them believe that the hot climate of Arabia is the cause of Hazrat Ayesha's maturity at the age of nine. This claim is against the law of nature and there is no real evidence found to support this claim to this day.

Maulana Muhammad Ali, in his book *Muhammad the Prophet*, published in 1924, and in a magazine called *"Pegham-I –Sulah"*, published in November 22, 1938, he wrote:

"The popular misconception as to Ayesha's age may be removed here. In the first place, it is clear that she had reached an age when betrothal could take place in an ordinary course and must therefore had been approaching an age of maturity. Again, the *Ashabah* (the companions of Holy of Prophet), speaking of the Prophet's daughter Fatimah, says that she was about five years older than Ayesha. It is a well-established fact that Fatimah was born when the *Ka'ba* was being rebuilt, i.e., five years before the Call or a little before it, and so Ayesha was certainly not below ten years at the time of her marriage with the Holy Prophet in the tenth year of the Call. This conclusion is born out of the testimony of Ayesha herself which is reported in the chapter entitled "The Moon" (54th chapter). She said she was a girl playing about and that she remembered certain verses then revealed. Now, the fifty fourth chapter could not have been revealed later than the fifth year of the Call, and therefore the report that states her to be six years old in the tenth year of the Call when her marriage ceremony took place cannot be correct, because this shows that she was born at the time of the revelation of 54th chapter. All these considerations show her to have been not less than ten years old at the time of her marriage. And as the period between her marriage and its consummation was not more than five years, because the consummation took place in the second year of the battle of Badr, it follows that she could not have been less than fifteen at that time. The popular account that she was six years old at marriage and nine years old at the time of consummation is decidedly not correct because it supposes the period between the marriage and its consummation to be only three years while this is historically wrong."

Despite the above-quoted criticism from Muhammad Ali, Nadvi not only contradicts himself about the age of Hazrat Ayesha. He also provides supporting evidence for Muhammad Ali's views when writing about the last days of the life of Hazrat Ayesha. He writes on page 111 of the 'Seerat-i-Ayesha' that, "Hazrat Ayesha was a widow and she passed 40 years of her life as a widow." Further, on page 153 he writes:

"The last days of Khilafat (Caliphate) of Amir Muawiyya were the last days of the life of Hazrat Ayesha and her age at that time was 67 years."

Now, if we deduct 40 years of her widowed life from 67 years, we find she was 27 years of age at the time of the passing away of the Holy Prophet in 11 A.H. and not 18 years old as reported by Nadvi in the earlier pages of the same book. Since the total period of the Call is 23 years, according to this account she was born about four years before the Call and not in the fourth year of the Call as Nadvi tried to make us believe in his earlier pages quoted above. Consequently, her age at the time of the Nikah in the tenth year of the Call works out to 14-15 years old and not 6 years old as Nadvi himself so assertively reported. According to this account, Hazrat Ayesha's age at the time of consummation of her marriage in 2 A.H. works out to 19-20 years old and not 9 years old as stated in earlier pages of Seerat-i-Ayesha. Further research is most naturally needed to find out which of the reports of Nadvi should be considered correct.

The first voice against the common misconception about the age of Hazrat Ayesha was raised by Hazrat Mirza Ghulam Ahmad of Qadian in 1895, in Ruhani Khaza'in, in Vol. 9, p. 377. And after that, in 1920, Sulaiman Nadvi wrote to Hazrat Mirza Bashir Ahmad:

"The second volume of *Seerat Khatamun Nabiyeen, sallalaho alehi wassalam* has been received. Thank you. Have read the selected arguments. May the God Almighty reward you for this service and bless you with more opportunities. Disagreements and agreements aside, you have, without a doubt, done much labor in this authorship."[7]

Holy Quran being the classics of Islam, no authority can supersede it. Even the Prophet was commanded to judge by it (4:104).

---

7 Seerat Khatamun Nabiyeen, sallalaho alehi wassalam, vol. 2, by Mirza Bashir Ahmad M. First published In Urdu, Qadian, India-1920.

What the Quran Says

———— ❦ ————

THE FIRST FOUNDATION stone of Islamic Teachings is the Quran. And the perusal of the Quran will reveal that marriage in Islam is a civil contract and message (4:21). As such, it can be finalized only between two individuals who are intellectually, emotionally and physically mature enough to understand and fulfill the responsibilities needed to understand such a contract. This can be further understood from a verse from the Quran:

> "And test the orphans until they reach the age of *Nikah* (marriage), and if you find in them *rushdin* (maturity of the intellect), release their property to them" (4:6).

Here, the Quran explains clearly that intellectual maturity should be observed (which always falls beyond puberty), and should be the basis to know when one arrives at a reasonable age to marry. The Quranic verses (7:189 and 30:21) describe marriage as emotional bondage between two mutually compatible persons through which they seek "to dwell in tranquility" in the companionship of each other which is not possible if either of them are not mentally and physically developed. Even in the Islamic countries unluckily, Muslim jurists and so-called scholars or muftis do not seem to understand these Quranic teachings. And Law Boards of various Muslim countries have not outlawed child marriage.

The second generally accepted source of Islamic faith is the Sunnah. The Sunnah is the summation of Islamic teachings related to faith and code of conduct as personally practiced and perpetuated by Muhammad (SAW) for all believers to implement and follow in their personal lives as well as for all proper Islamic governments to adhere to. The Sunnah is related to articles of Islamic faith and is continuous from the day of the Prophet. But many other aspects of Islam are derived from compilations of traditions of the Prophet, and consist of many books of compilations of reported accounts of Muhammad's sayings and actions. There are six books of *Hadith (Sihah Sita)* that are considered authentic by main stream Sunni Muslims. All of these books were written 200-300 years after the death of Prophet Muhammad (SAW). These books are based on collections of hundreds of thousands of stories from the living people who transmitted accounts about Muhammad and his companions as they heard from earlier generations. Therefore, the process of oral transmission made the basis for all these books. This act of narrators who heard from another and then passed the account to the next one is known as "chain of narrations." They would comprise a chain of more than 4-7 narrators going back to the life-time of the companions of Muhammad (SAW).

We cannot cast doubt on the veracity of the saying *Hadith*, used to assert Ayesha's young age. In Islam, Hadith literature (sayings of the Prophet) is considered secondary to the Qur'an. While the Qur'an is considered to be the verbatim word of God, Hadith literature was transmitted over time through rigorous but not incapable of error methodology. Considering all known accounts and records, Ayesha's' age at marriage can be estimated to have been anywhere from 9 to 19 years old. Being an embodiment of Islam, Muhammad's actions reflect the Qur'an's teaching on marriage.

Hazrat Mirza Ghulam Ahmad

———— ❧ ————

In 1895, Hazrat Mirza Ghulam Ahmad, founder of the Ahmadiyya Muslim Community, responded to the allegation against Holy Prophet Muhammad by the Pastor. Hazrat Mirza Ghulam Ahmad questioned the validity of the reports in Hadith that Hazrat Ayesha was nine years old at the time of consummation, and he wrote:

"Your knowledge of the Arabic language is subpar, but you have also proven to be unfamiliar with things of simple association with faith such as nature and healing. About the mention you have made about Hazrat Ayesha Sadeeqa (ra)'s marriage ceremony at the age of nine. Firstly, there is no mention of it by the Holy Prophet (SAW) himself anywhere, nor is there any revelation to this effect. Nor is it reported in any parallel narrations proving the age to be nine years. It is derived only from one narrator. Arabs were generally not known to keep written memorandums because they were illiterate."[8]

In a society without a birth registry and where people did not celebrate birthdays, most people estimated their own age and that of others. Ayesha would have been no different. What's more? Ayesha had already been engaged to someone else before she married Muhammad, suggesting she had already been mature enough by the standards of her society to consider marriage for a while. It seems difficult to reconcile this with her being 6.

---

8 Hazrat Mirza Gulam Ahmad, Ruhani Khaza' in vol. 9, p. 377, Qadian, India, published 1895.

Hazrat Mirza Bashir Ahmad writes:

"All though every sensible individual can understand that for a narration to be authentic is one thing, and for an approximation to be correct is quite another. In other words, although the narrations in which the estimate of Hazrat 'Ayesha being 9 years of age at the time of her *Rukhastanah* is given may well be authentic in terms of narration, this estimate of Hazrat 'Ayesha in itself may be incorrect, as many times the estimates of people with respect to their own age prove to be inaccurate."

Further, he writes "Any intelligent individual would concur that the most correct and easy method by which the age of Hazrat 'Ayesha may be discerned is to determine her date of birth on the one hand and the date of her Rukhastanah on the other. After the specification of both these dates are agreed upon, there should be no room for any uncertainty as to her age at the time of the *Rukhastanah*. First, we take up the question of her birth."[9]

Hazrat Ayesha (ra) has criticized *Riva'yat*, narrated by the Companions {*Sa'habah*}of the Holy Prophet (SAW), and commended, "I do not speak so that these persons tell lies, but often ears make mistakes in hearing." In the Bukhari and 'the Muslim', there are several such criticisms. This clarifies that sometimes the *Ra'vee* (narrator) is the most reliable. Even his stated narration may be wrong (the denied one).

Sometimes the reason is that the narrator has hurried a talk and ends with it incomplete. Sometimes the narrator comprehends a wrong meaning. And sometimes a narrator experiences forgetfulness. In accordance with Hazrat Ayesha, we also say that the narrator has made a mistake in listening. The phrase was spoken ("nineteen"), the narrator heard only the

9 The Life & Character of the Seal of Prophets, Vol. 2, by Mirza Bashir Ahmad M. First published In Urdu, Qadian, India-1920. English rendering by Ayyaz Mehmood Khan. Published by Islam International Publications, Ltd. UK. Page 238-38.

word "nine", and in this way the story came into being. Thus, at times ears make mistakes when hearing a talk.

Since the worthy companions of the Holy Prophet (SAW) might have committed mistakes, or since Hazrat Umar (ra), Abu Hura'rah (ra), ibn Umar (ra), etc., might have committed mistakes, 'Urwah ibn al-Zubayr and his son, Hisham, may certainly have made a mistakes. For example, nobody called Hazrat Ayesha (ra) the Negator, the one who denies a *Hadith*. Then, if we state a mistake of Hisham, how do we become a person who denies a Hadith? For, the denial of a *Hadith* is something else, and pointing out a mistake is another.

The well-known historian and scholar *'Allama* 'Imad-ud-Deen Ibn Katheer writes in his *Al-Badayah*, which is about Sayedah Asma', daughter of Hazrat Abu Bakr (and we hope *Mulana* Syed Abul Ala Maudoodi must have seen it as he referred to Al-Badayah' in his article), that Asma' died in 73 A.H. at the age of 100 years old. She was ten years older than Ayesha. Therefore, the age of Hazrat Ayesha would have been 17 or 18 years old at the time of *Hijrah*. Accordingly, her birth falls about four or five years before the Call, and her age at the time of the consummation of marriage in 2 A.H. works out to be 19-20 years old.

Author of *Al-Kamal fi Asma*, Abd al-Ghanī ibn Abd al-Wāḥid al-Jammā-īlī al-Maqdisi, writes "At the time of consummation of her marriage, Hazrat Ayesha's age was not less than 18-19 years old."

Hazrat Ayesha (ra) herself has been reported to have related that when the chapter entitled "The Moon" (chapter 54) was revealed she was a girl playing about and that she remembered certain verses revealed at the time. Now, the fifty-fourth chapter could not have been revealed later than the fifth year of the Call, and therefore the report which states her to have been six years old in the tenth year of the Call, when her marriage ceremony was gone through, cannot be correct because this would show her to have been born around the time of the revelation of the 54th chapter.

The compiler of the famous *Hadith* collection, *Mishkat al-Masabih*, *Imam*, Wali-ud-Din Muhammad ibn Abdullah Al-Khatib-Alumri, who died

700 years ago from the time of this publication, has also written brief biographical notes on the narrators of Hadith reports. He writes under Asma, the older daughter of Abu baker:

"She was the elder sister of Aisha Siddiqa, wife of the Holy Prophet, and was ten years older than her... In 73 A.H... Asma died at the age of one hundred years old."

This would make Asma 28 years of age in 1 A.H., the year of *Hijra*, thus making Ayesha 18 years old in 1 A. H. Further, it would make Aisha 19 years old at the time of the consummation of her marriage, and 14 or 15 years old at the time of her *nikah* (marriage). It would place her year of birth at four or five years before the Call. The same statement is made by the famous classical commentator of the Holy Quran, Ibn Kathir, in his book *Al-bidayya wal-nihaya*:

"Asma died in 73 A.H. at the age of hundred years old. She was ten years older than her sister, Ayesha."

In this regard, the following things have been written by many historians:

Asma was 10 years older than Ayesha.[10]
According to Ibn Kathir, Asma was 10 years older than her sister, Ayesha (ra).[11]
According to Ibn-Hajar Al-Asqalani, Asma lived a hundred years and died in 73 A.H.[12]
According to internationally acknowledged and well-versed historians, Asma, the elder sister of Ayesha, was 10 years older than Ayesha, such being in line with Ibn Kathir.

10 Siyar A/ Lama-nubala, Al-Zahabi, vol. 2, p. 289, Arabic, Muassasatu-risalah, 1992.
11 Al-Bidayah Wa- Nihayah, Ibn Kathir, vol. 8, p. 371, Dar al-Fikr al-'Arabi, Al- jizah, 1933.
12 Taqribu- tehzib, Ibn Hajar Al- Asqalani, p. 654, Arabic, Bab fi-nisa, al-harfu-alif.

Comparative analysis of both sisters and calculation of the data:

Asma died in 73 A.H. at the age of 100 years old (and 100 days).
Asma was 10 years older than Ayesha (ra).
73*355 (Islamic calendar) = 25,915 days.
25,915/365 = 71 years (conversion to Gregorian calendar).
(100*355)+100 (Hijrah years) = 35,600 days.
35,600/365 = 98 (Gregorian years).

Death of Asma:

693-98 = 595 C.E.
The marriage occurred after the Battle of Badrin.
622+2 =624 C.E.
624-605 = 19 years (a fully grown woman, not a 6 or 9-year-old girl).

Ayesha was a young girl during the revelation of Chapter 54 in 614 C.E.
According to another narrative in Bukhari Hadith, Ayesha is reported to have said:

"I was a young girl (jariyah) in Arabic" when Surah Al-Qamar was revealed.[13]

Chapter 54 of the Quran was revealed eight years before *Hijrah*.[14]
If Ayesha started living with the prophet at the age of nine in 623 C.E. or 624 C.E., she was a newborn infant (sibyah in Arabic) at the time that Surah Al-Qamar (The Moon) was revealed, according to the above tradition confirmed by all historians.

---

13 Sahih Bukhari, Kitabu'-tafsir, Bab QaulihiBal al-sa' atu Maw'idhum wa' 1-sa atu adha' wa amarr.
14 The Bounteous Koran, M.M. Khatib, 1985. This indicates that it was revealed in 614 C.E.

Ayesha was actually a young girl, not an infant, in the year of the revelation of Al-Qamar (614 C.E.).

Jariyah means "young, playful girl.[15] So Ayesha, being a *Jariyah* (young girl), not a *sibyah* (infant), must have been somewhere between 9-13 years old at the time of the revelation of Al-Qamar in 614 C.E., and therefore must have been 19-21 years old when she married the Prophet Muhammad (SAW).

If Ayesha was a young girl in 614 C.E., surely she couldn't have been 6 or 9 years old in 624 C.E. Thus, the tradition I mentioned earlier is flawed.

The reliability of the sources who narrated that Ayesha was 6 or 9 years old when she married is questionable. Most of such narratives are reported only by Hisham ibn'Urwah, who was the Great-grandson of Hazrat Abu-Bakr, who was reporting on the authority of his father. He was born in the year 61 A.H. and died in the year 146 A.H. Hisham Ibn Urwah was the son of Zubayr, and Urawa's mother was Asma, sister of Ayesha (ra).

Hazrat Abu-Baker's Grandson was Urwah ibn-Zubayr, and Asma was married to Zubayr, and Zubayr was the paternal cousin of the Holy Prophet.[16] Hisham Ibn Urwah reported an event as well known as the one being reported, and should logically have been reported by more than just one, two or three people. The following question has been raised by the majority of the scholars of Islamic history: why would anyone from Medina, where Hisham ibn Urwah lived the first 71 years of his life, have narrated the event despite the fact that in Medina his pupils included the well-known and well- respected Malik ibn Anas? Originally, reports of the narratives of this event are from people from Iraq, where Hisham is reported to have moved to after living in Medina for most of his life.

Tehzibu-Tehzib, one the most authentic books on the life and reliability of the narrators of the traditions of the Prophet (SAW), reports that according to Yaqub ibn Shaibah, "Narratives reported by Hisham are

---

15 Lane's Arabic English Lexicon.

16 Wiki sources. Also see The Life & Character of the Seal Of prophets, vol. 11. [Sirat Khatamun-Nabiyyin]. By Mirza Bashir Ahmad, published by Islam International publications, Ltd. Page 35.

reliable except what he narrated after moving over to Iraq."[17] It further states that Malik ibn Ans objected to those narratives of Hisham which were reported through people in Iraq. *Mizanu'l ai-tidal*, another book on the life sketches of the narrators of the traditions of the Prophet, reports:

"When he was old, Hisham's memory suffered quite badly."[18]

The references above clearly prove that Hisham's memory was failing. And his narrative while in Iraq, regarding Ayesha's age at the time of marriage, is unreliable. He was born in 61 A.H. and moved to Iraq in 131 A.H. He was quite old at that time and several tribes of Jews and Christians started to convert to Islam and were sent out of Makah and Medina, and settled in Iraq, causing harm to Islam.

"Unmarried female" in Arabic language is called *bikr*, and in the narrative reported by Ahmad ibn Hanbal,[19] after the death of the Prophet's first wife, when Khaulah came to the prophet suggesting him to marry again, the Prophet asked her about the choices he had to choose from. Khaulah said, "You can marry a virgin (*bikr*) or a woman who has already been married (*thayyib*)." When the Prophet asked about the identity of the *bikr* (virgin), Khaulah mentioned Ayesha's name.

All those who know the Arabic language are aware that the word *bikr* in the Arabic language is not used for an immature nine year old girl. It describes someone who is the equivalent of an English work maiden. Therefore, obviously a nine-year-old girl is not a lady (*bikr*). The literal meaning of the word, *bikr* (virgin), in the above Hadith, is "adult woman." Therefore, Ayesha was an adult woman at the time of her marriage.[20]

The narrative of the marriage of nine-year-old Ayesha by Hisham ibn Urwah cannot be held true when it is contradicted by many other narratives. Several other scholars, including Malik ibn Anas, who was a student

17 Tehzib-tehzib Al-asqalani, Dar Ihya as-turath al-Islami, 15th century. Vol. 11, p. 48-51.
18 Mizan-ai 'tidas, Al-Zahbi, Al-Maktabatu-athriyyah, vol. 4, page 301-02.
19 Musnad Ahmad ibn Hanbal, vol. 6, page 210, Arabic Dar Ihya al-turath al 'Arabi.
20 Ibid.

of Hisham ibn Urwah's, deems Urwah's narrative while in Iraq to be unreliable. Thus, the narrative of Ayesha's age at the time of the marriage is not reliable due to the clear contradiction seen in the works of classical scholars of Islam. First, we must consider that there is only one Hadith reported by Hisham bin Urwah that states Ayesha's age to be 9 when she moved into the Prophet's (SAW's) house. Although this information is widely quoted and found in many Hadith and history books, it must be noted that this information has come from a single person, i.e. Hisham bin Urwah, who is the last narrator in this Hadith's chain of narrators on the authority of his father. Thus, the Hadith is primarily a single Hadith. In general, a Hadith has more credibility if it is narrated by more people independently from diverse chains of narrators. In this case, there is basically one source. In one *Hadith*, in *Sahih Bukhari*, it is reported that Ayesha stated:

> "Since I reached the age when I could remember things, I have seen my parents worshipping according to the right faith of Islam. Not a single day passed but Prophet (SAW) visited us both in the morning and in the evening. When Muslims were persecuted, Abu Bakr set out for Ethiopia as an emigrant." This report sheds some light on the true age of Ayesha (ra). The mention of persecution of Muslims along with their subsequent emigration to Ethiopia clearly shows that Ayesha was referring to the fifth or sixth year of the Call. Ayesha was of an age that she could discern things, and so her birth could not have been later than the first year of the Call.

Also, Tabari (an authentic and early historian of Islam) reports that Hazrat Abu Bakr wished to spare Hazrat Ayesha the discomforts of a journey to Ethiopia 8 years before *Hijrah*. Soon after 615 C.E., he went to Muta'am with the son of the one Ayesha (ra) was engaged to and asked him to take Ayesha to his house as his son's wife. Mut'am refused because Hazrat Abu Bakr had converted to Islam. Subsequently, his son did not marry Ayesha (ra). But if Ayesha was already of marriageable age in 615 in C.E., she must have been older than nine in 622 C.E. If Ayesha (ra) was only seven years old at the time of her marriage, she could not have been born at the time Abu Bakr decided to migrate to Ethiopia, previously named Hubshah.

The statements above prove that Ayesha was not 6 or 9 years old when she got married. She was at least 19 years old. Moreover, the Qur'an rejects the marriage of immature girls and boys, as well as entrusting them with responsibilities.

Also, Imam Bukhari reported one Hadith, saying that that, "Umar [one teenager] states that the Prophet did not permit me to participate in the battle of Uhud, as at that time I was 14 years old. It may be added that on the earlier occasion of the battle of Badr, when some Muslim youth tried out of eagerness, to go along with the Muslim army to the field of battle, the Holy Prophet Muhammad sent them back on account of their young age (allowing only one such youngster, Umair ibn Abi Waqqas, to accompany his older brother, the famous Companion Sa'd ibn Abi Waqqas. It seems, therefore, highly unlikely that if Ayesha was ten years old, the Holy Prophet would have allowed her to accompany the army to the field of battle."

According to many Hadith in Bukhari, and Muslims, Ayesha participated in the battle of Badr and Uhud in 624 C.E. However, no one below the age of fifteen was allowed to accompany raiding parties. There is a report in *Sahih Bukhari* (a book compiled by Imam Bukhari) that reads as follows:

"On the day [of the battle] of Uhud when [some] people retreated and left the Prophet, I saw Ayesha, daughter of Abu Bakr, and Umm Sulmah, with their robes tucked up so that the bangles around their ankles were visible, hurrying with their water skins in another [in narration it is said, 'carrying the water skins on their backs']. Then they would pour the water in the mouths of the people and return to fill the water skins again, and came back again to pour water in the mouths of the people. It should also be noted that Ayesha (ra) joined the Holy Prophet's household only one year before the battle of Uhud. According to the common view, she would be only ten years of age at this time, which is certainly not a suitable age for the work she did on this occasion. This also shows that she was not so young at this time."

It was not an Arab tradition to give away girls in marriage at an age as young as nine or ten years old. Nor did the Prophet (SAW) marry Ayesha (ra) at such a young age. The people of Arabia did not object to this marriage because it never happened in the manner it has been narrated (that she was so young, that is).

Ibn Hisham's recension of Ibn Ishaq's *Sirat Rashul Allah*, the earliest surviving biography of Hazrat Muhammad (SAW), records Hazrat Ayesha as having converted to Islam before Hazrat Umar ibn al-Khattab (ra), during the first few years of Islam, around 610 C.E. In order to accept Islam, she must have been walking and talking, hence at least three years old, which would make her at least fifteen years old in 622 C.E.

Reports regarding Ayesha's death also must be carefully reviewed to better understand this matter. The year she died is listed as the 55th, 56th, 57th, 58th, or 59th year after *Hijrah*, [21] and her age at that time is listed as 65, 66, 67, or 74 years old.[22] Just as there is no agreement regarding her date of birth, there is no agreement regarding her date of death.

Reports saying that she died in the 58th year after the *Hijrah* and that she was 74 years old when she died give the impression that they are sounder than others because they give detailed information, such as the day she died (they say Wednesday), that it corresponded to the 17th day of *Ramadan*, that upon her request she was buried at night after the *Witr Prayer* in the *Jannat al Baqi* graveyard, that upon her last request the funeral prayer was led by Abu Hurayra and that she was lowered into the grave by persons like her sister, Asma's two sons, Abdullah and Urwah, her brother Muhammad's two sons, Qasim and Abdullah, and her brother Abdurrahman's son, Abdullah.[23] Therefore, when calculations are made according to this date, we see she lived 48 years after the Prophet's death (48+10=58+13=71+3=74). This would mean she was born three years before Muhammad's prophet hood and that she was 17 when she married (74-48=26-9=17).

---

21   Ibn Abdilbarr, Istiab, 2:108; Tahzibu'l Kamal, 16:560.
22   Ibn Sa'd, Tabaqat, 8:75; Nadvi Siratu's Sayyidati Ayesha, 202.
23   Ibn Abdilbarr, Istiab, 2:108; Dogrul, Asr-1 Sadet, 2:142.

Many things show strong support for the idea that Ayesha must have been older than official history claims her to have been when she married the Prophet (SAW): that she was on the battle front at Uhud, in the third year after the *Hijrah*, when even boys were turned away; her depth in scholarly matters and the mature attitude and statements she put forth in regard to the matter of slander; the age difference between her and the Prophet's daughter, Fatima; her knowledge and awareness of the *Hijrah* and later developments after arriving in Medina; her marriage being consummated after her father's suggestion and after the *Mahar* had been paid;[24] the position of the Prophet as a guide in the society; the sensitivity of the Prophet and his fatherly compassion; the differences in reports regarding the date of marriage, such reports having no finality to them;[25] Ayesha using a doubtful and estimated expression referring to her age; dates of birth and death not being as clearly determined in that society as they are today. All of this concludes that she was engaged at 14 or 15 years old and was married to the Prophet (SAW) at the age of 19 years old. The evidence in favor of this conclusion is too strong to be ignored.

It should also be noted that Ayesha (ra) joined the holy Prophet's household only one year before the battle of Uhud. According to the common view, that would make her only ten years old at that time which is certainly not a suitable age for the work she did on this occasion. This also shows that she was not so young at this time.[26] If, as it is documented in the previous section above, Ayesha was 19 years old at the time of consummation of her marriage, then she would be 20 years old at the time of the battle of Uhud.

I have explained only some of the major points that go against accepting the commonly known narrative regarding Ayesha's (ra) age at the time of her marriage. Now, I will enter into a new discussion, still regarding marriage.

---

24 Tabarani, Kabir, 23:25; Ibn Abdilbarr, Istiah, 4:1937; Ibn Sa'd Tabaqat, 8:63.
25 Bukhari, Manakibu'l Ansar, 20, 44, 36.
26 Fadl-ul-Bari, vol. 1, p. 651.

Child marriage In Jewish communities:
The law of the Talmud and the Bible
on the Marriage of Young Girls

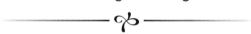

IN JEWISH ASHKENAZI communities in the Middle Ages, girls were married off very young. Child marriage was possible in Judaism due to the very low marriageable age for girls. A *Ketannah* (literally meaning "little [one]" referred to any girl between the age of 3 years old and 12 years and one day old. A *Ketannah* was completely subject to her father's authority, and her father could arrange a marriage for her without her consent.[27]

It is Christian evangelists and other believers in the Bible who have been bitterly reviling the Holy Prophet Muhammad (SAW) partly because they believe his marriage to Ayesha (ra) was immoral. The main accusations regarding his marriage to Ayesha are that she was too young in age while the Holy Prophet was a much older man, fifty years old, and that her consent to the marriage was either non-existent or she was not capable of giving it. This claim is a recurring one among critics of Islam, so its foundation deserves close scrutiny. The Qur'an states that marriage is void unless entered into by consenting adults. Ayesha defiantly entered puberty before her marriage to the Prophet (Saw), as documented earlier. Critics allege that in seventh-century Arabia, adulthood was defined as when one reaches the onset of puberty. But, they forget that in Europe, five centuries after Muhammad's marriage to Ayesha, 33-year-old King John of England married 12-year old Isabella of Angouleme. There is Islamophobia inherent in the depiction of Muhammad's marriage

---

27 Wiki sources.

24

to Ayesha as motivated by misplaced desire and it fits within a broader Orientalist depiction of Muhammad as a philanderer. This idea dates back to the crusades. According to the academically well-known scholar, Kecia Ali, "Accusations of lust and sensuality were a regular feature of medieval attacks on the Prophet's character and, by extension, on the authenticity of Islam."

Hazrat Maryam (Mary, the mother of Christ), may Allah bestow peace on her, was 11 years old, or, according to some scholars, 12 years old, when she married Joseph, who was 90 years old [Reference of work on the Constitution, Doctrine, Discipline, and History of the Catholic Church, New York: Robert Appleton Company, Vol. V111, p. 505]. And this, the most famous marriage in Christianity, is not in the canonical Gospels of the Bible; it appears in other early Christian writings (known as apocryphal writings). The husband was selected and Mary was handed over to him, and she played no part in his selections.

These accounts are summed up in the Catholic encyclopedia, the 1913 edition, which is available online.

The Holy Quran states, "O Mary, Allah gives thee glad tidings of a son through a word from Him; his name shall be the Messiah, Jesus, son of Mary, honored in this world and in the next, and of those who are granted nearness to God" (Ch3:46). In the same chapter, the Holy Quran states, "O People of the Book! Why do you deny the Signs of Allah while you are witnesses thereof? O People of the Book! Why do you confound truth with falsehood and hide the truth knowingly?" (3:71-72).

The Old Testament states that the Prophet David had 100 wives and that Solomon had 700 wives and 300 concubines. The word "concubine" is very much familiar to 21st century progressive women. The word echoed from Buckingham palace to the White House in the last decade. The Qur'an has established the complete innocence and moral integrity of all Biblical prophets, even when the Old Testament and the New Testament leave us to our assumptions and imaginations.

Hazrat Abraham (Abram) was eighty-six years old when he married Hagar (Hazrat Hajrah) (Genesis, chapter 16, verses 1-4 and 15-16).

Islam is the first religion to put restrictions on the number of wives one can have. Someone getting a second marriage is only allowed under certain conditions (Holy Qur'an, Ch. 4:4).

In the Holy Qur'an, God revealed to Muhammad (SAW) that, "Allah chooses His Messengers from among angels, and from among men. Surely, Allah is All-Hearing, All-Seeing (Ch. 22: 76).

To sum up the Qur'anic verses about all Prophets of God, we can conclude that all the Prophets received revelations from Allah, faith in God, obeyed Allah's commands, were bestowed pure hearts, were humble natured, peaceful, trustworthy, truthful, gave Allah's commandments and offered Allah's love to mankind.

In the Holy Quran, the Prophet David is known as Hazrat Daud (ah), such being in Arabic. His story starts around 1,000 B.C. During this time, King Saul's army went to fight the Philistines. Prophet David (ah) was a youth in this army. Goliath was most likely a leader or commander of the Philistine army. Goliath challenged any man from King Saul's army for one-on-one combat as was done in those days. All the men were too frightened to except the challenge. No one dared to volunteer, except for David (ah). The Holy Quran tells us that, "David slew *Jalut* (Goliath), and Allah gave him sovereignty and wisdom, and taught him of what He pleased" (Holy Quran: Ch. 2: 252). David (ah) became a prophet and King of the Israelites. He sang the praises of Allah. Prophet David (ah) is mentioned in several chapters of the Holy Qur'an for his unique qualities. God almighty also gave Prophet David a son named Solomon who also became a prophet and a King and was famous for his piety, wisdom and justice.

Mecca's Memoirs

―――――――――― ∞ ――――――――――

LIFE WENT ON. Every morning Mecca became luminous with news of new believers entering the faith, but every night Mecca became dark with the hardships forced on believers. Meccans were experiencing joy and difficulty at the same time. Ayesha watched everything, and she had described such precisely to future generations. Her natural curiosity led her to record every development she experienced; it is almost like a photographic record of her life. She knew where verse was revealed, who became Muslim and when, etc. Well-known historians recorded that one day, many years later, a man from Iraq came to Medina and asked questions about the Mecca period. In her reply, Ayesha related an insightful analysis of the time.

The Meccan period was full of unforgettable and sad memories for Ayesha. The only brightness in their lives was the Messenger of God. He visited the house of Abu Bakr frequently and comforted them. Ayesha expressed her pleasure with this and said:

> "Ever since I can remember, I saw my parents as practicing believers. The messenger of God used (ra) to visit us almost every day in the morning or in the evening."[28]

Death of Abu Talib (ah) and Hazrat Khadijha

In his tenth year of prophet hood, the Holy Prophet (SAW) experienced several sorrowful events. The hardships endured by Muslims during the blockade and confinement in *Shi'bi Abi Talib* gravely affected the health

―――――――――――――――――――――

28 Ahmad ibn Hanbal, Musnad, 6/198; Bayhaqi, Sunan 6/204.

27

of both Hazrat Khadijha and the Holy Prophet's uncle, Abu Talib. Hazrat Khadijha passed away a few days after the lifting of the blockade and Abu Talib passed away a month later. Thus, the Holy Prophet lost his most faithful, loving and caring wife, Hazrat Khadijha, and his uncle, Abu Talib, who at the critical time in his life, gave him protection. The Holy Prophet patiently bore the grief caused by all these tragedies.

The Marriage Proposal

The Holy Prophet's first wife was Khadijha, daughter of Khuwaylid. Khadijha lived with the Holy Prophet for twenty-five years, until her death at the age of sixty-five. And according to other narrations, she was 60 years old at the time of her death. She died during Ramadan, three years before the *Hijrah*. At that time, the Holy Prophet was fifty years old. Khadijha was the second person to adopt Islam and had always given unstinted support to her husband during his trials and difficulties. She sympathized with him and comforted him during every challenge he faced, and never failed to extend her helping hand to him. After the death of such a loving companion, the Prophet's life became very sad.[29] His faithful followers were worried about him.

Two years had passed since the death of Hazrat Khadijah, and the Prophet of God was living alone with his three daughters. One day, the wife of Uthman ibn Maz'soon, Khawlah bint Hakim, went to God's Messenger respectfully and she asked him:

"Do you not want to marry?"

The Prophet of God was fifty years old. Feeling sad due to Khadija's death, he responded, "Alright, but with whom?"

Khawlah responded, asking the Holy Prophet whether he preferred to marry a widow or someone who hadn't married before. Khawlah's attitude was that of a woman capable of finding both.

---

29 Bukhari: Sahih-Chapter Inspiration.

The Holy Prophet asked about the latter option. He said, "It is Ayesha, daughter of Abu Bakr, a friend whom you love the most among people." Then he asked Khawlah about the other option. It turned out to be Sawdah bint Zam'a, one of the earliest Muslims.

Sawdah accepted Islam during the most difficult days in Mecca and even migrated to Abyssinia to escape persecution. Her husband, as-Sakran ibn 'Amir, died in Abyssinia. Thus, she returned. Both of them were possibilities so the Holy Prophet told Khawlah to find out hoped to lessen the Prophet's troubles ladies' opinion. The Prophet authorized Khawlah to carry out the necessary negotiations. Khawlah was happy because she hoped to lessen the Holy Prophet's troubles. According to some historians, Khawlah first approached Abu Bakr who gave his consent to the marriage. Ayesha, however, had already been betrothed to Jubayr, son of Mut'am. Before conveying his consent to the Prophet, Abu Bakr said that if Ayesha became a member of their family, their son, Mut'am, would forsake their religion which was not acceptable to Abu Bakr. Thus, this engagement was broken. Some historians have noted Umm Ruman, mother of Hazrat Ayesha, to be the first person in Abu Bakr's family who Khawlah spoke to. She conveyed the message of the Prophet Muhammad:

"The prophet Muhammad sent me to ask for your daughter Ayesha's hand in marriage."

Umm Ruman was speechless and filled with pleasure. Abu Bakr said to Khawlah, "Now, you can go and inform the Prophet of God and invite him.

It was the month of *Shawwal* in the twelfth year of revelation and an engagement was made between the Prophet and Ayesha.

There are some references in books of several well-known Islamic histories about the first approach of Khawlah, which referred; that it was to Sawdah's family, not Ayesh's family because she was mature at time.

Being a widow, Saudah was still mourning for her husband in her heart. This offer was of a nature that could cease her pain. Saudah had an elderly father and she decided to receive his blessings first. This duty was also given to Khawlah. So, Khawlah went to Saudah's elderly father and told him that Muhammad, the son of Abdullah, was asking for his daughter's hand in marriage.

When the old man heard the name "Muhammad, son of Abdullah," he straightened up and said:

"He is a generous man and a good match. But how does your friend feel about this?"

Khawlah quickly responded:

"She likes the idea too."

Even though Sawdah consented, some of her relatives opposed the marriage. Her brother, Abdullah ibn Zam'a, who heard the news later on, protested his father's decision.[30] Sawdah's uncle also screamed in poetic verse, objecting to this marriage.

According to Zarqani (Vol. 3, page 261), Hazrat Saudah (ra)'s father, Zam'a, announced her marriage with the Prophet for 400 Darham dowry during the month of Ramadan in the tenth year of *Nubuwah*.

Some narrations state that after the death of Khadijah, Sawdah was the next to marry the Prophet. However, other narrations report that it was Ayesha. Historians dispute this, largely because of the short time between the two events. Ibn-e-Ishaq believes Sawdah was the first to marry the Prophet after the death of Khadijah, but according to Abdullah bin Muhammad bin Aqeel, Ayesha was the Prophet's next wife after the death of Khadijah.[31]

It is reported in various narratives that in the month of *Shawwal*, in the twelfth year of revelation, an engagement was made between the Prophet and Ayesha. Ayesha herself states that her dowry was of the value

---

30 Later on, Abdullah ibn Zam'a became a Muslim and expressed his regret for the reaction he had that day.

31 Tabqaat ibn-Saad, Vol. 8, page 36-37, Zarqani vol. 3, page 260.

of 500 Dirham. That day marked a new period for Ayesha and she was fully developed in both mind and body. She was the happiest of young women because she would become the wife of the most beloved servant of God. At that time, a huge responsibility, being a mother of believers,[32] was placed on her shoulders, and at a young age.

Ayesha (ra) was aware of her responsibilities. The process of revelation, which she had followed carefully until that day, would now be approached even more meticulously by her. She would record every event, like a photograph, in her mind.

---

32 It is stated in the Qur'an (Ahzab 3:6) that the Prophet's wives were mothers of believers.

The Holy Prophet's Advice to Umm Ruman

AYESHA'S MOTHER, UMM Ruman, felt a heavy burden on her shoulders because her daughter was going to become the wife of the Holy Prophet. She became very sensitive to her daughter's energetic behavior. When she saw something she did not like, she condemned Ayesha, sometimes quite harshly. God's messenger, who came to visit after such an incident had taken place, felt the chilly atmosphere in the home and asked the reason for it. Umm Ruman was embarrassed but explained what had happened between herself and her daughter. The Prophet turned to Umm Ruman and said:

"O, Umm Ruman! Treat Ayesha properly and preserve her rights. Please, for my sake."[33]

Before his marriage with Ayesha, the Prophet had a dream in which an angel had presented something to him that was wrapped in silk. The Prophet asked the angel what it was and the angel said it was Umm Ruman's wife. When Umm Ruman removed the silken cover, he saw that it was Ayesha.[34]

After the marriage ceremony, Ayesha (ra) continued to live with her parents, as this marriage was not consumed yet. During that time, the Holy Prophet (SAW) visited tribes and invited them to Islam. He was looking for open hearts that would submit to God. The opponents of the Holy Prophet (SAW) had made it almost impossible for him to leave his house to carry his message to any section of the people of Mecca. Because of these circumstances, the Holy Prophet (SAW) decided to convey the

---

33 Hakim, Mustadrak, 4:5 (6716).
34 Bukhari: Sahih-Chapter Inspiration.

message of Islam to the People of Ta'if, a city approximately forty miles east of Mecca. During this trip, Zaid bin Harith accompanied him. First, the Holy Prophet (SAW) met the important people of the town and conveyed to them the message of Islam. However, all of them refused to accept Islam and insulted him. Not only that, they also asked the vagabonds and street thugs to follow him and force him to leave the town. They followed him and pelted him with stones. His legs and feet were bruised and blood filled his shoes. Thus, they forced him to leave the town. The Holy Prophet (SAW) and his companion dragged themselves along a short distance, and when they were away from the town, they stopped in a vineyard belonging to two Meccans.

Hazrat 'Abdullah bin Ja'far relates that after the sad demise of Abu Talib, the Holy Prophet (SAW) went to spread the message of Islam to the people of Ta'if. However, they did not accept him. The Holy Prophet (SAW) offered two rak'at prayers under the shade of a tree and most humbly supplicated to God Almighty.[35]

Both the *Isra* and *Miraj* events are called night journeys; these events took place in the above-described days of hardship.

The Holy Prophet's night journey is the story of his transportation from one city to another.

This Night Journey took place in the 5th year of the Call. The Prophet's journey from Mecca to Jerusalem is called *Isra* and his Ascension to Heaven is known by the name of *Miraj*.

One night, the Holy Prophet (SAW) had a vision that he should make a trip from Mecca (Mecca's Sacred Mosque to the Distant Mosque that refers to Prophet Solomon's Temple at Jerusalem, now known as Aqsa Mosque) to Jerusalem (and indeed did so). This trip is commonly called *Isra*. The details of this event is given in the Holy Quran (Ch.17:2.).

On another occasion (2BH), he made a journey to heaven. This journey is commonly called *Miraj* (the ascension).

---

35 As-Siratun Nabawiyyah ibn Hisham, vol. 2, page 61-62; Sirah Ibn Hisham Biography of the prophet, Abridged by 'Abdus Salam Harun, p. 90, Al-Flah Foundation, Cairo, Egypt.

Holy Prophet's Night Journey from Mecca to Jerusalem (*Isra*)

One night, when the Holy Prophet (SAW) and the others present in the house of Hazrat Umm Hani went to sleep after offering their prayer, the Holy Prophet was taken away by the angel Gabriel on a visit to *Aqsa* Mosque in Jerusalem, and then to the seven heavens. In the morning, the Holy Prophet (SAW) said to them, "Last night I offered my evening Prayer with you. Then I went to Jerusalem where I offered Prayer and now I am offering the Dawn Prayer with you."

Hazrat Umm Hani as Hind bint Abi Talib was called and begged him not to tell the people, "Because they will regard you as a liar and harm you."

The Prophet responded by saying, "By God, I will tell them."[36]

When the Holy Prophet (SAW) told the *Quraish* that he had visited Jerusalem during the night, the *Quraish* mocked him and mentioned it to Abu Bakr Hazrat. Abu Bakr responded by saying, "If he says so, then it is true." This earned Hazrat Abu Bakr the title of *Sidique* (the truthful) from the Holy Prophet.[37]

The journey of the Holy Prophet from Mecca to Jerusalem is called ISR, and his ascension from Jerusalem to heaven is called the *Miraj*. Both of these events are known as the Night Journey. The Night Journey of the Holy Prophet (SAW) to Jerusalem is described in the Holy Qur'an (Ch. 17:2 and Ch. 53:8-18).

The idolaters of Mecca continued persecuting the believers. The persecution of Muslims at the hands of pagan Meccans led to their emigration to Medina in large numbers. Even before the migration of the Holy Prophet (SAW), the migration process slowly accelerated. Sometimes, a whole lane of houses were emptied in the course of a night. In the morning, a Meccan would find out that the occupants of the houses had migrated to Medina. After enduring thirteen years of unimaginable suffering at

---

36 As-Siratun Nabawiyyah, Ibn Hisham vol. 1, p. 267.
37 As-Siratun Nabawiyyah, ibn Hisham vol. 1, p. 399; Usdul Ghabah, Ibn Athir, vol. 3, p. 21, Dhikr 'Abdullah bin Uthman bin'Amir Abu Bakr.

the hands of the fledgling religion's enemies, the Holy Prophet (SAW) left Mecca under Divine guidance. He migrated to Medina, where the first Muslim community was already established by some of his followers who had migrated there earlier. From then on, the Holy Prophet (SAW) visited Hazrat Abu Bakr and informed him that Al-Mighty God had allowed them to leave Mecca and to emigrate. Hazrat Abu Bakr was delighted because he knew that he was going with the Messenger of God on his trip. Hazrat Abu Bakr shed tears of joy.[38]

According to Hazrat Ayesha, when the Prophet decided to migrate he used to visit Hazrat Abu Bakr daily, either in the morning or in the evening. She further relates about her father, Hazrat Abu Bak:

"Ever since I reached the age of discretion, I found my parents to be Muslim. There was not a single day when he Holy Prophet did not visit our house, either in the morning or in the evening."

When Muslims experienced severe trials and oppressions by the infidels that made the lives of Muslims unbearable, like many others, Hazrat Abu Bakr also left his home, with the intention to migrate to Abyssinia. When he reached a place called 'Bark al- Ghim`ad', Ibn Daghinah, a leader of the Q`arah tribe, met him. He asked, "Abu Bakr! Where are you going?"

Hazrat Abu Bakr responded by saying, "My people have expelled me. So, I wish to travel around the world and worship Allah."

Ibn Daghinah said, "O, Abu Bakr, you should neither leave the city nor be expelled by others. You try to establish lost virtues, strengthen the ties of kinship, help the poor and week; you are hospitable to guests and you are always ready to help the people in need. I give you my protection. Go back to your home and worship Allah."

After this, Hazrat Abu Bakr returned home with the company of Daghinah. In the evening, Ibn Daghinah roamed around the town and met elders and revered people of Quraish. He told them, "Such a valuable person like Abu Bakr should not leave town. You are expelling a

---

38 Tabari Tarikh, 1:569; Ibn Hisham Sira, 3:11.

person who reestablishes lost virtues, strengthens the ties of kinship, helps the poor and the weak; he is hospitable to guests and is always ready to help people in need."

The *Quraish* did not belie what Ibn Daghinah said about Hazrat Abu Bakr and accepted his guarantee of protection for Hazrat Abu Bakr. However, they asked him to tell Hazrat Abu Bakr that he should worship, offer prayers and recite whatever he likes in his home. He should not hurt their feelings with it and should not do it in public. They feared that he may influence their women and children.

Ibn Daghinah told Hazrat Abu Bakr what the *Quraish* had said to him. Hazrat Abu Bakr worshipped Allah at home and did not offer his prayers in public; nor did he recite the Holy Qur'an outside his home. After some time, Hazrat Abu Bakr reflected on the situation. He built a mosque in his home and started to offer his prayers and recite the Holy Quran in his mosque. Soon, women and children of polytheists started to gather around him in large numbers. They were amazed to see him. Hazrat Abu Bakr had no control over his emotions while reciting the Holy Qur'an, thus he wept profusely. Seeing this occur, the leader of the *Quraish* became nervous, and they talked with Ibn Daghinah about it. They told him, "We had accepted your guarantee of protection on the condition that he would worship and offer prayers and recite the Quran in his house and not in public. However, he has failed to follow the conditions of the protection. He has built a mosque in his house and worships his lord openly. We fear that our women and children will be affected by this. Ask him to refrain from worshipping in his mosque. If he agrees to worship within his house, he can stay under your protection. Otherwise, ask him to surrender your guarantee of protection of him. We do not want to disgrace the guarantee of protection given to him by you. At the same time, we cannot let Abu Bakr practice his beliefs openly."

Hazrat Ayesha says, "Ibn Daghinah came to Abu Bakr and said, 'You know the conditions under which I have given my protection. Either adhere to the conditions or surrender my protection, because I do not like people saying that my protection has been dishonored.'"

Hazrat Abu Bakr told him that he was surrendering his guarantee of protection and that he was happy to be under the protection and security of Allah.

In those days, the Holy Prophet (SAW) was in Mecca. He told Muslims that in his dream he saw the place of migration. The place had date orchards and was between two valleys. Thus, a few Companions of the Holy Prophet migrated to Medina, and some of those who had migrated earlier to Abyssinia also moved to Medina. Hazrat Abu Bakr also started to prepare for migration to Medina around this time. When the Holy Prophet (SAW) came to know that Hazrat Abu Bakr intended to migrate to Medina, he told him to wait because he thought Hazrat Abu Bakr would also be given permission by God Almighty to migrate. Hazrat Abu Bakr said, "May my father and mother be sacrificed for you!"

"Do you really hope so?" the Holy Prophet (SAW) asked.

"Yes," Hazrat Abu Bakr responded. Thus, Hazrat Abu Bakr stopped making preparations for migration so that he could migrate along with the Holy Prophet. Furthermore, he made ready two camels in excellent conditions for travelling by keeping them at home for four months and feeding them leaves of the acacia tree.[39]

---

39 Ibn Sad's Al-Tabaqat Al-Kabir. Translation by Mo' in-ul Haq, Kitab Bhavan, New Delhi, India, vol. 1, p. 263-66; Sahih Bukhari, Manaqibul Ansar, Bab Hijratun Nabi WA Ashabihi Ilal. Medina.

The Covenants of Aqabah

———— ⚬⚬ ————

AT THE TIME of Hajj, while preaching, the Holy Prophet (SAW) met a group of people who had come fromMedina.. He conveyed to them the message of Islam and asked them to accept it. They accepted his invitation to Islam and became Muslims. When they returned to Medina, they conveyed the message of Islam to other members of their clan and urged them to accept the new faith. In 621 A.D., twelve people came from Medina at the time of Hajj. The Holy Prophet (SAW) conveyed the message of Islam to them and entered into agreement with them. The agreement occurred at a place called Aqabah. Thus, the agreement became known as The Covenant of Aqabah. According to this agreement, they were to worship one God and to obey His commandments. They further agreed not to steal, tell lies, commit adultery, kill their children, commit any evil act or disobey the Holy Prophet (SAW). The Holy Prophet sent Hazrat Mus'ab Ibn Umair with them to teach the Holy Qur'an and the teaching of Islam. Soon, the inhabitants of *Yathrib* started to accept Islam at his hand. The next year, Hazrat Mus'ab came to Mecca and gave the good news that many people belonging to both the *Aus* and the *Khazraj* tribes had entered the fold of Islam.[40] The next year, in 622 A.D., a second covenant was signed at Aqabah with the people from Medina. This time, 73 Muslims, out of which 62 belonged to the *Khazraj* tribe and 11 to the *Aus* tribe, came from Medina. They included two women, Nusaybah, the daughter of Ka'b, and Asma, the daughter of 'Amr. They were taught Islam by Hazrat Mus'ab and were full of faith and determination. They

---

40 Sirah Ibn Hisham, Biography of the Prophet, abridged by Abdus Salam Harun, p. 84-85, Al-Falah Foundation, Cairo, Egypt.

also met the Holy Prophet (SAW). During the night, they reached the appointed place and waited for the Holy Prophet (SAW). The Holy Prophet (SAW) came with Hazrat Abbas, who was the head of *Banu Hashim* and *Banu Abd Manaf* at that time. They swore allegiance to the Holy Prophet (SAW). This was basically an extension of the earlier agreement. In this agreement, they agreed to Protect and help the Holy Prophet under all circumstances as they protect their own family members. All the drawbacks of signing this agreement were fully explained to them. They listened to all the drawbacks of the agreement and agreed to bear all the adverse consequences wholeheartedly. This Covenant included clauses about wars they might have to face. Under all circumstances they would protect the Holy Prophet (SAW). The Holy Prophet told the party that he would go to Medina if they would hold Islam as dear to their hearts as they did with their wives and children. All members of the party unanimously said, "Yes, yes."

There were some conditions for the last pledge of Aqabah. Hazrat 'Ubad ibn as-Samit said, "We gave a pledge to the Holy Prophet (SAW) that we would listen and obey in time of plenty as well as in scarcity, under favorable and unfavorable circumstances, and that we would not prefer ourselves to other Muslims, and that we would not disgrace those who are in authority, and that we would speak the truth wherever we are, and that we would never fear the blame of the blamers."[41]

---

41 Sirah Ibn Hisham, Biography of the Prophet, abridged by Abdus Salam Harun, p. 85-89, Al-Flah Foundation. Cairo, Egypt.

Hijrah and a Plan to Assassinate the Holy Prophet (SAW)

FROM THAT POINT on, Hazrat Abu Bakr's household collected the necessary provisions for the journey and prepared themselves for upcoming migrations to Medina. Hazrat Abu Bakr's daughters, Asma[42] and Asma's younger sister by ten years, Ayesha, with their mother, Umm Ruman, were the first witnesses of this migration. They were the first to know the travel plans of their father and the Holy Prophet (SAW).

They followed the scheme closely. It included issues such as the route, the arrangement of guides, the places on the *Thawr* Mountain where they would hide and wait for three days until everything became calm, as well as information about who would visit them and what responsibilities they would take. When the unbelievers in Mecca heard that the community of the Holy Prophet (SAW) was migrating to Medina, they attempted to stop it from happening in a variety of ways. They kept watch of various routes to Medina and made some of them return. They physically barred the people from leaving. They kept watch on some believers and they divided some believers from their families. They did these things, but in the end they were not able to make the Muslims give up their migration plan. Eventually, the non-believers got together and made a final decision to kill the Holy Prophet (SAW). When the *Quraish* of Mecca realized they could not stop the tide of conversion or the migration of Muslims to Medina, they became furious, and when they could not catch and kill the Holy Prophet (SAW), they promised a

---

42 Asma was twenty-seven years old and married to Zubayr ibn Awwan.

reward of one hundred camels to anyone who could bring the travelers to them, dead or alive. Not surprisingly, the leaders of these pagans were Abu Jahl, Abu Lahab, Abu Sufyan and Utbah. All of them gathered at *Darun-Nadwah* and, after rejecting suggestions to imprison or banish Muhammad (SAW), they planned to assassinate him. God Al-Mighty informed the Holy Prophet about their hideous plans. When the Holy Prophet (SAW) learned of such evil intentions, he made a plan to leave the house at a time when the enemy would least expect it. The Holy Prophet told his plan to Hazrat Ali and made him cover himself with his mantle, and told him to sleep in his place on the bed.

Abu Jahl, who was one of the leaders of the Pagans, went angrily to Abu Bakr's home and asked where their father was. They said they did not know, but this was no excuse for Abu Jahl. Furious at the response, he slapped Asma who was six months pregnant at the time.[43]

Three months had passed and yet there was no news of Abu Bakr and the Holy Prophet (SAW). One day, Ayesha and Asma saw their brother Abdullah happily coming toward them. Instantly, they understood and ran to him in joy. Their father Abu Bakr had sent a letter which invited the family members to Medina.[44] The letter was brought by Zayd ibn Harith and Abu Rafi. Abdullah ibn Urayqit, the guide of the Holy migration, also joined these two in their journey. At the end of the letter written to his son, Abdullah was told by his father to take his sisters and mother to Medina.

The tasks of Abu Rafi and ibn Haritha were defined; it was the Holy Prophet (SAW) who had sent them. He had given them two camels and five hundred drachmas and assigned them to bring the Holy Prophet's household together with Abu Bakr 's family to Medina. But their path was full of surprises. When they left Mecca and went to Mina, where they came across Tallha ibn Ubaydullah who was migrating too, they found this man to be trustworthy; he was involved in the mission of the Holy Prophet

---

43 Abu Nuaym, Hilyatul Awliya 2:56; Ibn Hisham, Sira, 3:14.

44 It is stated that the Prophet took five drachmas as a debt from Abu Bakr. When they came to the place named Qadid, Zayd bought the three camels to be used during the journey. See Abu Nuaym, Hilyatul Awliya 9:227; Dhahabi, Siyar 2:152.

(SAW) since the first days. Hazrat Ayesha's camel became nervous, refusing to follow the caravan. This concerned Umm Ruman because the camel was carrying the future wife of the Prophet (SAW). The camel kept going the way it wanted to go. Umm Ruman, whose fear increased with every step the camel took, pulled her daughter away, fearing for their lives, and screamed:

"Give up its halter."

She hoped her advice would help where her actions could not. She hoped that the halter would get caught up in a branch while it dragged on the ground. Such would keep the camel from going further.[45]

And that is exactly what happened. The camel that Ayesha was riding, after she tossed the rope for it following her mother's advice, stopped before going much further. Its halter tangled itself in a branch, keeping the intractable camel from wandering away. Other members of the caravan ran over and made the camel follow the route. Everything was on the right track and their steps toward Medina were speeding up once more. Ayesha's sister Asma was pregnant and her labor pains increased gradually, and when they came to Quba, she had no more endurance left. Although they were very close to their destination, they had to stop. Asma then gave birth to a baby boy. They took the baby to the Holy Prophet (SAW) and he held the infant in his hands, naming him Abdullah.

---

45 Tabarani, al-Mujamu'l Kabir, 23:183 (296); Haythami, Majmutu'z Zawaid, 9:366; Tahmaz, As-Sayyidatu Ayesha, 27.

The Medina Pestilence Ended

———— ✿ ————

Their three-month long journey ended and the small caravan reached Medina. By this time, the Holy Prophet (SAW) was busy with the construction of his mosque, *Masjid al-Nabawi*, and some surrounding houses.

The Holy Prophet's two daughters, Fatima and Umm Kulthum, and his wife Saudah, daughter of Zama'a, took refuge in one of the houses. They reached Medina on the twelfth of *Rabi-ul-Awwal* in the fourteenth year of the prophet hood.

Their problems in Mecca seemed like they had ended. Yet, they were about to experience a scene that would overshadow their happiness. Emigrants, who were not accustomed to Medina's conditions, were suffering from an unfamiliar disease. Abu Bakr was one of them; he slept feverishly, awaiting a merciful hand that would guide him to health. They had fallen ill with the Medina pestilence. Some of them did not even have the energy to stand and for this reason they did their daily prayers, which they had never given up, while sitting down.

The Holy Prophet (SAW) turned to them and said:

"You should know that the one who prays while sitting gets half of the good deeds than the one who prays while standing."[46]

After getting permission from the Holy Prophet (SAW), Ayesha went to visit her father who was very sick. Bilal al-Habashi and Amir ibn Fuhayra were sharing the same room with Abu Bakr. Ayesha went toward her

---

46 Tirmidhi, Slat, 247; Ibn Maja, Slat, 141; Ahmad ibn Hanbal, Musnad, 2:192, 203, 214, ibn Kathir, Al-Bidaaya, 3:224.

father but her heart was deeply grieved by the scene that she saw. It was as if her father had gone and someone else had come in his place. The active man was now writhing due to a fever, and was sleeping unconsciously. She went closer to him and said:

"O, my dear father, how are you? How do you feel?"

Abu Bakr gave a meaningful look to his daughter whom he had been away from for months, and said:

"Every family is being dispossessed and death is closer than ones shoelaces."

Ayesha was shocked. Yes, death was always near, but life still continues for a sick man, she thought. Abu Bakr wanted to give advice about the language of sickness, first to Ayesha, then to everyone else. She thought, "Surely my father does not know what he is saying."

Amir ibn Fuhayra and Bilal al-Habashi were not fully conscious either. Homesickness had placed a permanent mark on their hearts, making their sickness in their new home worse.

Ayesha left them, feeling quite sad. She couldn't pretend nothing happened. Ayesha went to the Holy Prophet (SAW) and told him what she had seen and heard, for he had always solved every problem.

Ayesha said, "They are delirious due to high fevers and they are talking to themselves unconsciously."

The Holy Prophet (SAW) was very upset. He held his hands up to the sky and prayed against those who had caused this situation by persecuting Muslims for years:

"My Lord! I leave Utbah ibn Rabi'ah, Shayba ibn Rabi'ah and Umayya ibn Khalaf to you. As they made us leave our city and come to this place where sickness has spread, you too give them what they deserve!"

Then he turned and prayed for his society, saying:

> "My Lord! Make us love Medina as much as, or more than, you made us love Mecca. Make this city a land of health and grant abundance. Then take this disease and send it toward Jufa.[47]

The Holy Prophet (SAW) had a dream that night. He dreamed that a gloomy woman with a messy appearance was traveling from Medina toward Jufa. The dream meant that his prayers were accepted. After that time, the emigrants never again suffered from high fevers or any other sickness caused by Medina's environment. [48]

The Marriage of Ayesha

Ayesha, who had migrated with her family members, had naturally settled in her father's home. The house was in the *Bani Harith ibn Khazraj's* neighborhood. At that time, the Holy Prophet (SAW) was staying in the house of Khalid ibn Zayd as a guest.

In the meantime, Ayesha fell ill. Her body was weak and the conditions of the journey and Medina were difficult for her. She had lost a lot of weight and her hair started to fall out. Her mother, Umm Ruman, tried everything to make her daughter regain her health. Abu Bakr, who was well by this time, visited his sick daughter and stroked her head with compassion. He prayed to God for his daughter's health to return.

After a month of sickness, Ayesha started to feel better and she even gained some weight as a result of her mother's special attention.

By this time, the Holy Prophet (SAW) had been constructed and the civilization would grow around it as it started to flourish in Medina. Before his marriage to Ayesha, the Holy Prophet had a dream in which an angel had presented something to him which was wrapped in silk. The Holy Prophet (SAW) asked the angel what it was and he said it was his wife.

---

47 Bukhari, Fadailu'l Medina, 11, Fadilu's Sahaba, 75, Marda, 8.
48 Ibid.

When he removed the silken cover, he saw that it was Ayesha. In that dream, the angel Gabriel gave the message of God to marry Ayesha.

When Abu Bakr knew about this dream of the Prophet, he asked the Prophet:

"O, the Holy Prophet of God, is there a reason preventing you from marrying Ayesha?"

The Holy Prophet (SAW) responded:

"*Sadaq* [Dower]."

Sadaq was the money that needed to be given directly to the bride upon marriage. For Abu Bakr, no material value could be compared to the Holy Prophet (SAW). Abu Bakr offered to the Holy Prophet and gave the necessary amount to him. The Holy Prophet then gave the money directly to Ayesha without delay.[49] Previously, women's rights were disregarded completely. The money sent by the groom was customarily used by the bride's father and not the bride. Every passing day, the Holy Prophet's practices corrected wrongs and established Islamic principles.[50]

At the same time, Hazrat Abu Bakr initiated the construction of a one-bedroom house near the mosque, with his own money. Then a small room was finished for Ayesha. This room was so small that when the Holy Prophet (SAW) stood up, his head nearly touched the ceiling. And, it was unadorned. But spiritually, the room was large enough to enlighten the world. For the Holy Prophet (SAW), this meant the end of being a guest visitor. For seven months, he stayed in Khalid ibn Zayd's home.

Eight months had passed since *Hijrah*, and Umm Ruman invited the ladies of the *Ansar* (Helpers, the native of Medina Muslims) into

49 Tabarani, al-Mujamu'l Kabir, 23:25 (60); Abdilbarr, Istiab, 4:1937; Ibn Sa'd, Tabaqat, 8:63.
50 Tabarani, al-Mujamu 'l Kabir, 23:25 (60); Ibn Abdilbarr, Istiab, 4:1937, Ibn Sa'd, Tabaqat, 8:63.

her house. Umm Ruman bathed and dressed her daughter and then brought her before the ladies who said, "Your coming has been a blessing and is auspicious."

And another lady said, "May her good deeds and blessing be in abundance, and may her happiness increase."[51] After this, they adorned the bride. Shortly after, the Holy Prophet (SAW) came. There was nothing to offer him except a bowl of milk. The Holy Prophet took a sip of the milk and passed the bowl to Ayesha who was too shy to drink it. The ladies advised her not to refuse the gift of the Holy Prophet (SAW). Accordingly, she took a sip and put down the bowl. The Holy Prophet asked her to pass it on to her friends, but they declined and said that they did not feel thirsty. The Holy Prophet (SAW) again insisted and said:

"Lies and hunger cannot be together."

Hearing that, one of Ayesha friends, Asma bint Yazid, said:

"O, Messenger of God, if someone says, 'I do not want something,' when he does want it, is this considered a lie?"

The Holy Prophet (SAW) answered:

"Yes. While a lie is recorded as a lie, a little lie is recorded as a little lie.[52]

Choosing the month of *Shawwal* for the marriage was also meaningful since people thought marrying in that month was a cause of ill fortune. Many years later, Ayesha recommended marrying in the month of *Shawwal* in order to eliminate one of the remaining pre-Islamic superstations and said:

---

51 Bukhari, Fadailu's Sahaba, 73 (1423).
52 Ahmad ibn Hanbal, Musnad, 6:438 (27511).

"The Holy Prophet (SAW) and I were engaged in the month of *Shawwal* and we married in the month of *Shawwal*." This marriage changed a number of harmful customs.

Firstly, the Arabs did not give the hands of their daughters to those whom they called their brothers (though they were not actual brothers). This objection was raised by Abu Bakr, but the Holy Prophet (SAW) said that a brother in faith is not an actual blood brother to be placed in the prohibited category. Secondly, the Arabs considered the month of *Shawwal* as inauspicious for the departure of a bride. The marriage ceremony of Ayesha took place during this month, such starting to shatter the fear of such occurring. It was also an Arab custom to take flaming torches before the party, and the husband used to first meet his bride in a palanquin. All of these pagan customs were abolished during this marriage.[53]

It was a simple ceremony, bereft of ostentation or extravagance of any kind. According to Ayesha's narration, the Holy Prophet (SAW) sacrificed neither a camel nor a sheep that day. Instead, *Khazraj's* leader, Sa'd ibn Ubadh, brought a meal to the Prophet's home, such becoming their wedding dinner.

By this time, Ayesha was living in the Holy prophet's house and following the Holy Prophet (SAW) closely when he was apart from society and attained decisions for mankind. She was a woman of her time who helped things progress, a brilliant mind who followed incidents and understood them, a wonderful storyteller who explained what she had seen and heard in the home of the Holy Prophet (SAW). God's most beloved and merciful Prophet, who was sent as a guide to mankind, was followed closely by a talented person who opened doors that may have stayed shut, particularly about family life and issues related to women. He was a guide for all, male and female, and a gracious adviser everyone should follow.

---

53 Bukhari: Sahih, chapter: Marriage.

Her father's attitude after the wedding was in accordance with Qur'anic injunctions. In the Holy Qur'an, God stated the privilege of those who were married to the Prophet:

"O, wives of the Prophet! You are not like any of the other women (*Ahzab* 33:32). This specialty was a merit, but if unfulfilled, carried many risks. While great rewards could be gained for putting forth effort, sins could result in punishments twice as worse. Yet, the wives of God's Messenger were poised to fulfill their duties, and would die in purity and go to Paradise.

He heard that Mistah ibn Usasa had said negative things about Ayesha when she was slandered. Jews were disappointed and stopped sending money that he had formerly given to Mistah for his daily needs. A short time later, when the verse about giving charity to needy people in every circumstance, and about forgiving people by blinding yourself to their faults as being the most significant invitation for Holy forgiveness (Al-Nur 24:22) was revealed, he changed his attitude, made repentance and said:

"I swear to God I surely want the forgiveness of God."

He then started to give Mistah the money that was necessary for his daily bills.

Abu Bakr made an oath to himself:

"I swear to God I am going to continue to give this money without delay."[54]

---

54 Bukhari, Shahadat 15 (2518). Ayman, 17.

Ayesha's House

AYESHA WAS LIVING in her small house in the Holy Prophet's home around the Prophet's Mosque (known as Masjid-Nabvi). Hers was a small room, enough only for her needs. Her place was on the eastern side of the Holy Prophet's Mosque. Her door opened toward the west side of a courtyard. The Holy Prophet (SAW) used to enter through this door. The Mosque was like a garden of Ayesha's house. When the Prophet stayed for days at a time in the mosque (particularly during *Ramadan*), he put his head inside the house for Ayesha to comb his hair and would extend his hand for getting anything.[55]

This house was no longer than six to seven cubits; its walls were plastered with mud and had an arm's length of six or seven. It had a ceiling that anyone could touch. Its roof thatched with date palm leaves, was filled with wool and was covered by a blanket as protection against rainwater leaking down. The house's only wooden door was never closed to anyone.[56] A blanket served as a curtain. Adjacent to it was a top floor where the Holy Prophet (SAW) had spent a month during his absence from his wives.

Hazrat Ayesha (ra) explained the size of her room in these words:

"If the Messenger of God were performing prayer when I was sleeping, he used to touch my foot when he was about to prostrate. I would pull my legs in and only then the Messenger of God could perform his prostration."[57]

---

55 Bukhari: Sahih, chapter: Hadith and Bukhari, Itiqaf, 4 (1926).
56 Bukhari, Adab al-Mufrad, 1:272 (776).
57 Bukhari, Salat, 21 (375).

The household also comprised of matting, a divan, a bed, a leather pillow filled with fiber, a water pitcher, a bowl, a piece of leather hung to a hook, and a bucket to put water and dates in. In this abode, of a beacon of light and guidance, the owner didn't have the means to light even one lamp at night. Ayesha says that sometimes forty nights would pass without the lamp being lit.

Ayesha once said:

"At the time of the Messenger of God, we would spend forty nights in succession without a burning lamp or anything to give light."[58]

In those days, the oil used for lighting was also used for cooking. Ayesha said:

"Surely if we had an oil lamp, then we would have used it for cooking."[59]

Besides the Holy Prophet (SAW) and his wives, there was a maid servant called Barira. When the Holy Prophet (SAW) had only two wives, Saudah and Ayesha, he lived alternately with them. When the number of his wives increased, he stayed with Ayesha for two days out of a period of nine days.

The homes of other wives were not different than Ayesha's, except their doors opened outward and not into the mosque. Describing the simplicity of their rooms, Hasan said:

"I was visiting the wives of the Holy prophet (SAW) during the Caliphate of Uthman and when I raised my hand a little, I could reach the ceiling.[60]

---

58 Tayalisi, Musnad, 207 (1472).

59 Harith ibn Abi Usma, Musnadu'l Hadith, 2:996; Tabarani, al Mujamu'l Awsat. 8:360 (8872); Ishaq ibn Rahuya, Musnad, 3:1000.

60 Ibn SA'd, Tabaqat, 1:506; Tahmaz, as-Sayyidatu Ayesha.

When it was necessary to enlarge the Prophet's Mosque, and the deconstruction of Ayesha's house was discussed, famous *Imam* Saeed ibn Musyyab stood up and said to the Caliph, Walid ibn Abdulmalik:

> "I wish you didn't have to destroy this room and that people could be content with what kind of life he, the Messenger of God, was pleased with, even though he had in his hand a key to the world's treasures."[61]

According to Ayesha, the members of the Holy Prophet's (SAW's) household never ate wheat bread three days in a row[62] until he passed away and reached his Merciful Lord. Most of the time, they did not eat bread or bake food in the oven, or cook food over a fire, for a month at a time.[63]

Sometimes three full moons would pass and they would eat only dates and drink *Zamzam* (*Zamzam* is a well located within the Masjid-al-Haram in Makha, Saudi Arabia) water.[64] When they ate, they sat together at a table and ate from the same bowl. Sometimes their relatives shared in what they ate as well. The reality was that nothing changed in this house of felicity; neither the booty received in later years nor the gifts sent by his supporters altered the simplicity of his life. While he passed away (died) through the veil between this world and the hereafter, the Messenger of God remained the purest and most humble of people.

Regarding the day he passed away, Ayesha said:

> "On the day that the Messenger of God passed away, there was only a little barley on the shelf for food. There was nothing more. I ate it and thus managed to stand on my feet. But after weighing how little was left over, the blessing of abundance was lost and it finished soon."[65]

---

61 Ibn Sa'd, Tabaqat, 1:500, 8:167; Suyuti, ad-Durru'l Mansur, 7:554.
62 Bukhari, At'ima, 73 (5059); Muslim, 3: Zuhd, 20 (2970).
63 Ahmad ibn Hanbal, Musnad, 6:217.
64 Bukhari, Riqaq, 17 (6094).
65 Bukhari, Khums, 3 (2930).

For 50 years she lived as a widow; she distributed charity to others. She kept herself content. The Holy Prophet advised her, as related in the tradition:

"O, Ayesha. Save yourself from hellfire even if it means giving just half a date in charity, since it would both ease one's hunger and serve an enormous need."[66]

Once a poor and needy person came to Ayesha's home and she gave whatever she had as charity to her. Later, she asked the people around her to bring back the person that she helped. When the Messenger of God saw this, he interrupted and said:

"Give and do not calculate. This is so that calculation will not be made against you."[67]

The Greatness of Hazrat Ayesha

Ayesha's greatness and extraordinary ability had
been revealed during her childhood. Ayesha was like
all extraordinary people who display their talents
and intelligence when they are young, things they
are destined to reach in fullness in the future.

Further, her manners were sublime.

Ayesha had a fair complexion with a tinge of pink. She was beautiful and charming. In her youth she was slim, but in her later years she had become somewhat plump. As a measure of austerity, she only had one dress which she used to wash herself. She would color it occasionally in saffron. Once in a while, she put on ornaments including a necklace of beads of Yemen and gold rings, which she put on her fingers.

---

66 Ahmad ibn Hanbal, Musnad, 6:79 (24545).
67 Ibn Hibaan, Sahih, 8:151; Bayhaqi, Sunan, 2:38 (3436).

She was fond of games. Ayesha often got the girls her age in her neighborhood together and played with them. Early in her life, she revered the Holy Prophet and if he ever chanced to pass by their merriments, they would hide their games and conceal themselves. The Holy Prophet would then ask them to resume their play.

Ayesha was particularly fond of wings. The Prophet asked her what the artwork she had with her was and she replied that it was a horse. The Prophet said that horses do not have wings. But she explained that Sulaima's (Solomon's) horses had wings which elicited a smile from the Holy Prophet. This reply is an indication of her quick wittedness, acquaintance with religious traditions and sharpness of intellect. Ayesha's memory was impressive. She could explain any verse of the Holy Qur'an that was recited in her presence; she used to memorize it (the Qur'an).

Ayesha's Personality and Traits

———— ✶ ————

Ayesha spent the most impressionable period of her life in the company of the Holy Prophet (SAW) who had come to lead his people. Ayesha had reached the stage of development which is the pinnacle of spirituality. She was exalted in character, extremely sober, generous, content, pious and kind-hearted. Contentment is a virtue generally lacking in women. The Holy Prophet (SAW) once said that he had found a larger number of women in hell than men. He was asked to give a reason for it and he said, "This was due to their ungratefulness to their husbands."

But Ayesha was an exception. She spent her married life in austerity and privation. Expensive dress, costly ornaments, imposing residence, and delicious food she had never known at her husband's house, but she never complained. Spoils and tributes filling the state coffers were only to be distributed to the needy. After the death of the Holy Prophet (SAW), whenever she ate full meals, her tears would flow from her eyes. Whenever anyone asked about this, she said she cried because she remembered the days when the Holy Prophet (SAW) never ate a full meal. She did not have any child but she used to bring up poor children, particularly orphans, and would arrange their marriages when they came of age. Whenever ladies approached the Holy Prophet (SAW) with any request, she put their cases to him and helped them. She implicitly obeyed the Prophet and worked hard to please him. If his face ever showed any anxiety or sorrow, she grew restless. She gave all her attention to his friends and relatives. She once got angry with Abdullah bin Zubair and vowed never to meet him, but when the relatives of the Holy Prophet (SAW) put in a word for him, she relented.[68]

She never spoke poorly about any other person. The number of her narrations are in the thousands but there is not a word in them ridiculing anyone. A wife is not generally well disposed toward her co-wife but she paid tributes to them all.

The name of a man was mentioned during the course of a conversation. She observed that the man was not a good person. Somebody pointed out that the man died. She immediately began to pray for him. One from the audience asked her to account for her sudden change in behavior. She said that the Prophet stated that one should not speak ill of a dead person.

She did not like people to praise her but in spite of her modesty, she was self-respecting and high-minded. Small talk irritated her. She got angry with her nephew Abdullah bin Zubair when he said that her hands were too open and that whatever he gave her she would give away to the poor.

Imam Muslim's book of tradition [*Muslim Saheeh*], [Imam Muslim bin Al-Hajjaj] records that an Egyptian visited her and she asked him about the conduct of the governor of Egypt. The man said that his conduct was un-reproachable. She narrated a saying of the Prophet who had prayed, "O God, if he who is a keeper of my community transgresses against it, Thou be hard on him, but one who treats it well, Thou be benevolent towards him."

On another day, she heard God's Messenger praying:

"My Lord! Enable me to live as a poor man. Take my life as a poor man and resurrect me with poor people on the Day of Judgment."

Ayesha asked:

"Why, O Messenger of God?"

---

68 Bukhari: Sahih.

56

He replied:

> "Because the poor will enter heaven more than forty years before the rich. O Ayesha! Love the destitute and needy people and always keep them nearby, because on the Day of Resurrection God will exalt you."[69]

One day, the Holy Prophet (SAW) entered Ayesha's room and noticed that she was wearing silver rings. He asked in a displeased tone:

> "What are those, O Ayesha?"

Ayesha said:

> "I wore them to look nice for you, O Messenger of God."

In the same tone, he asked:

> "Then did you pay *Zakat* (prescribed purifying alms) for them?"

She knew that Zakat was not obligatory for such rings which were worth very little. But it seemed this was another situation in which being close to the Prophet meant being different from others. Deeply grieved, she replied in the negative.

After her reply, the Messenger of God, who wanted those around him to live an ascetic life like he, stated that this minor incident could be enough to lead her to Hell.[70]

The Holy Prophet (SAW) hit her very hard, depriving her of her senses. After that, Ayesha never kept any possession, no matter how small, without thinking about the afterlife. She gave away whatever she had. She learned that her most vital wealth, in this world and the Hereafter, was her

---

69 Tirmidhi, Zuhd, 37 (2352); Bayhaqi, Sunan, 7:12 (12931).
70 Abu Daud, Zakat, 3 (1565), Hakim, 1:547 (1437); Bayhaqi, Sunan, 4.

closeness to the Messenger of God; to lose this wealth was unthinkable for a woman so clever. One day, the Messenger of God asked her to do something after his death:

> "If you want to reunite with me, be in this world like a traveler! Keep away from being near the rich and do not think about buying a new dress before the present one becomes so old that it cannot be used anymore."[71]

The Messenger of God was a man of moderation who balanced the needs of this would and the next in the best possible way. Through the message that was revealed to him, God Almighty made him realize that he must continually seek rewards in the afterlife without forgetting his duties in this world (Qasas, 28:77). There is not a satisfiable degree of ambition in human nature; humans were created to remain dissatisfied with the world and everything in it. The resulting ambition is meant to be used to earn the Hereafter, for the Qur'an indicates that individuals who live for this world and do not consider the Hereafter will lose everything. God's Messenger was well aware of this and when he came home, he turned to his wives and encouraged them to embrace the same sensitivity:

> "If a man had two valleys filled with wealth, he would ask for a third. Only soil can fill up his mouth. Nevertheless, wealth is given to make daily worship possible and to fulfill the requirements of *zakat*. There is no doubt that God accepts the repentance of the people who ask."[72]

While his wives never considered their poverty as a problem, the Messenger of God, too, tried to be comforting about it. When he visited their rooms, he asked:

> "Is there anything to eat at home?"

---

71 Tirmidhi, Libas, 38 (1780); Hakim, Mustadrak, 1:547 (1437).
72 Ahmad ibn Hanbal, Musnad, 6:55, 5:218 (24321), 21956.

Upon learning that there was nothing for them to eat, he would say, "I am fasting" and direct himself again toward worship.[73]

The helpers of Medina sometimes tried to lessen the worries of the Holy Prophet (SAW) by sending him food and drink.[74] But he preferred to live in an ascetic way. What the Companions did, however, exemplifies a type of kindness that would be rewarded. The Holy Prophet (SAW) was sensitive; he never wanted to risk consuming even a tiny blessing in this world that belonged to the Hereafter. He only had a plain mattress filled with rough fibers. When a female Companion from the helpers noticed it, she presented Ayesha with a new mattress filled with wool as a gift. When the Holy Prophet (SAW) came home, he immediately asked:

"What is this, O Ayesha?"

Ayesha answered:

"O Prophet of God! A woman from the helpers saw your bed when she came to our home and sent this after going back to her house."

Although the kindness of the woman of Medina was nice, his preference of a plain bed was unwavering. He turned to Ayesha and said:

"Send it back. I swear to God, if I wanted, God would put mountains at my disposal and turn them into gold and silver.[75] Although silk and gold are allowed for women, the Holy Prophet (SAW) wanted the women closest to him to be more careful and asked them to remain distant even from everyday blessings.

---

73 Ahmad ibn Hanbal, Musnad, 6:49 (24266); Ibn Hibaan, Sahih, 8, 393 (3630).
74 Bukhari, Hiba, 1 (2428); Ibn Maja Zuhd, 10 (4145).
75 Bayhaqi, Shuabn 'l Iman, 2:173 (1478); Tabrani, MuJamn'l Awat, 6:141.

One day, he saw two golden bracelets on Ayesha's wrist and said:

"Do you want me to tell you what is better than these? If you take them off and buy two silver bracelets instead, and then color them with saffron, that would be better."[76]

The Holy Prophet (SAW) not only gave advice. He also followed the changes happening around him, closely. It was obvious from the simplicity he had chosen for himself, that he also wanted similar things for the people who were closest to him. He wanted them to keep away from anything that bounded them to this world or caused them to forget about the afterlife. When he and his army went to Tabuk, the meeting place in the Byzantine Empire, the most supreme kingdom of the era, Ayesha procured a piece of cloth that had a picture on it and hung it up as a curtain, on one side of the house. When the Holy Prophet (SAW) returned form Tabuk and saw it, he ordered:

"Take it away from my sight. Change it because when I enter the house and see it, I remember this world."[77]

After the battle of Khyber, the Holy Prophet (SAW) allocated eighty *wasks*[78] of dates and twenty *wasks* of barley to be given annually to his pure wives. But because of Ayesha's generosity and their large number of visitors, the amount allocated was not enough to meet the need.

On the day that God's Prophet (SAW) passed away, there was nothing more than half a bowl of barley in his home. And even that he had borrowed from a Jewish neighbor after giving the Messenger's armor as collateral.[79]

---

76 Nasai, Zina, 39 (5143).
77 Ibn Hibban, Sahih, 2: 447 (672); Nasai, Sunanu'l Kubra, 5:502 (9781).
78 One wask is the equivalent of 165 liters.
79 Bukhari, Jihad, 88 (2759), Tirmidhi, Buyu, 7 (1214).

Ayesha was living in this house under austere conditions. Her simplicity, showing that real pleasure and happiness does not stem from worldly wealth, was sustained meticulously after the passing of the Holy Prophet (SAW). Her room, tiny in terms of area, continued to serve the generation of Muslims, like a spring that flows into many rivers. In latter days, just like those when the Holy Prophet (SAW) was alive, Ayesha's first responsibility was to feed the hearts and minds of people.

The Austerity of Ayesha

———— ✿ ————

AFTER THE HOLY Prophet (SAW) passed away, Ayesha (ra) spent her nights in prayer and fasted regularly. Her devotion and routines were clear. She observed every detail of asceticism and piety. Qasim, one of her closest pupils and a leader of the following generation of Muslims, said that she fasted the whole year except during *Eid al-fitr* and *Eid al-Adha*[80] (the feast of Ramadan and the feast of Sacrifice respectively). Ayesha spent every day in repentance, asking for forgiveness from God, thinking of the previous day with remorse. Her example was the Holy Prophet (SAW) and she believed in her heart that it was necessary to use given opportunities to make progress every day.

Ayesha (ra) also thought that continuing every single act of worship was obligatory for her. She was quite determined no one was able to deter her. One day, when someone found her enthusiasm strange, Ayesha said:

> "If my father rose from the grave and told me not to do even one supererogatory prayer that I had begun to perform in the time of God's Messenger, I still would not quiet."[81]

Ayesha barely met her own needs, but she still gave whatever she had to the needy.

One day, Jabir went to visit her. She wore a worn-out dress, parts covered in patches. Wanting to fulfill her responsibility, Jabir said:

> "Why don't you wear another dress?"

---

80 Ibn Jawzi, Sifatu's Safwa, 2:31.
81 Ibn Jawzi, Sitatu's Safwa, 2:31.

62

As mother of believers, Ayesha did not think like Jabir, and said:

"One day, the Messenger of God said, 'If you seek a reunion with me, do not change your dress until it becomes unusable, and do not think about what you need more than a month in advance.' Tell me, do you think I should change what he ordered me to do until the time I meet with him again?"[82]

In her life history, recorded by various historians, it is told that she was not content and that whenever she (ra) saw or heard about the wrenching state of the poor, she gave whatever she had to such people, or sold something of some worth at the market and sent the money from such transactions to the needy. While she was giving, she never thought about her own needs, but always tried to lessen the troubles of others. One day, she literally gave everything she had to the poor and had no more money for that day. She still did not quit giving. She sold some of her belongings at the market and without hesitation gave that money as charity. In the evening, the time for her to break her fast, she only had a piece of barley bread to eat.

Hazrat Ayesha's intentional humility represented a singular type of lifestyle for the people around her and she continued to live the same way after the Holy Prophet (SAW) passed away. Genuine freewill is that of a person who is powerful and has limitless opportunities. It was this willpower that Ayesha, until the end of her life, chose to carry in the same humble way she shared with the Holy Prophet (SAW), with delicacy and sensitivity.

Hazrat Ayesha could have lived however she wanted to. Yet, she chose to follow the Holy Prophet's advice, and this choice led to her other choice to live humbly, just as he had.

Surely this was a voluntary choice. Hazrat Ayesha was one of the closest people to the Holy Prophet (SAW), yet their closeness was different to others. Even after his death, Ayesha (ra) followed his ways though she had many opportunities to do otherwise. But she never changed the lifestyle they had shared. Her wealth was in her Muslim asceticism and piety.

---

82 Ahmad Ibn Hanbal, Musnad, 6:138 (25122).

Ayesha's Humility and Asceticism

HAZRAT AYESHA DID not spend her time uselessly. She leaned the golden rule of life from the Holy Prophet (SAW) and did not meddle in any issues other than those which had religious decrees, and did not spend time nagging on the mistakes of others. It is impossible to find a distorted or negative expression within the hundreds of thousands of Hadith that she narrated. She warned those who abused others, and did not shy away from pointing out what was clearly wrong. When Hassan Ibn Thabit, charged for violating a religious law, started to condemn himself, Ayesha consoled the old Companion by saying:

"Yet you are not as bad a person as you are saying."[83]

She comforted him even though Hassan hurt her years ago with similar statements. Ayesha did not return slander and did not hold grudges. Until her death, she was an example of forgiveness toward those who openly worked against her. One day, when her nephew and student, Urwa, denounced Hassan Ibn Thabit, Ayesha became angry and said:

"Do not condemn him. He was an important man who defended the Messenger of God."[84]

When people around her engaged in gossip or backbiting, particularly about someone who was deceased, Ayesha flew into a rage and then

---

83 Malik, Muwatta, Haj, 43 (836).
84 Bukhari, Maghazi, 32 (3915).

prayed to God for the forgiveness of the person that had been talked about. Ayesha said:

"The Messenger of God said, 'only speak well of your dead.'"

She practiced her religion precisely. One day, while walking on a road, she heard a bell ring and stayed where she was. The ringing of a bell was an unwelcome sound and so she tried to avoid it. A little while later, she heard it behind her and began to walk faster to escape the sound disliked by God's Messenger.[85]

On another day, she heard that the orphans staying with her in her home had brought a game similar to backgammon with them. She became angry and sent a message, saying:

"Either you throw it out or I will come and take you out."[86]

Hazrat Ayesha even felt anxious about her dreams. She never thought they were meaningless and thought that perhaps they contained important messages about the interpretation of Hadith. A single nightmare either made her give *sadaqa* (voluntary charity) or emancipate a slave the next day.[87]

She habitually used any small excuse to emancipate a slave. Once, she gave in to the demands of others and broke a certain oath. That is, she emancipated forty slaves as expiation, instead of one, but she still did not forgive herself and shed tears over it for the rest of her life. Upon realizing that her female slave was of the Tamim tribe, a tribe that God's Messenger said descended from the linage of the Prophet Ishmael, Ayesha gave the slave freedom.[88]

---

85 Ahmad Ibn Hanbal, Musnad, 6:152 (25229).
86 Bukhari, Adabu'l Mufrad, 1:435 (1274).
87 Haythami, Majmuatu'z Zawaid, 1:484 (419).
88 Bukhari, Itq, 13 (2405).

Ayesha once fell ill and people told a man from the Zatt tribe about the illness because said man had some knowledge of it. Once at Ayesha's house, the man spoke about what the jinn told him:

"They are saying a female slave with a baby in her arms has performed witchcraft on a woman. They're even saying that the baby has urinated on the slave woman."

Some went, found the slave and brought her to the man. Ayesha knew her and asked:

"Did you cast a spell on me?"

The slave had no choice but to confess because apparently everyone knew what had happened. She said yes.
Then Ayesha asked:

"Why did you do that?
"In order to be set free," the slave girl said.

The slave related her own freedom to the life of Ayesha, declaring that she would be free on the day that Ayesha died.
Ayesha became angry and said:

"I swear to God that I will never set her free."

So, Ayesha sold her and bought a new slave, then setting the new slave free.[89] There was no one who did not know of her unwavering resolve on this issue. Ayesha emancipated a total of sixty-seven slaves.[90] She spoke to everyone and did not look down on anyone. One day, she gave a small bag of bread to a man who asked for food. After he had gone, an-

---

89 Bukhari, Adabu'l Mufrad, 1:68 (162).
90 San'ani, Subulu's Salam, 4:139.

other man, who was destitute and who appeared to be mentally ill, came. Ayesha called for him to be closer to her and offered him her own food. When the man had satisfied his hunger and left, Ayesha was asked why she behaved this way, and she answered:

"How could I act differently when the Messenger of God said, 'Treat people in accordance with their condition?'"[91]

Despite every hardship she experienced, Ayesha lived frugally and never thought of obligating someone to show her kindness she rendered. She hesitated to waste anything. Ayesha wanted the people around her to exercise the same discipline. She never complained about her ascetic life because she had chosen it out of her own free will and lived a life that centered on the Hereafter.

This choice was not a result of poverty, because even in times of plenty, she chose the same lifestyle. When Hazrat Umar sent a bag of gold to her, she could not hold back her tears and immediately gave away the gold to those around her. She still did not think she had done enough so she prayed to God that she should never be subjected to such a blessing again. [92]

A special student of hers, Ayesha bint Talha, said:

"Those of us who were close to her based on our position, young and old, came from all around and wrote letters and brought armfuls of gifts. I would present them to her, saying, 'O dear aunty! This is so and-so's letter and this is her gift.' And she would tell me, 'O my dear girl! Write a letter and send a gift in response. If you do not have a gift, I will give it to you.' And then she would give me a gift to send."[93]

Ayesha had amazing willpower. Neither the people around her nor the changing times were able to change her. She never gave up treating

---

91 Abu Daud, Adab, 23 (4842).
92 Hakim, Mustadrak, 4:9 (6725).
93 Bukhari, Adabu'l Mufrad, 1:382 (1118).

others justly, even those who hurt her or gossiped about her. She never based her actions on the wrong doings of others.[94]

Ayesha had only one dress. When it was dirty, she washed and dried it and then wore it again. Such was a general practice among the wives of the Holy Prophet (SAW).[95] But, during her first years in Medina, when she first began to live in the house of felicity with Holy Prophet (SAW), Ayesha owned a high-quality garment worth five drachmas. She made Median women happy by lending it to them for weddings or special occasions, in rotation.[96]

She never thought to buy a new dress until the one she wore became completely worn-out.

Her nephew Urwah confirmed:

"Ayesha did not replace the garment that she wore with a new one until the one she had was threadbare and covered in patches."

In those days, many people said to her:

"God gave you much. Why do you not benefit from it?"

Ayesha gave a short and direct answer when this question was asked:

"The new will not fit the ones who are not created for the new."[97] Ayesha said she would not give up her habit. When a gift was sent to her, Ayesha remembered the plain lifestyle of the Holy Prophet (SAW) and his statements on the issue. As a result, she would shed tears and allocate the gift to the needy. During his Caliphate, Muawiyya sent Ayesha garments, silver and other things that she could use. When she saw them, she started to weep and said:

---

94 Muslim, Imara, 19 (1829).
95 Bukhari, Hayd, 11 (306).
96 Bukhari, Hiba, 32 (2485).
97 Bukhari, Adabu'l Mufrad, 1:166.

"The Messenger of God was not able to have any of these."

Ayesha separated them into parts and gave them to needy people. By night time, nothing of what the Caliph had sent remained in her possession.[98]

One day, baskets full of grapes were brought to her as a gift. Ayesha Immediately started to give them to the poor. The female slave who helped with her house work accompanied her. By nightfall, the woman came over to her with some grapes. Ayesha was surprised because she thought that she had given away all the grapes. Thus Ayesha asked:

"What is this?"

The slave did not know what to say. She had kept the grapes without Ayesha's knowledge in order to offer her them at night.

Ayesha scolded her and said, "One bunch, huh?"

Her attitude surprised the slave, who then understood the sensitivity of her mistress. Ayesha added:

"I swear to God that I will neither touch nor eat it." Then she went away.[99]

Ayesha continued to give away gifts brought to her throughout her life, always helping the poor. Ayesha knew that when she gave even a little, she would receive abundant blessings from God. Who has infinite treasures to bestow? Ayesha never thought about her own benefit. Caring for the destitute, she hoped to supply their needs. There was nothing that pleased her more than a smile from a needy person.

At times when she had no money, Ayesha sold her belongings and gave the money as charity. Ayesha's nephew Abdullah ibn Zubayr said:

---

98 Abu Nuaym, Hilyatu'l Awliya, 2:48.
99 Ibid.

"I swear to God, either our beloved mother Ayesha will give up her attitude or I will stop her."

Someone told Ayesha what Abdullah ibn Zubayr said, causing her to ask:

"Did he really say this?"

Then she said:

"I swear not to talk with ibn Zubayr until the afterlife."

So, she did not speak to him. This hurt Abdullah ibn Zubayr and he looked for a solution to restore their past relationship. Although he came to Ayesha's door many times, he did not hear anything other than:

"No! I swear that I will not go back to this issue. I won't give up my promise."

The passing of time hurt his conscience. Abdullah asked two leaders, Miswar ibn Mahrama and Abdurrahman ibn Abd al-Aswad, to intercede on his behalf. It was a duty for every believer to make peace between two believers.

Thus, the two leaders stated above went to Ayesha's door and said:

"May God's mercy and blessings be upon you. Are we allowed to come inside?"

Abdullah ibn Zubayr was with them but the two did not say that.
A voice from inside was heard:

"Welcome. Come."

They were happy and said:

"All of us?"

"Yes, all of you."

Their plan got Abdullah ibn Zubayr inside. As soon as he entered, he begged her for forgiveness from the other side of the curtain. Miswar ibn Mahrama and Abdurrahman ibn Abd al-Aswad supported him and asked for Ayesha to forgive him. Despite all their pleading, Ayesha did not change her mind and forgive Abdullah, in tears at this point. The two intercessors, as part of their plan, said:

"You know that the Messenger of God said it is not allowed for one Muslim to stay angry at another Muslim for more than three days."

Then Ayesha started to cry, remembering the statement of the Holy Prophet (SAW), and replied:

"But I swore an oath, and you know that swearing an oath is serious."

Her heart was softening and she had no option but to follow the Messenger of God's statement. She did not reject the requests of the intercessors and accepted Abdullah ibn Zubayr's apology. From then on, she spoke to him. But, this cost Ayesha forty slaves because she had broken an oath. Ayesha cried when she remembered her oath and what she had experienced. The people witnessed that her scarf became wet with her tears.[100]

One day during the lifetime of the Holy Prophet (SAW), a woman came to Ayesha with her two daughters in her arms. It was apparent that they were needy and that their life was full of hardships. Ayesha did not have much in her home but it was her nature to be content with what she had and not to worry about what she did not have. She brought them three dates from her home. The mother gave two of the dates to her daughters.

---

100 Bukhari, Adab, 62, (5725).

The children, who had long felt the absence of food, ate the dates with pleasure. Their mother watched them with grief as Ayesha looked on. When the children finished their dates, their eyes focused on the remaining date in their mother's hand. With maternal love, she divided the date that she had kept for herself into two and gave half of the date to each daughter. They ate happily. Nothing remained for the mother who was satisfied with her daughters' joy, daughters whose eyes were shining.

As soon as the Messenger of God came home, Ayesha shared the incident with him. She was touched and expressed the mother's sacrifice. The Holy Prophet (SAW) said the following good news:

"For what she did, God bestowed heaven to that woman or saved her from hell."[101]

Most of the time, Ayesha's eyes were filled with tears and her heart was delicate. She was not able to keep herself from crying and wept until her tears dried up. She always sobbed when she did not do her duty or when she was not able to keep her word, and paid atonement for such. Ayesha spent her days and nights in lamentation when she was treated unjustly.

But her tears were not restricted to herself. Disappointed with Muslim society, she wept for future generations as well. One day, she remembered the Antichrist (Dajjal) and started to weep, thinking of the troubles and disasters that Muslims would experience. Ayesha cried so fervently that she did not realize that God's Messenger had come to her side. He asked her:

"Why are you crying?"

Ayesha turned to God's Messenger and said sadly:

"O Messenger of God! I remembered the Antichrist."[102]

---

101 Ahmad ibn Hanbal, Musnad, 6:92 (246550).
102 Ahmad ibn Hanbal, Musnad, 6:75 (24511).

Ayesha's Generosity

---❦---

Hazrat Ayesha (ra) learned from the Holy Prophet (SAW) to live for others. Whenever she saw needy people, she forgot her needs and gave whatever she had to them. She knew the Hadith well and said:

"Save yourself from the hell-fire even by giving half a date in charity."[103]

Ayesha was also the daughter of Abu Bakr, the most generous of men. Being generous was a general characteristic of her family members. When Ayesha's nephew Abdullah ibn Zubayr described the characteristics of his mother Asma and his aunt Ayesha, he said that they were like competitors when it came to giving charity.[104] "When Ayesha had nothing to give, she sometimes borrowed from someone else and gave it as charity."

Ayesha once referred to a Hadith, saying:

"Any servant of God, who had the intention and effort to repay his debt, will be given help by God Almighty."[105]

Her nephew Urwah said:

"I witnessed that she gave seven thousand drachmas of charity while she was wearing a patched garment."[106]

---

103 Bukhari, Zakat, 8, 9 (1351).
104 Bukhari, Adabu'l Mufrad, 1:106 (280).
105 Ahmad ibn Hanbal, Musnad, 6:99 (24723); Hakim, Mustadrak, 2:26 (2202).
106 Ibn SA'd Tabaqat, 8:67, Dhahabi, Siyar, 2:187.

Ayesha sold her house to Muawiyya for one hundred and eighty thousand or two hundred thousand drachmas. Before getting up from where she sat, she had given everything to the poor, with nothing remaining for herself.[107]

A needy person once came to her and asked for a bite of food. Ayesha had some grapes and asked a woman nearby to give them to the needy person at the door. The woman looked at her strangely, implying that Ayesha needed the grapes for herself. Ayesha reminded her that even the tiniest of good deeds will be rewarded:

"Why are you hesitating? Do you know how many atoms are in this grape?"[108]

She was alluding to the verse that says, "Whoever does an atom's weight of good will see it" (Zilzal, 99:7).

One day, a needy woman with two daughters came to Ayesha and asked for something to eat. There was nothing. Ayesha looked everywhere but found only one date. She gave it to the woman who looked embarrassed. Then her eyes were caught by the woman's reaction. The woman divided the date into two and gave half to each of her daughters. Ayesha was reminded of the mother who had divided her own share for her daughters.

Ayesha was deeply moved by what she saw. After the woman left, she continued to think about her. When the Messenger of God came home, Ayesha shared the story with him. The Messenger of God was also affected and said:

"There is no doubt that such daughters will be a shield against Hellfire for those who treat them kindly."[109]

---

107 Ibn SA'd Tabaqat, 8:165, Abu Nuaym, Hilyatu'l Awliya, 2:47, 48.
108 Malik, Muwatta, 2:997 (1811).
109 Bukhari, Adabu'l Mufrad, 1:59 (132).

Another day, a poor woman came to Ayesha who searched everywhere and found only a piece of bread. It was the bread she was going to break her fast with but Ayesha gave it to the woman without hesitating. Ayesha's housekeeper tried to warn her:

"But there is nothing for you to break your fast with."

Still, Ayesha ordered:

"Give the bread to the woman."

The housekeeper had no choice but to give it to her. Close to sunset, some gifts of lamb meat and bread were brought to Ayesha. God blesses those who give for his sake. When it was time to break the fast, Ayesha joked with the housekeeper:

"Take this and eat. It is better than your dried bread."[110]

Something similar happened when one of her nephews, Abdullah ibn Zubayr, brought gifts valued at one hundred thousand drachmas and saw her giving it all away. It was a day of fasting for Ayesha. She gave until nothing remained. When it was sunset, Ayesha asked her housekeeper, Umm Dharr:

"O Umm Dharr. Why don't you bring something for us to break our fast?"

Umm Dharr brought some olive oil and bread, saying:

"O mother of the believers, why didn't you keep something, even just one drachma, from what you gave away so that we could buy some meat?"

---

110 Malik, Muwatta, 2:997 (1819).

In the housekeeper's words, there was embarrassment about being unable to set a good table for Ayesha and bewilderment that she never benefitted from so many opportunities. Ayesha understood and said gently:

"Do not pressure me. If I had remembered at that time, I might have done that."[111]

Ayesha knew that she would benefit from what she gave away and so she gave endlessly. She learned this from God's Messenger.

One day, they scarified an animal and Ayesha gave away meat from the entire animal until only its shoulder blade remained in her hands.

When the Messenger of God came home, he asked:

"What did you do with scarified animal? What remains for us?"
"I distributed all of it. Only its shoulder blade remains," Ayesha replied.

What Ayesha did was what the Messenger of God expected her to do because God the Almighty had promised that He would increase the value of anything given for His sake. The goodness inherent in giving for charity for God's sake will never be removed and is permanent. The Messenger of God said, "No, dear Ayesha. On the contrary, every part of it except its shoulder blade remains as an eternal reward."

---

111 Ibn Sa'd, Tabaqat, 8:67; Dhahabi, Siyar, 2:187.

Ayesha's Education and Upbringing

LITERACY AMONG ARAB men, not to mention Arab women, was rare. At the time of the advent of Islam, only seventeen people were literate in the whole clan of the *Quraish*. Among them, only one was a woman, Shafaa, daughter of Abdullah Adwiya. It is significant that Islam ushered in an era of education and literacy along with the propagation of Faith. The terms of the ransom of the prisoners of the battle of Badr, who were poor, was that each prisoner should teach ten Muslim children. One hundred Companions of Shafaa were taught to read and write. Among the wives of the Holy Prophet (SAW), Hafsa and Umm Salama were literate, Hafsa having learned from Shafaa bint Abdullah under the direction of the Holy Prophet (SAW). Many men had come into personal contact with the Holy Prophet (SAW) and the Prophet's majestic company had inspired them to un-precedented heights of spiritually. Such opportunities were not previously available to women. His wives came into close personal contact with him and obtained the benefit of learning which gradually spread far and wide. A large number of women were taught by prophet's wives and these women had served in many radiating centers. Except for Ayesha, all the wives of the Holy Prophet (SAW) were widows. Ayesha alone enjoyed the advantage of being brought up under the benevolent and inspiring care of the Holy Prophet. During this period of training and upbringing, God's design took her far away from what could be only a Pagan surrounding and brought her to the abode to flourish and acquire radiance like a well-cut gem, so she could see light and bring guidance to Muslim women.

Among the *Quraish*, Abu Bakr was an expert in genealogy and poetry. Ayesha acquired these arts as her family inheritance, but her real upbringing began after her marriage. She started learning to read and write and soon was able to read the Qur'an. Reading and writing are, however, only external manifestations of education. The standard of real learning and education is much higher. It encompasses within its ambit, development of human values, perfection of conduct and knowledge of essentials of religion, the sacred law, the commands and injunctions of the Prophet, and the knowledge of the Word of God. Ayesha was taught all of this and acquired a high degree of proficiency in terms of following such teachings. Apart from religious learning, she acquired knowledge of history and literature. She learned a little bit about medicine too. She learned history and literature from her father, and medicine from numerous physicians of Arabia who visited the Holy Prophet (SAW). Due to the teaching of these physicians, she became acquainted with the descriptions of various diseases and their remedies.

The Holy Prophet (SAW) used to deliver a sermon daily, near the house of Ayesha, where she became an avid listener of such sermons. Whenever she was unable to understand something, she consulted the Holy Prophet after his lectures. She used to give weekly lectures to ladies who would assemble at her house to hear her lectures. Day and night, she used to hear the precepts of religion from the Holy Prophet and then pose problems before the Holy Prophet (SAW), wanting a solution to such problems and not content until the matter became clear to her. Once, the Holy Prophet (SAW) said, "Whosoever was subject to accounting in the Hereafter, chastisement was his lot."

Ayesha said that God states, "And he in whose right hand is given his record, shall have an easy reckoning" (Holy Quran Ch. 84: Verse 10-11). The Holy Prophet explained that this relates to the presentation of accounts, but if anybody was subjected to cross examination and searching questions, he was doomed. Once she said to the Prophet that, "God states, 'Think of the day when the Earth shall be given a different form and the Heavens also, when men shall appear before God, the One, the Overpowering' (Ch. 14:48). But, in another verse He says, 'On the day of

Resurrection, the whole earth shall appear but a handful for Him, and the entire heavens shall seem lying folded together in His right Hand' (Ch.39: 67). Where would mankind be in the absence of earth or heavens?"

The Prophet replied, "On the road in-between."

During the lecture, the Prophet said, "On the Day of Resurrection, people will arise naked from their graves."

Ayesha asked, "O Prophet! If men and women will be raised together, will their glance not waver in that case?"

The Holy prophet replied, "It will be so terrible that no one will have thought about another."

Ayesha then enquired, "Will anyone remember others on that Day?"

The Holy Prophet answered, "Not on three occasions: when people's actions will be weighed, when their scroll will be handed over to them and when Hell will roar that it is reserved for three types of men."

She wanted to ask if the righteous deeds of infidels and polytheists will be recompensed. Abdullah bin Jad'aan, for example, was a kind hearted and well-behaved polytheist of Mecca who had called a congregation of the *Quraish* to put down lawlessness and bloodshed. The Holy Prophet (SAW) participated in that meeting. Ayesha enquired, "O Prophet. During the days of ignorance, Abdullah bin Jad'aan used to treat the people well and feed the poor. Will his generosity merit any reward?"

The Holy Prophet (SAW) replied, "No, Ayesha. He has never begged God to forgive his sins and shortcomings on the Day of Judgment."[112]

For marriage, the consent of the girl is also necessary but maidens are too modest to give it. Ayesha asked the Holy Prophet (SAW), "Shall the consent of the bride be asked for before marriage?" When the Holy Prophet (SAW) answered in the affirmative, she said, "But the brides, due to their shyness, keep quiet when the question is asked."

The Holy Prophet (SAW) said, "Their silence is to be reckoned as their consent." In Islam, neighbors have great rights. But, if one has two close neighbors, then who shall be given preference? Ayesha

112 Musnad: Ayesha.

posed this question before the Holy Prophet (SAW), who answered, "The one whose door is nearer."[113]

Once, a foster uncle of Ayesha came to meet her, but Ayesha did not meet him, saying, "If I have been sucking by a woman, what have I to do with the brother of her husband?"

When the Holy Prophet (SAW) came, she asked him about what was said above, and he said, "He is your uncle, so call him in."

There is a verse of the Holy Qur'an that says, "And who give [to others] what they give, sincerely believing that they who hasten after good… (Ch. 23:60). Ayesha had doubts that it would cover thieves, drunkards and evil-doers who do not fear God. The Holy Prophet (SAW) stated that it only covers the cases of those who observe prayers, properly fast and fear God.[114]

The Holy Prophet (SAW) once said, "Whoso likes to meet his Lord, God also likes to meet him."

Ayesha said, "None of us like to meet death."

The Holy Prophet (SAW) said that this was not the meaning of the verse: "It means that when a believer hears of the mercy and good pleasure of God and Paradise, his heart yearns to meet Him. God is also eager to meet him. And when an infidel hears about God's chastisement and displeasure, he abhors meeting Him and God detests him."[115]

Scores of questions and discussions on the part of Ayesha are noted in the book of Hadith which formed an integral part of her education and training.

There was a man who wanted an audience with the Holy Prophet (SAW). The Holy Prophet permitted that man to come in even though he knew the man was wicked. The Holy Prophet (SAW) talked to him gently and gave him his full attention. When the man left, Ayesha asked the Prophet why such courteous treatment was given to him when it was well known that he was an evil man. "The worst man is

---

113 Ahmad: Musnad, page 175.
114 Bukhari: Sahih, page 159.
115 Tirmizi: Al-Jam'I, book of burials.

he who is shunned by people due to his uncivil behavior,"[116] was the response given by the Prophet.

On one occasion, the Holy Prophet (SAW) said, "Exercise moderation, endear yourself to people and give them tidings that their deeds [alone] will not take them to Paradise." This seemed strange to Ayesha since she thought that sinless people will be exempted.

She asked, "O Prophet, will not your acts ensure admission into paradise?"

The Prophet replied, "Not even me, except if God encompasses me in His mercy and forgiveness."[117]

Once, the Holy Prophet wanted to sleep without having said his prayers. Ayesha reminded him about his need to pray. The Holy Prophet (SAW) said, "My eyes sleep but not my heart."[118] Apparently, Ayesha's remark was indiscreet, but if she had not been vigilant, the community might have remained ignorant of the reality of Prophethood.

Beside these questions and discussions, the Prophet used to keep an eye on what Ayesha did, and if she ever erred, he would correct her. A few Jews came to the Prophet, and instead of saying As Salam Alaika (mercy on you), they said, "AS-Sam alaika [death be upon you]."

The Holy Prophet (SAW) replied by saying, "WA alaikum [on you also]."

But Ayesha, who was listening, could not control herself and said, "Death and curse on you." The Holy Prophet (SAW) advised her to show gentleness, for God loves gentle treatment to all.

Once, someone had stolen something belonging to Ayesha. In her rage, she cursed the thief. The Holy Prophet (SAW) remarked, "By cursing, do not lessen your reward and the other man's sin." Ayesha was accompanying the Prophet in a journey on a camel's back. The camel became restless and Ayesha cursed it. The Holy Prophet (SAW) sent the camel back, saying, "An accursed thing cannot go with him."[119]

---

116   Bukhari: Sahih-Chapter: Backbiting.
117   Bukhari: Sahih-babul Qasd.
118   Ahmad: Musnad, page 517.
119   Ahmad: Musnad, page 517.

Generally, people, and particularly women, do not think about small sins. The Holy Prophet (SAW) told Ayesha, "Abstain even from small sins, for they must also be accounted for." During the course of a conversation, Ayesha described a woman as short. The Holy Prophet (SAW) interrupted her and said that her comment amounted to back biting.[120]

Safiya, another wife of the Holy Prophet (SAW), was somewhat short, and Ayesha referred to such during a conversation. The Holy Prophet (SAW) remarked, "If you are to mix up the water of an ocean with what you have said, it will acquire a sour taste." Ayesha said that she had only narrated a fact. The Holy Prophet (SAW) said that he would not say such a thing even for all the treasures of this world. A beggar once arrived at the Prophet's door, after Ayesha hinted for the beggar to do so. A maid servant took a small quantity of something, to give to the beggar. The Holy prophet (SAW) said, "Do not count alms before giving, or else God will also give you restricted measure."[121] On another occasion he said, "O Ayesha, even if you have a bit of a date, do not refuse a beggar. By giving it, save yourself from the fire of Hell. A hungry stomach will welcome anything."[122]

Once the Prophet prayed, "O God, keep me needy in this world. Grant me death in that state and raise me among the poor on the Day of resurrection." Ayesha asked what the reason for such a prayer was. The Holy Prophet said, "The needy and the poor will enter Paradise forty years ahead of the rich. O Ayesha! Do not refuse a beggar. Even you have only a date to offer. Love the poor and give them a place near you."[123] Beside these counsels relating to good behavior, the Holy Prophet (SAW) used to teach her prayers, supplications and other spiritual matters. She listened to them avidly and observed them all scrupulously.

---

120 Ahmad: Musnad, page 170.
121 Abu Daud: Sunnah Chapter: Manners.
122 Ahmad: Musnad, Ayesha.
123 Tirmizi: Jam'l, chapter: Righteousness.

Ayesha Inside the Home of the Holy Prophet

THE HOUSE OF the Holy Prophet (SAW) was one of felicity, a place of serenity and reciprocal love. In that house, there was a tenacious bond constructed on sacrifices. The Holy Prophet (SAW) followed the precepts of the Holy Qur'an. Quranic teaching described husbands and wives as a perpetual source of comfort and consolation to each other:

> "And one of His signs is that He hath created for you mates of your own kind that ye may find comfort in their company, and hath put between you love and tenderness" (Ch. 30:21).

The married life of Hazrat Ayesha (ra) is a mirror of the Holy Prophet's behavior towrd his wives. In one of the narrations, he says, "The best among you are those who treat their wives well, and I am the kindest towards my wives." Relationships did not exist merely in the present and future, but were considered the journey toward eternal life.

In her home, Ayesha scarified herself to fulfill every wish of God's Messenger. Hers was absolute obedience. She was only satisfied in fulfilling his wishes, and at the same time, tried to anticipate his feelings before he stated them. She continued to do this even after his death, until her last breath. Ayesha evaluated her every step before she took it and made decisions according to what she knew of him. One day, she bought a pillow for the Prophet to sit on. Yet she did not know his opinion about its decorative painting, or perhaps the painting on the pillow did not grab her attention. But everything that happened had a purpose. Through this incident, an unknown fact would be revealed and his thoughts on the issue would be clarified. When the Messenger of God arrived, he stayed in front of the door and did not enter. The mother of believers became anxious and asked immediately:

"O Messenger of God! I repent God, and ask forgiveness from His Messenger. Did I commit a sin?"

The tone of her voice indicated that her heart was melting with worry. She feared she had done something that God and His Messenger were against. The Messenger of God stated that he did not like the new pillow she bought and explained:

"The painters of these pictures will be tormented and be asked to bring to life what they tried to create. Angels do not enter into a house in which there are such pictures [depicting living beings]."

When his feeling became clear, Ayesha took away the painted pillow that prevented angels from entering their house.[124]

Ayesha did house work on her own. With effort and hardship, she grinded flour by hand and cooked her own meals. She lifted all the bed linens and pillows and prepared the water for the Prophet's ablution, all on her own. Ayesha spun the string used for his sacrificial camels, laundered his clothes, combed his hair and would sometimes sprinkle a fragrant odor on it. She softened and prepared the *miswaq* (natural tooth brush, i.e. a soft branch of a tree) that the Holy Prophet (SAW) used, and always kept it clean.

She hosted their visitors, trying to supply their necessities and please the people of the Suffah[125] at Ayesha's home, the house of felicity.

Then he asked Ayesha, "Why don't you offer us something to eat?"

---

124 Muslim, Libas, 87 (2107).
125 The people who stayed in the antechamber of the Prophet's Mosque were devoted to fully obtaining religious knowledge.

The only thing cooked in the house was from the *hashesha* plant and she offered it to the visitors. The Messenger of God addressed her again:

"O Ayesha, bring some more things to us."

Pleasing the visitors meant pleasing the Messenger of God, and pleasing God's Messenger meant pleasing God. How could she not do whatever the Messenger of God wanted? But it was like trying to create a meal from nothing. Finally she made a meal by mixing cottage cheese, dates and oil. When the people of Suffah had satisfied their hunger a little, the Messenger of God said:

"O Ayesha, serve us something to drink."

Ayesha brought milk to the visitors, in a large bowl. But it was clear there wasn't enough milk for all of them. So, God's Messenger asked for more milk. There was a tiny amount remaining and it would have been odd if she served it in the large bowl. So, she served it to the visitors in a small bowl.[126]

Ayesha came from such a home where she knew very well that giving the little amount in one's possession for the sake of God would be a means for an eternal reward, so she behaved accordingly.

The Holy Prophet (SAW) joined in his family members' social lives and watched their entertainment. He even took them on social outings. From time to time, he encouraged playful competitions among them. He was the ideal husband and father. One day, Ayesha was narrating something to him and she used the word *hurafa* (superstition). He asked:

"Do you know what *hurafa* means?"

But he knew that she did not know the meaning of the word and added without waiting for her response:

---

126 Abu Daud, Adab, 103 (5040); Ahmad ibn Hanbal, Musnad, 5:426 (3666).

"Hurafa was a man from the Uzra community. He was kidnapped by demons during the era of Ignorance. He stayed with them for a long time and one day they set him free. He started to explain the strange things that he had witnessed while the demons and the people who heard his stories began to call them 'Huraf's statement.'"[127]

In the days before the Holy Prophet (SAW) passed away, his head started to ache. He knew he would leave this world soon. He began to make amends for all that had passed, not only with those who were living, but also with those Companions he had buried before. Visiting their graves in the cemetery, he returned with the hope that he would meet them tomorrow. One day, Ayesha's head also started to ache and she moaned, "Oh, my dear head."

God's Messenger responded, "Why are you moaning like that?" He meant, compared to my ache, what can you be?

His words rang true. The Messenger of God continued:

"What will you gain if you die before me? I will wash you, shroud you, perform your funeral prayer and bury you in your grave."

Hearing such unexpected words, her eyes opened wide. She wondered if he was telling a joke or expressing a truth. Recognizing that his attitude was gentle and full of mercy, she understood that he was teasing her. So, she teased him back, saying:

"Yes, I should die so that when you are done with my burial, you can do whatever you want with your other wives after I am gone, right?"[128]

Her words made the Messenger of God smile as they conveyed the depth of her love.

---

127 Ahmad ibn Hanbal, Musnad, 6:157 (25283).
128 Bukhari, Marda, 16 (5342).

Ayesha sometimes felt distressed. On one such day, her father Hazrat Abu Bakr came to her room. She was cranky and spoke loudly. Although Abu Bakr considered her as the mother of believers since the time she had been betrothed to the Messenger of God, he could not consent to anything she might do that would hurt the Messenger. As soon as he saw her condition, he took her aside and scolded her:

"O, so and so's daughter, how can you talk so loudly in the presence of God's Messenger?"

Abu Bakr spoke; he held up his hand to indicate that she must endure his lecture. He felt he had the right to scold her since she was his daughter. For nothing could hurt him as much as his own daughter causing sadness to the Messenger of God. Then Abu Bakr realized that the Messenger of God witnessed his scolding, and he felt ashamed for intervening in the private matters within the Prophet's home. He knew that he had been wrong but he felt he had to do it to prevent something worse. Still, the anger he felt toward Ayesha did not lessen. He wondered how she could talk to the Messenger of God in such a tone. He remained annoyed but the presence of God's Messenger prevented him from saying anything else, causing him to leave quietly.

After his departure, the Holy Prophet (SAW) went to Ayesha who was feeling ashamed. Her father had told the truth: nobody should raise their voice in the presence of God's Messenger. She looked at him with embarrassment.

It was time to end the moment happily. Because the matter was understood, the Messenger of God took a step to turn grief into pleasure. Indicating where Abu Bakr recently stood, he said:

"See how I interfered with the issue between you and this man, and how I rescued you from his anger?"[129]

---

129 Abu Daud, Adab, 92 (4999); Nasai, Sunanu'l Kubra, 5:139 (8495).

That day, Abu Bakr left, full of sadness, but when he went back a short time later, he saw an entirely different situation. The Messenger of God and Ayesha welcomed him with smiles on their faces. The previous situation had been temporary and left only pleasure. Abu Bakr was an expert on expressions and guessed how the mood had softened, but he wanted to hear such a change in their voices. With a smile on his face, he said:

"Why not share your pleasures with me just like you shared your troubles?"[130]

Sometimes, there were arguments among the wives which the Messenger of God reconciled with humor. But sometimes verbal quarrels turned into physical attacks. One day, Ayesha cooked a meal using flour and milk, and offered it to the Holy Prophet (SAW) while Sawdah was sitting next to him. But Sawdah did not want to eat her food.

Ayesha threatened:

"You will eat this meal or I will spread it on your face."

Sawdah still refused to eat, possibly because they were similar in age. It was the perfect chance to turn the threat into a joke. So, Ayesha did what she threatened to do. She spread some of the food on Sawdah's face.

Sawdah's action made the Messenger of God smile. Then he, one who always tried to heal the disagreements that sometimes happened between his wives, used the scene as a pretext for solidarity. He took some of the food in his hand, and holding it up toward Sawdah, he said:

"Why don't you do the same thing to her?"

Sawdah spread the flour meal on Ayesha's face, which made everyone smile.

---

130 Ibid.

Outside, they heard Umar's loud voice calling his son:

"O Abdullah! O Abdullah!"

Umar, who was nearby, would never leave without seeing the Prophet. Since the Messenger of God thought he might come inside, He said:

"Let's get up so you both can wash your faces."

Although it was a joke, it happened in the privacy of their family and did not need to be shared with anyone else, even with Umar who had a special place at the side of God's Messenger. Ayesha made the following remark about a memory:

"After I saw the attitude of God's Messenger toward Umar that day, I held Umar in awe."[131]

There were even times when the Messenger of God was angry, and sometimes the reason for his anger was Ayesha. One day he came home with a captive who he left in Ayesha's room. At that time, there were other women visiting and talking to Ayesha. As their conversation deepened with time, they forgot about the captive. Seizing the chance, the man escaped.

Sometime later, the Messenger of God came back and the slave was missing. He became very angry. Granting slaves their freedom was something he did often and he probably planned to set this one free as well. But the timing was important. Turning to Ayesha, he asked:

"O Ayesha. What happened to the captive? Where is he?"

There was nothing Ayesha could say. With enormous sadness, she said:

"I was lost in conversation with the other women."

---

131 Abu Ya'la, Musnad 7/449; see also: Tahmaz, as-Sayyidatu Ayesha, 42, 43.

As there was no chance to catch the captive, the Messenger of God said:

"Shame on you. May your hands break."

The Messenger of God's anger was enough to make Ayesha distraught. She knew she should have been more careful with what had been entrusted to her, no matter the circumstances. Then the Messenger of God left and started to ask people to find the captive. He was found and brought to God's Messenger. The problem was resolved. Sometime later, the Messenger of God went home. Ayesha was gazing at her upturned hands and then flipped her palms down, over and over again. When God's Messenger saw Ayesha in that state, he asked:

"What is wrong? Do you need to take ablution?"
"You curse me, so I am waiting to see which of my hands will break."

It was like the return of a child to his mother after he was chastised. She was scared of his curse, but at the same time hoping to turn his curse into a prayer for herself. The Messenger of God opened his hand to heaven and after many prayers exalting God, added:

"O My Lord! I am human and I become angry like a human. Whichever believer, man or woman, I cursed, please consider the curse as a reason for them to be cleaned of their material and spiritual sins."[132]

Like in any family, there were times when Ayesha was discontent or times when the Messenger of God was angry. God's Messenger understood her displeasure and immediately intervened to settle the matter amicably. One day, he said:

---

132 Ahmad ibn Hanbal, Musnad, 6:52 (24251).

"You understand immediately whether I am pleased or angry with you and I understand immediately whether you are pleased or angry with me."

Ayesha was surprised and asked:

"How do you know that?"

The Messenger of God said:

"While you use the expression, 'I swear to Muhammad's God' when you are pleased with me, you prefer to say, 'I swear to Abraham's God' when you are angry with me."

Ayesha responded:

"That's true, O Messenger of God. I swear to God, you tell the truth. I promise you that from now on I will not take any name other than yours to my mouth."[133]

One day, eleven women sat down and they promised to tell each other their real opinions of their own husbands. Each of them, in order, talked first about the most well-known feature of her husband. Some honored their husbands while others listed their husbands' bad habits. Ayesha listened carefully, sometimes smiling, and other times feeling sad. When Umm Dharr's turn came, she explained that she was the daughter of a shepherd when Abu Dharr married her. She said he did many kind things for her and that she had tasted every type of pleasure with him. She also listed the favors of her mother-in-law, as well as the virtues of her stepson from Abu Dharr's previous wife, and of her maid. But her beloved husband had divorced her and she then married another man. Her new husband was good and generous, but his kindness and generosity did

---

133 Bukhari, Nikah, 107 (4930).

not equal Abu Dharr's. Although Abu Dharr divorced her, she still could not forget him, for her new husband's benevolence did not overshadow that of Abu Dharr.

Though the other women told their stories, what Umm Dharr said stuck with Ayesha and she later shared it with God's Messenger. The Messenger of God turned to Ayesha and said:

"You see, you and I are like Abu Dharr and Umm Dharr, with one difference: he divorced his wife but I will not do that."

Such was a compliment that pleased Ayesha and she said:

"May my mother and father be sacrificed for you. You are better for me than Abu Dharr."[134]

Moderation in Entertainment

The holy prophet allowed moderate levels of entertainment. When he saw Ayesha come to his place without any show or ceremony on the day they joined in marriage, he asked:

"O Ayesha. Haven't you got any amusement? The Helpers like amusement."[135]

There were certain instances when the Prophet let his family members watch some games. Latter Ayesha explained:

"I remember God's Messenger was screening me with his clothes when the Habashi (Ethiopian) people came to do a display in the mosque. I watched them until I got tired."[136]

134 Bukhari, Nikah, 82 (4893).
135 Bukhari, Nikah, 53 (4868).
136 Bukhari, Iydayn, 2 (907).

On the festival of *Eid*, a group came with shields and spears to entertain the crowds. People gathered and were watching, and Ayesha came near to see what was going on. Because she was at the back of the crowd, she wasn't able to see the action. Turning to God's Messenger, Ayesha said she wanted to see what was happening. The Prophet asked:

"Do you really want to see?"

Ayesha nodded.

So, the Prophet lifted her behind his shoulders, her cheek resting against his cheek, and the Messenger of God called:

"Come on, O Bani Arfida!"

After some time passed, the Prophet asked:

"Are you satisfied?"

Ayesha became tired and replied in the affirmative.
So, God's Messenger said:

"Then you can go."[137]

However, it is true that the Messenger of God also intervened when limits were exceeded and kept to the boundaries of reasonable entertainment. One day, a female musician came to play for Ayesha. The Prophet asked:

"Ayesha, do you know her?"

Ayesha looked at the unknown woman and responded in the negative.
He explained that she was a musician from some tribe and added:

---

137 Ibid.

"Do you want her to play for you?"

Naturally, as no one says no to an offer from God's Messenger, she said yes.

Taking out her instrument, the woman started to play and Ayesha noticed some signs of discontent on the Prophet's face. Ayesha had seen this look before when the Messenger of God found two girls dancing in Ayesha's room. When people got out of hand, a warning came. Today, both the voice and the attitude of the musician did not coincide with the seriousness of belief. Soon, the Messenger of God turned to Ayesha and said:

"Satan has made his way to the vocal cords of this woman."[138]

The Messenger of God sounded out the people around him and took steps according to theirs. It was his general attitude and he advised his people to do the same:

"Walk in step with the weakest among you."[139]

He was a person of moderation and knew how to act in every environment. As a prophet, he was occupied with the most sensitive work and carried out his duty with care. He did not, however, hold his family to his own standards of sensitivity. As regular people, it would have been impossible for them to endure. And he was there to make life easier.

Once, when there was a military expedition, Ayesha was drawn by lots.[140] At a certain point in the journey, the Messenger of God told his army to continue on while he stayed back with Ayesha.

---

138 Ahmad ibn Hanbal, Musnad, 3:449 (15758); Tabarani, Mujamu'l Kabir, 7:158 (6686).

139 Ajluni, kashf al-khafa, 2:50.

140 When there was a military expedition, the people decided which wife would accompany him by drawing lots, in order to not break their hearts.

The Messenger of God said:

"Let's race."

Ayesha was small and naturally more agile, so she won the race. Years later, they were on a different journey together. The time that had passed made her forget about their earlier competition. But the Prophet had not forgotten and again told others to keep going while he stayed behind with Ayesha. He said:

"Let's race."

As before, Ayesha accepted the Challenge. They started to run again but this time the Messenger of God won. Ayesha had gained some weight and lost some of her speed. God's Messenger turned to Ayesha and, with a smile, said:

"This is pay-back for our earlier race!"

Ayesha's Request for a Nickname

ONE DAY, AYESHA asked for a new nickname from the Holy Prophet (SAW). Mature people in Arabian society were not called by their birth name. It was common practice and an important sign of rank and honor to do this. There was competition in virtue among people in terms of their names. Some people became so well-known by their nicknames that people forgot their real names. Generally, these names were given in relation to their first-born child; a father became Abu (father of) so and so, and a mother became Umm (mother of) so and so. People without children were called ibn (son of) someone or binti (daughter of) someone, the name given depending on if the person was a son or daughter.

The Holy Prophet used to call her by a number of names such as Humayra, Aish, Binti Siddiq, Muwaffiqa and Binta Abu Bakr. But none of them could be a permanent nickname. Since everyone she knew had a nickname, Ayesha expected to have one too. She repeatedly requested a nickname. She would say, "O, Messenger of God, my friends have nicknames!"

Though this was all she said, the Messenger of God understood her silent requests. Most likely, this was the polite way to ask for something. Perhaps Ayesha was asking for a baby who would automatically supply her with a new name and who would continue the progeny of God's Messenger. But perhaps the Prophet concluded from his own experiences that having a child was not his destiny. All three of his sons died in early childhood and three of his four daughters would die before him. Ruqiyya died during the Battle of Badr, and neither umm Kulthum nor Zainab outlived him.

A discerning and Godly guided wise person such as the Holy Prophet (SAW) would have drawn a conclusion from such events. Perhaps God did not want any of his children to live on the earth after him. It was necessary to explain all of it to Ayesha in a kind and delicate way. He chose a response that neither made Ayesha sad nor avoided a reply. He said:

"Then you should take the nickname of your sister's son, Abdullah."

His words probably hinted, "That path is closed to you." The astute Ayesha understood immediately and never made the same request again. After that moment, Ayesha was called by the nickname of her sister's son, Abdullah ibn Zubayr and was known as Umm Abdullah.[141]

---

141   Abu Daud, Adab, 78 (4970); Ahmad ibn Hanbal, Musnad, 6:260 (26285).

Hazrat Ayesha's Moral Model

THE HOLY PROPHET (SAW) was sent to perfect morality. His wives were most influenced by his moral instructions. Witnessing all of his declarations, and all of his actions and behaviors, they learned his good manners and shared them with others. They gained new wisdom and learned a new path to high morals. Every person who went to the house of felicity, every gift that was brought there and every incident that happened there resulted in novel judgments from God's Messenger, the representative of the morality taught in the Qur'an.

One night, Ayesha baked a small bun of barley for the Messenger. But when he came, he closed the door as soon as he entered which meant he wanted to rest. He always covered the rim of the water jug and the top of the food bowl and turned off any lights that were on, when he wanted to rest.

As he rested, Ayesha too became sleepy and fell asleep. Then, the Holy Prophet (SAW) felt a little cold and went close to Ayesha, warming himself by putting his head in her lap and falling back to sleep.

Meanwhile, a sheep that belonged to their neighbor came inside the room and took the barley bun. Ayesha tried to frighten the sheep from where she was sitting but it did not work. Her movement wakened the Prophet. Ayesha jumped up and started to run after the sheep. Looking on, the Messenger of God shouted after her:

"If you catch it, take only the bun. Don't hurt our neighbor for what the sheep did."[142]

---

142 Bukhari, Al-Adabu'l Mufrad, 1:54 (120).

In those times, many ate the meat of *keler,* a type of lizard the Messenger of God did not choose to eat because of its nature. However, eating lizards was *halal* (permitted) and the Prophet made it clear to his Companions that it was permissible to eat them.[143] One day, a gift of *keler* meat was brought to their home. The Prophet did not eat it. Ayesha asked:

"Should I give it to needy people?"

Her intention was sincere; others could eat what they chose not to since there was no statement that banned the meat's consumption. But the Messenger of God did not share Ayesha's opinion because he thought of aspects that Ayesha was not considering. He felt he should not discriminate against others because if it was to be known that he disliked this meat, other people would not like it either. He would be giving meat that he did not like to someone else. So, he turned to Ayesha and said:

"No, never give the things that you do not eat to others."[144]

143 Bukhari, Tamanni, 15; Muslim, Sayd, 42.
144 Ahmad ibn Hanbal, Musnad, 6:123 (24961); Bayhaqi Sunan, 9:325 (19208).

Ayesha's Love for God

AYESHA'S HOME WAS the sanctuary of the Holy Prophet (SAW). Whenever the Prophet entered the house, he would audibly recite, "If the son of Adam has two fields filled with wealth and treasure and he desires a third, only dust can fill the chasm of his greed. God says I have conferred wealth for My remembrance and assistance to the poor. If it returns toward God, God turns toward the man." The daily repetition of these sentences was to instill into the hearts of the hearers the transitory nature of the world and the insignificance of wealth. Ayesha was an avid listener. By following the Holy Prophet, she was living an exemplary life in every regard.

The Holy Prophet (SAW) used to sleep after the *Isha* prayer (night prayer) and get up well before dawn, and say the *Tahajjud* prayer (prayer before Dawn). He used to wake up Ayesha who would join in on the prayers. When dawn broke, he said *Sunnah* (not obligator) prayers and again lied down and talked to Ayesha. He went to the mosque to lead morning prayers. At times, both he and Ayesha would pray throughout the night. The Holy Prophet (SAW) would recite long chapters of the Holy Qur'an and if he came across any verse calculated to engender fear of God, he would beseech God's protection. And if he came to a verse giving glad tidings, he would pray for its conferment and his prayers would continue throughout the night.

Beside the five daily prayers and *Tahajjud* prayer, she would follow the Prophet in saying the "mid-morning prayer" and in keeping fasts. In the last ten days of Ramadan, the Prophet would seclude himself in the mosque for constant prayers. Ayesha used to have a tent pitched in the courtyard of the mosque for the *Itkaf* prayer. The Prophet would visit the tent for a short while after the morning prayers.[145]

Ayesha was at the height of her service to God. She was consistent during the life of the Messenger of God and after his death. She saw God's Messenger as a man who loved worship and who served with the attitude of a lover. Ayesha spent the most fruitful times of her life with the person who was closest to God, a man who reached new heights in his knowledge of God, who was the most beloved servant of God. He prayed during the nights until his feet were swollen. During just one *rakah* (Prayer cycle), he stood long enough to recite hundreds of pages of the Qur'an. His bows and prostrations at prayer were as long as the time he spent standing. Ayesha said:

"Neither can you ask nor can I explain the beauty of his prayers."[146]

Ayesha witnessed hundreds of thousands of miracles; she even saw the revelation of the Qur'an, when God's Messenger and the Angel Gabriel met. She considered the life of the world like the shade under a tree where people rest for a while and then continue on their way. She directed her earthly life toward the life of the Hereafter. The world and everything it held had no value for her, for God's Messenger had taught her to value the other world. During the nine years that she lived with the Messenger of God, Ayesha followed him and attempted to live like he did.

The Holy Prophet (SAW) went to his room after he finished the *Isha* (night prayer), brushed his teeth and went to bed. At midnight, he got up and performed the *Tahajjud* prayer which was obligatory only for him. After two-thirds of the night passed, he awakened Ayesha and asked her to pray. Ayesha also got up and performed the *Tahajjud* prayer followed by the *witr* prayer.[147]

---

145 Bukhari: Sahih, I'tkaf of women.
146 Bukhari, Tahajjud, 16; Manaqib, 21.
147 Ahmad ibn Hanbal, Musnad, 6:55 (24320).

Sometimes Ayesha joined the Messenger of God and prayed with him all night, until sunrise. On such a night, God's Messenger recited Ch. 2, Ch. 3 and Ch. 4 of the Holy Qur'an in just one *raka*. When he recited a verse that made someone quiver with fear, he prayed to refuge God's wrath, and when he recited a verse of good news, he again turned toward God and asked for mercy.[148]

Before the morning prayer, the Messenger of God performed a short *rak'ah* prayer and slept on his right side if he needed rest, or talked to Ayesha until the call to prayer. Ayesha followed the congregational prayer from her room adjacent to the mosque. Basically, her nights were brighter than her mornings.

At the Farewell Pilgrimage, Ayesha was with him and witnessed the large crowd where the Messenger of God said farewell to his society. During the pilgrimage, he fell ill and his society learned how to perform the pilgrimage rites in illness. Having learned how to worship directly from the most beloved servant of God, Ayesha knew, explained and continued to perform all the recommended prayers.

One day, Ayesha took Abdullah ibn Qays to her side and said:

"Do not neglect to get up at night and pray. The Messenger of God never abandoned the night prayer. When he was sick or very tired, he prayed while sitting, but he never gave it up."[149]

Even for non-obligatory, recommended prayers, Ayesha made them up if she missed performing them on time. After witnessing God's Messenger performing the Zuhar prayer, she considered it indispensable and would not abandon it.[150] Once, early in the morning, Ayesha's nephew Qasim ibn Muhammad came to her home while she was praying. It was not yet time for the morning prayer and the time for the night prayer had passed. He asked:

"O Ayesha. wich one is this prayer?"

148 Ahmad ibn Hanbal, Musnad, 6:92 (24653).
149 Ahmad ibn Hanbal, Musnad, 6:125 (24989).
150 Ahmad ibn Hanbal, Musnad, 6:138 (25112), Nasai, Sunanu'l Kubra, 1:181 (482).

With the attitude of one who seeks to hide their good deeds, she replied reluctantly:

"I missed my habitual prayer tonight so I am performing a make-up prayer."

Abdullah ibn Abu Musa once came to ask her the principal points of Islam while she was, again, performing the *duha* rayer.

When he said, "I will wait until you are finished with your prayer," in a voice loud enough to be heard by others, the other residents of the house who were familiar with the length of her prayers said:

"Alas!"[151]

This meant that the one who intended to wait for the end of Ayesha's prayer should expect to wait for a very long time. When she started to pray, it was as if she lost her connection with the world and everything in it, such being due to her deep reverence for God Almighty.

Ayesha led a humble and ascetic life from a young age. During the recitation of the Holy Qur'an, when she recited a verse that included a warning or threat, she hesitated, then went back to the beginning and recited it again in order to feel deeper grief. The people around her witnessed that her scarf often became wet with her tears. One day when she recited the verse, "Then God bestowed his favor upon us and protected us from the punishment of the scorching fire," (Ch. 52:27) she could not hold back her tears and began to sob. The verse is an explanation of the state of those who had left the world and lived in the peace of salvation in the hereafter. But she remained concerned about her position in the afterlife and never thought of herself as the guaranteed recipient of such mercy. During the reading of such verses, she always said the prayer in the following words:

---

151 Ahmad ibn Hanbal, Musnad, 6:125 (24989).

"O Lord, please bless me and keep me away from the hell fire."[152]

Her nephew and student Urwah grew tired of waiting for her to finish her prayers and left to work at the bazaar. He said:

"When I came back from the bazaar after finishing my business, I swear to God, I found her continuing the same prayer in tears."[153] She always tried to perform her prayers in congregation following the *imam* (prayer leader) from her room which was adjacent to the mosque, or pray with women who came to her room.[154] Sometimes, she ordered Zekvan, her emancipated slave, to lead her in prayer.[155] Her sensitivity about fasting continued; she spent almost every day in fast.[156] On the day of *Arafa* one year, which was before *Eid al-Adha*, it was very hot, to the point that it started to cause people to suffocate. Ayesha was fasting. Her brother Abdurrahman visited her and when he saw that she was fasting despite the weather and that she looked tired and was soaked in sweat he said, concerned:

"Why do you not break your fast?"

But Ayesha, who aimed to follow the Holy Prophet (SAW), said:

"How could I break my fast when I heard God's Messenger say, 'Certainly, the fast of the day of *Arafa* is atonement for the sins of the year before?'"[157]

---

152 Ibn Abi Shayba, Musannaf, 2:25 (6036).

153 Ibid.

154 Tahmaz, as-Sayyidatu Ayesha, quoted in Abdurrazzaq, Mussannaf, 2:82, 125, 141.

155 Bukhari Jama'a, 26 (659).

156 Ibn SA'd, Tabaqat, 8:68.

157 Ahmad ibn Hanbal, Musnad, 6:128 (25014).

Ayesha fasted during the days in Mina, though eating and drinking during those times were permitted.[158] She never gave up her fast, even during journey when breaking one's fast was allowed.[159]

The pilgrimage Ayesha went on with the Holy Prophet (SAW) was his last pilgrimage. She went to Mecca several times after he died and showed a different sensitivity on those pilgrimages. During the early years, the Ka'ba was not crowded. In later years, because of the increasing crowd of believers, Ayesha circled the Ka'ba very carefully to avoid mixing with men, doing her rotation on a wider scale. It took longer and increased her hardships, but despite that, she looked for chances to be alone. When she saw that it was crowded around the *Ka'bah*, she left and circled the *Ka'bah* from as far away as the middle of Sabir Mountain.[160] She tried her best to follow the Holy Prophet (SAW). She also did when performing pilgrimage. In the early years, she took a break in *Mina*, in a place called Namira. But later, because of the crowds, she set up her tent in a deserted region called Erak. Sometimes she even set up her tent in the region of Sabir Mountain.

She was meticulous about the minor pilgrimage too. So much so that even before she saw the moon for the month of *Muharam*, she went to Juhfa and prepared for the minor pilgrimage by reciting the invocations, and then without losing time, she went to Mecca.[161] When it was time to break her fast on the night of *Arafa*, she requested only water.

---

158 Bukhari, Sawm, 67 (1893).
159 Abdurrazzaq, Mussannaf, 2:560-61 (4459-446); Bayhaqi, Sunan, 4:301 (8266).
160 Malik, Muwatta, Hajj 13 (750).
161 Ibid.

Ayesha's Dedication to Follow the Qur'an's Commandments

———— ✂ ————

SINCE THE REVELATION of the Quranic verse relating to Purdah, Ayesha paid strict attention to the Qur'an. All well-known historians have recorded that if she wanted some young students to come before her for their education, she would get them breast fed by any sister or niece to become their foster aunt or grand aunt. Other students were taught behind the curtain. She would not go to the *Ka'ba* in a crowd of men. She would put on a veil during circles of *Ka'ba* or get the circle cleared of men to enable women to do this homage. Ishan Tabaii, a leader of the Tabiun and who was blind, visited her. She kept the curtain in between Ishan Tabaii and herself. He asked why she was observing Purdah when he could not see her.

She replied, "If you can't see me, I can see you."[162] There is no *Purdah* in *Shariah* for dead persons, but as a measure of extra caution she would put on a veil, after the burial of Hazrat, whenever she visited the Prophet's tomb. As a wife of the Prophet, she was a mother to other Muslims. In spite of this, she behaved carefully and kept a distance between herself and men who were not close relatives of hers.

Once Ayesha's wet nurse's husband came inside. He was considered an uncle who she did not have to observe Purdah in front of. Some women asked her the reason why she used a curtain to separate them. She replied:

---

162 Ibn Sa'd, Tabaqat, 8:69.

"His wife was the one who breast fed me, not him." Perhaps it was not clear to her what she was supposed to do in this situation. When the Holy Prophet came, she said:

"He is your uncle. Allow him into your place."[163]

It was reported by ibn Abbas that Ayesha used to cover even when the Prophet's two grandsons Hasan and Husain visited her home. Hasan and Husain, because of her caution, did not always go near the wives of the Holy Prophet (SAW) and behaved more carefully as well.[164]

Even while worshiping, she did not mix with the crowed and circled the Ka'ba. A woman asked her to go together to the *Hajr-e-Aswad* (the holy Black Stone):

"O mother of the believers, why do we not kiss or touch the *Hajr-e-As wad*?"

Hazrat Ayesha told the woman to stay away from her and expressed that it was improper for women to move into such a crowd.[165] Knowing her cautious ways, people often tried to make her more comfortable while she was circling the *Ka'ba* by clearing the area of men. The circling area was prepared for Ayesha in this way. She even covered her face while circling the *Ka'ba*, never wanting anyone to see her face.[166] She was meticulous even during a visit to the cemetery. After Hazrat Umar was martyred and buried, Ayesha conducted her visits more carefully to the graves of the Holy Prophet (SAW) and her father Abu Bakr.[167] Her sensitivity was even reflected in her lectures. Ayesha allowed everyone to come and benefit from her knowledge and had students from every region. Her foremost students were her nephews

---

163 Bukhari, Shahadat, 7 (2501).
164 Ibn SA'd, Tabaqat, 8:59.
165 Bukhari, Hajj 63 (1539).
166 Ahmad ibn Hanbal, Musnad, 6:85 (24592).
167 Hakim Mustadrak, 4:8 (6721).

and her relatives. Though it was easier for them to visit her home, she kept a curtain between herself and distant relatives and strangers, and taught lessons from the other side of that curtain. If she had to interfere, Ayesha corrected mistakes by signaling with her hands. Her disciple *Imam* Masruq said:

> "I used to hear the noise of her clapping from the other side of the curtain."[168]

Hazrat Ayesha constructed a beneficial environment for classes very carefully. She made sure the ones who always came to lectures had been breast fed by those she had the closest relations to, so she could see them more for the sake of knowledge. She knew that the Holy Prophet (SAW) had given similar permission to Abu Hudayfa's wife Sahla bint Suhayl, and although Salim had been an adult, she had given milk to him, so they became close relatives.[169]

It was necessary that she taught, through practice, what she knew, to her students who had the status of her relatives. One of her close relatives had a servant named Salim who wanted to learn how to perform ablution himself. Since Salim was the slave of one of her close relatives, she accepted him like a relative.

After some time had passed, the same man came to Ayesha again and told her:

> "O mother of the believers, please pray for me."

Ayesha asked why.

Wanting to share his happiness with her, he said:

> "God Almighty bestowed me freedom."

---

168 Bukhari, Adahi, 15 (5246).
169 Muwatta, Rada, 2 (1265); Abu Daud, Nikah, 10 (2061).

She responded:

"May God give you blessing."

As soon as she said this short prayer, Ayesha hid herself behind the curtain. From then on, he did not have the status of a close relative, and so she talked with Salim from the other side of the curtain.[170]

---

170 Nasai, Tahara, 83 (100).

Conveying the Message of
Quranic Teaching

───── ✃ ─────

CONVEYING THE MESSAGE of Quranic teaching and guiding others, truly constituted the center of Ayesha's life after the days of the Holy Prophet (SAW). She intervened in mistakes she saw, to explain how an issue was resolved during his life time. Ayesha enjoined the good and forbade the evil in every circumstance; she did whatever she could to guide her people. The motive behind her efforts was her serious concern for putting the teaching of the Qur'an and the *Sunnah* into practice. Ayesha once saw a woman wearing a *hijab* with pictures painted on it while she was walking between Safa and Marwa. Ayesha warned the woman:

> "Get rid of these pictures on your clothing. The Messenger of God got angry when he was clothing like that."[171] Ayesha insisted on sharing the knowledge that she had and felt anxious that something would remain restricted only to her. Among them, there were things that she felt ashamed to share because of her modesty, so Ayesha told wives to share them with their husbands. One day she said:

> "Since I feel ashamed to say this to them, tell your husbands, that they should use water to clean themselves after using the restroom. This is what the Messenger of God did."[172]

---

171 Ahmad ibn Hanbal, Musnad, 6:225.
172 Tirmidhi, Tahara, 15 (19); Nasai, Tahara, 41 (46).

She warned girls, even little ones, who wore jewelry on their hands and feet when they visited her, explaining that excessive adornment would invite Satan and deprive their houses of angels.[173]

Whenever she saw a fault, she wanted it to be corrected. One day, she saw her brother Abdurrahman performing ablution in a hurry, hurrying because he wanted to attend the funeral prayer of Sa'd ibn Abi Waqqas. Ayesha warned him:

"Abdurrahman, be more careful washing your feet while performing ablution. I heard the Messenger of God say, 'what a pity for heels [burning] in fire!"[174]

---

173 Abu Daud, Hatam, 6 (4231).
174 Muwatta, Tahara, 35.

Performing Ablution with Sand or Earth

———— ⚭ ————

IN AYESHA'S SITUATION, the verses about *tayammum* (using earth for ritual purity in the absence of water, Ch. 4:43) were revealed. Ayesha realized she lost a necklace belonging to her sister Asma. She felt she should do whatever she could to find it and return it to its owner. She looked around in the darkness but could not find it. She went to God's Messenger and together they started to look for the necklace. When others saw God's Messenger was looking for something, they joined in the search. But the necklace was nowhere to be found. When everyone understood they would not be able to find it, they started to rest again. The Messenger of God put his head on Ayesha's lap and closed his eyes. Some went to Ayesha's father Abu Bakr and said:

> "Do you see what your daughter did? She kept God's Messenger and his people in this place without even a sip of water!" It was true. There was no water in their water skins, or any sign of a well or spring nearby. They would rise at dawn to perform the morning prayer, but wondered how they could perform their ablutions without water. They thought about it and were not able to solve the problem.

Abu Bakr became angry. If his daughter's necklace had not been lost, they would not have stayed there, and would have likely rested near a spring. Angry, he entered Ayesha's tent prepared to lecture her. Then he saw the Messenger of God resting in her lap. So he stopped and then went close, slowly. Angrily, but quietly, he said:

> "You made people and God's Messenger stay here, and they neither have a sip of water nor a chance to find water."

Ayesha was in a difficult situation, as she had no reply and could not move because the Messenger of God was still resting. But suddenly he woke up and quickly realized there was no water. He thought of his people who were suffering and who had to pray but did not have any water. Just then, the state of revelation descended on God's Messenger. The Angel Gabriel came and brought a verse revealed from God. It declared a different way of performing ablution in the absence of water.

"...If you are ill or on a journey, or if any of you have just satisfied a call of nature, or you have had contact with women, and can find no water, then betake yourselves to pure earth, sprinkling it lightly over your face and hands [and forearms, up to and including the elbows]. Surely God is one who grants remission, is All-forgiving" (*Surah Nisa* Q. Ch. 4:43).

This new revelation solved their problem. Now when they were without water, they would not feel anxiety. For they Knew they could perform ablution with clean dust until water was found, and do their prayers.

Abu Bakr witnessed what God had bestowed on them. He had scolded and had been angry, but now he looked on with great admiration. It was her mistake that created an opportunity for revelation.

Abu Bakr said:

"O my daughter, what a blessed person you are. As a result of the delay that you caused, God bestowed Muslims with ease and blessings."[175]

"This was not your first blessing, dear family of Abu Bakr."[176]

After the prayer was performed, their journey started again. As Ayesha's camel stood up, she noticed a shiny object that had been underneath it. She bent over and looked at it closer. She saw, with joy, that it was the necklace she had borrowed from Asma.[177]

---

175 Ahmad ibn Hanbal, Musnad, 2:272 (26384); Ibn Maja, Tahara, 90 (565).

176 Bukhari, Tayammum, 1 (327, 329).

177 Bukhari, Fadilu's Sahaba, 5 (3469).

Ayesha's Attendance on Various Military Campaigns

———— ❦ ————

AYESHA'S BRAVERY WAS immense and she did not shy away from being on the front lines even when others did. Though she was a woman, she was often found on the battlefield with the Messenger of God. She never hesitated even in fierce battles. Ayesha was beside the Messenger of God during significant turning points at Uhad, the Battle of Khandaq (also known as Ghazwah Khandaq and The Battle of Ditch), the Mecca conquest, Bani Mustaliq and Hudaybiya.[178] She supported the ones who were fighting in battle, and at the same time, served God's Messenger. Ana ibn Malik said:

> "At the Battle of Uhud, I saw Ayesha, binti Abu Bakr and Umm Sulmah carrying water on their shoulders. They competed with each other when carrying water in a hurry for wounded soldiers. They went back and forth to Medina from Uhud to refill their water skins.[179] Ayesha was on the battle ground at Khandaq, when the Meccans laid siege to Medina. She served the Prophet and carried water for men, together with other Muslim women.

In the sixth year after *Hijrah*, the Holy Prophet (SAW) saw in a dream that he, along with his Companions, was performing the *Tawaf* (circling

---

178 Nadawi, Siratu's Sayyidati Ayesha, 170.
179 Bukhari, Fadailu's Sahaba, 48 (3600).

of Holy Ka'bah). Accordingly, he announced his plan to perform *Umrah*. In some reports, it is recorded, that it was pilgrimage. Any way, the Holy Prophet left for Mecca, with fourteen hundred of his followers. They were strictly told not to carry any kind of weapons, except their sheathed sword, the customary companion of the Arab traveler. The *Quraish* of Mecca did not want the Muslims to enter Mecca, and their top generals, Khalid bin Walid and 'Ikrimah, had prepared their army and were ready to stop the Holy Prophet and his Companions from entering Mecca. When Muslim caravans reached a place called Hudaybiya, they found out that Meccans were ready to fight to stop them from entering Mecca. And Muslims were prohibited from entering Mecca with force. Budail bin Warqa' of the *Khuza'* (also known as the *Huzaa* tribe) conveyed the message of the Holy Prophet that they had come to perform a pilgrimage and not to fight with Meccans. The *Quraish* sent 'Urwah to the Holy Prophet with the message that under no circumstances would they let them enter Mecca.

Moments away from the conquest of Mecca, the Holy Prophet said:

"O Ayesha. Something important happened with the Huzaas!"

When Muslims made the peace Treaty of Hudaybiya with the Messenger, the *Huzaa* tribe was among Muslim allies. Immediately, Ayesha guessed that the *Qurais* had violated the Treaty of Hudaybia. Ayesha knew that the Meccans were not powerful enough to do that and also be granted impunity; it would be foolish of them. So, she asked whether the Prophet thought that the *Quraish* would venture to violate the treaty. But it was true. The Meccans had attacked the *Huzaa* tribe (also known as the Khuza tribe) by night and killed twenty-three people including children. It was a gross violation of the Hudaybiya Treaty. Still, the Messenger of Allah drew attention to the divine wisdom behind the happenings and stated that the *Quraish* violated the treaty because God willed something else to be realized.

115

Ayesha knew that if God willed something to happen, the result of such a will would be good. Still, she asked:

"O Messenger of Allah, will the result be good?"

"Yes, it will be good."

After some time had passed, God's Messenger told Ayesha to prepare for journey and keep this issue secret.

The journey would be different than previous ones. It would be to their birth place, a place God Almighty gave particular value to. As she was preparing for their journey, Abu Bakr came and asked the reason for her activity. Since Ayesha was determined to do as the Prophet told her, she did not say one word even to her father. Ayesha also strived to find financial support when necessary. The Muslim women gave whatever jewelry they had: earrings, anklets, bracelets and gold, in charity, to serve God and his Messenger's cause.[180] Before a *Tabuq* (small table) in her room, Ayesha laid a blanket down, and the women competed to bring valuable things from their houses to place on the blanket.

---

180 Waqidi, Maghazi, 1:992. Resit Haylamaz, Ayesha, he Wife, the Companion, the Scholar, p. 83.

The Slander Against Hazrat Ayesha

———— ✛ ————

THE MUSLIMS OF Mecca had to face open enemies, but in Medina they had to face hypocrites, ones who only professed to be Muslims. The Holy Qur'an repeatedly refers to them. While the *Aus* and *Khazraj* railed around the banner of Islam, a sizeable group of hypocrites had been formed. These groups were alarmed at the growing power of the Muslim State and were in an alliance with the *Quraish*.

On *Sha'ban*, 6 A.H., the Prophet received information that *Al-Mustaliq* were preparing for an assault on him. The Prophet led a force to meet the enemy at the spring of Bani Al-Mustaliq near Al-Murasyi, where he ousted the enemy. As a result, a large number of Hypocrites, along with their leader AbdullahIbn Ubayy, joined the Muslim army.

While the army was still at this place, a hired servant of Bani Ghifar, belonging to the emigrant, quarreled with another man of the tribe of Juhinah, an ally of Al-Khazraj. He called out, "O ye Muhajiroon [Emigrants]."

The other man shouted, "O ye Ansar."

Abdullah ibn Ubayy, who was nearby, shouted to his associates, "Did they dare it? They set themselves against us in our own city and tried to outnumber us. By God, had you held back and had not been so generous, they certainly would have gone elsewhere."

Hazrat Ayesha experienced her greatest sadness. The leader of the hypocrites and the conspiracy against her, Abdullah ibn Ubayy ibn Salul, was on the lookout for an opportunity to reinstate the esteem he had lost after the migration of Muslims to Medina. He sought revenge against the Muslims, especially against Allah's Messenger and Hazrat Abu Bakr. The Meccans had sent many letters to provoke him to turn

117

against the Medina Muslims. Ibn Salul replied that he was prepared to give support via soldiers and weapons, things that were wanted. He had planned to shatter the spirits of the Muslim army during the Battle of Uhud by leaving the battleground with a throng that constituted one-third of the army. He helped and harbored the Meccan army by joining with several Jewish tribes such as *Bani Quray*. Many of his plans had been executed but he had not been able to reach his goal. Every passing day worked against him and his followers. His allies such as *Bani Nadir, Bani Qaynuqa* and *Bani Qurayza*, had not obeyed the Medina Treaty and had been forced to leave Medina. Eventually, when Abdullah ibn Ubayy ibn Salul started to lose his base support, he saw his power diminish quickly, day by day.

These events deeply affected the hypocrites and seeing the successes of Muslims produced hatred and rancor in their hearts. Although unexpected in words, Ibn Salul's real goals were to weaken the reputation of the Messenger of Allah and keep people away from him. Hazrat Abu Bakr, the closest Companion of Allah's Messenger, was his first target.

He found his chance in the region of the Muraysi Spring. Abdulla ibn Ubayy and his closest friends voluntarily attended the Battle of Bani Mustaliq though they had looked for excuses to stay in Medina during previous battles. They hoped to exaggerate small tensions that erupted by chance at the Muraysi Spring, to cause a rift in the bond between the helpers and the emigrants. Still not satisfied, Abdullah ibn Salul then took careful steps to offend the Messenger of Allah. The helpers and the emigrants, who had scarified their lives for each other without hesitation until that day, were nearly made into enemies because of their plotting. If the Messenger of Allah had not intervened, an unending feud would have been ignited.

Ibn Salul, seeing that his first attempt had failed, continued to plot. About the emigrants, among who was the Messenger of Allah. The Messenger of Allah went so far as to talk about biting the hand that fed them.[181] He also made threats publicly and privately:

---

181   ibn Hisham, Sira, 2:290; Ibn Sa'd, Tabaqat, 2:107.

"I swear to God, when we return to Medina, the dignified one will get the despicable one out of Medina."[182] This meant himself and the Messenger of Allah. When some perceptive Companions recognized his plotting and it seemed as if he could not continue, he denied what he said and behaved as if he were as pure as snow. It came to the point where Umar proposed to kill him. But the Messenger of Allah said:

"No, Umar. Why? Then wouldn't people say, 'Muhammad is killing his friends?'"

So, it was best to set off immediately on their journey. And the Prophet ordered for that to happen. Despite the high temperatures, they would return to Medina without having rested.

The Angel Gabriel came and informed the Messenger of Allah about what the hypocrites had done and said, and then revealed a chapter of the Holy Qur'an called *Munafiqun* (The Hypocrites).

Ibn Salul, who thought he would walk away with all his plotting, was then ostracized by his tribe and he abandoned all hope after the verses were revealed. Sincere people from his tribe, who he had convinced to follow him, reproached him sharply and left him. His own son Abdullah was among them. Abdullah felt ashamed of what his father had done. But when a man told him that his father was going to be killed, Abdullah became upset. He waited for a time and then came to Allah's Messenger with sorrow and said:

"O Messenger of Allah. I heard that you want to kill Abdullah ibn Ubayy ibn Salul because of the information you got. If you plan to do that, please order me to kill him instead, and I will bring you his head. The *Khazraj* tribe knows that no one is as sensitive as I about doing well to his father. If you give this order to a man other than me, I could not endure seeing he

---

182 Ch. 63:8. Holy Quran (Al-Munafiqun).

who executed Abdullah ibn Ubayy ibn Salul living among my people, and I might kill him. Then I would be killing a believer in exchange for an unbeliever, and I am worried that I would be thrown into the hellfire."

This suggestion was enough to freeze blood in one's veins. Even though he was his father, he would kill the man who had hurt Allah's Messenger. But the Messenger of Allah was merciful and said:

"No! On the contrary, as soon as he is among us we will treat him well and try to make him content."

Despite the reassurance from Allah's Messenger, Abdullah's heart was not yet satisfied. He waited for his father and first made his father's camel lie down, and then held his father by the shirt and said:

"I will not let you go until you say, 'The Messenger of Allah is dignified and I am despicable.'"[183] After this chain of negative events, they continued on their journey without resting until they were exhausted by the severity of the heat. Finally, a break was given. It did not last long and soon after, the Messenger of Allah gave the order to keep going. They rapidly approached Medina. Nothing disturbed Allah's Messenger or his Companions until they saw ibn Muatta[184] catching up from behind with Ayesha on his camel. Ayesha had been forgotten in the region where they had rested. She left to attend the call of nature and again noticed her sisters' necklace was lost; thus, she had searched for it. Because Ayesha was very slender, the palanquin that she traveled in had been placed on her camel without anyone noticing the difference in weight. When she went back, there was no

183 Bukhari, Manaqib, 9 (3330).
184 Safwan ibn Muattal was praised by the Prophet with the words, "I know nothing but goodness about him" and, "The person [Safwan ibn Muattal] God clothed in clothes of Paradise."

sign of the army. At first, she heard no one. She had no choice, so she squatted and started to wait for her people to notice her absence and come back for her. Before much time passed, Safwan ibn Muatta al-Salami, who left behind the army, came at day break. He asked if anything had been left. When he saw an indistinct figure in the distance, he led his camel closer to it and was surprised to see that the figure was the mother of believers, Ayesha. He surprisingly said:

"Allah's Messenger's family has been left behind!"

Safwan could not understand how the wife of Allah's Messenger and the mother of believers had been left behind alone. He asked:

"May God grant His mercy on you. Who left you here?"

He seated her on his dromedary, took hold of its halter and briskly walked to catch up with the army. By the next halt, Safwan overtook the army. Nobody noticed the incident, which was not unusual considering the situation, for their caravans were in the vast emptiness of the Arabian wilderness.

Abdullah bin Ubayy ibn Salul came to know about Hazrat Ayesha's arrival with Safwan. It was precisely a scene that someone could use to cause discord. He wanted to make use of it to vilify Ayesha. This was a golden chance for him and a pretext to slander the Prophet and his family, and to erode the sentiments of love and admiration the Muslims had for the Prophet and his household. He started a campaign of vilification and three gullible Muslims lent their ears to the slander.

According to the report of ibn Hisham, Ayesha alone remained unaware of the slander circulating about her. But the hypocrites worked with speed. The Holy Prophet and the family of Abu Bakr heard about the slander and were grieved, perhaps because neither the Messenger of Allah nor Abu Bakr's family believed what had been said. They did not feel it was necessary to tell Ayesha about the slander. But Ayesha sensed a difference in the behavior of the Messenger toward her. During her illness, he had not fussed over her as he had during previous sicknesses she faced. Once, when her mother Umm Ruman was with her, he asked, in a discrete way, about her health.

Ayesha felt hurt and said:

"O Messenger of Allah, why don't you let me go to my mother's during my illness so she may take care of me?"

The Holy Prophet said:

"You know what is best."

Though Ayesha did not understand why the Prophet was behaving coldly toward her, her feelings led her to her family's home. She stayed with her mother Umm Ruman. Twenty days later, she was able to pull herself together. She rose from the bed but remained ignorant about what was being said about her.

Some people visited her during her illness and one night she went outside with one such visitor. This was Umm Mistah who was their close relative; she left the house with her to answer a call of nature. Just then, Umm Mistah's foot got struck and she stumbled and fell. When she got up and tidied herself, she cursed:

"Damned, Mistah!"

Ayesha was shocked, wondering how a woman could curse her own son, one who was virtuous. Ayesha, known for her depth of Islamic knowledge, felt she should intervene regarding the mistake. She said:

"For God's sake! What a terrible thing to say about a man who is among the emigrants and the soldiers of the Battle of Badr."

Umm Mistah looked at Ayesha with confusion and surprise. Her son Mistah was among those spreading the slander. A moment later, Umm Mistah replied:

"O daughter of Abu Bakr. Don't you know what he said about you? Is it possible that you are among the believing women who consider situations naively? Or do you really not know what happened?"

Even the question was confusing. Ayesha was genuinely ignorant of all that had happened. She asked:

"What has he said? What situation? I am not informed about anything."

And she looked into Umm Mistah's eyes. Her look said, "Tell me as soon as possible what is going on.'

So Umm Mistah began to speak:

"There are some rumors about you."

Umm Mistah then spoke at length about the situation. She explained the slander and resulting discord, from the beginning.[185]

It was impossible for Ayesha to believe. Before, she felt the blood running in her veins. Now, her blood froze. Her sickness which was about to end was doubled, her eyes were filled with tears and her heart was filled with sorrow. She had difficulties breathing and her sobs were suffocating her.

She didn't have the energy to move her legs and she was about to faint.

She asked:

"Is it true that all this has happened?"

---

185 Ibn Hisham Sira, 4:464.

It was her last sentence before she fainted.

After some time, with great effort, she regained consciousness. Yet, she was not fully in control of herself. She said:

"Glory be to You, O God! How can people talk like that?"

She got up with the help of Umm Mistah and went back to her father's house. She was exhausted, and though she wanted to arrive quickly by taking fast steps, her legs did not comply with that hope.

When she arrived home, she went to her mother and said:

"May God bestow mercy on you. Why didn't you tell me people were talking amongst themselves about me?"

Umm Ruman was a calm and mature person with a strong character. Under these circumstances, it was necessary to be cool-headed.

She began to console her daughter tenderly:

"Oh, my dear child. Slow down a little. God will show you ease. I swear to God there is no woman as beautiful as you, who is as loved by her husband as much as you. Further, many have fellow wives who are against them and slander to disgrace them. Of course there is much gossip in such a situation."[186]

Despite all the consolation and prayers of Umm Ruman, Ayesha was depressed and plunged into deep sorrow. The scandal was even more distressing to the Apostle of God. Ascending the pulpit of the mosque, he said, 'O ye believers, who would punish the man who I have come to know, who has caused this trouble to my family? What I know of my family is nothing but good. They say good things about a man I have known well."

---

186 Bukhari, Shahada, 15, (2518).

The people of the *Aus* were filled with rage at the slander. They said, "We are prepared to behead the man who has given tongue to this calumny, whether he belongs to *Aus* or *Khazraj*."

Abdullah bin Ubayy belonged to the *Khazraj* tribe. SA'd bin Ubadh took such as an affront on the honor of his tribe. He said to Sa'd bin Muadh, "I would have spoken about my tribe. You cannot kill the man. You do not have that power."

A cousin of Sa'd bin Muadh said, "What is this hypocrisy? You are siding with the hypocrites." Feelings ran high and the dying members of the tribal feud were likely to be rekindled, but the Prophet pacified both of them and the matter ended there.

When Safwan learned that Hassan composed a derogatory couplet, he took out his sword and went in search of Hassan and attacked him saying, "Now receive this cut. I am not a poet, but a warrior." Hassan was caught and brought before the Prophet who had Hassan compensated for.

It was systematic slander. Before they had reached Medina, there was no one left who had not heard about it. If the same lies were spoken everywhere, people would not know what to believe. The hypocrites sought revenge, such wishes growing for years in their hearts, and dreamed of the pleasure they would experience in the future from the opportunity that had fallen into their hands.

When Hazrat Ayesha came to know about the slander against her, she went to her parents' house and stayed there untill she was cleared of the slander, by God Almighty, through revelation to the Holy Prophet (SAW).

Ayesha was confident that God would protect her honor and put to shame the slanderers. But she could not imagine that God would send a revelation to attest her chastity and to safeguard the chastity of pious women of all times, a revelation which would be read in mosques and prayers until the end of time. She hadn't been wailing for long when the revelation to prove her innocence came.

"Lo! They who have raised this slander are a gang among you. Deem not [O Prophet] that it will do you any harm. On the other hand, it will give you an advantage [over the accusers]. Unto every one of them will be paid what of sin he hath earned. And for him who played the leading part: he shall be severely chastised. Why didn't the believing men and believing women among you, when they heard of this, think well of their own people and say, 'This is manifest slander!'?"

The verse means to say that God is merciful to mankind in as much as He has laid down in the Quranic injunctions. By acting upon such, they can save themselves from those most dreadful social evils which are likely to undermine the whole social structure. The verse also implies a warning to Muslims to beware of these evils. It is, however, to be regretted that the Quranic injunctions in regard to these social evils have been honored more in the breach of them than in the observance thereof.

According to Bukhari Ktab al-Nikah, it is stated that:

"The extremely painful incident referred to in the Quran in Ch. 24: 12; It took place during the Holy Prophet's return from the expedition against Bani Mustaliq in the 5th Hijrah. The Muslim army had to halt for the night at a place a short distance from Medina. During this expedition, the Holy Prophet was accompanied by his noble and talented wife Hazrat Ayesha. As it happened, Ayesha went out some distance from the camp to attend to the call of nature. When she returned, she discovered that she had dropped her necklace somewhere. The necklace itself was of no great value but as it was a loan from a friend, Ayesha went out again to search for it. On her return, to her great grief and mortification, she found that the army had already marched away with the camel she was riding on, her attendants supposing that she was in the litter as she was then very young and light weight. In her helplessness, she sat down and cried until sleep overpowered her. Safwan, a *Muhajir* who was coming to her rear, recognized her (he had seen her before the verse enjoining 'Purdah' was revealed) and brought her onto his camel to Medina, himself waking behind the animal.

"Verily, those who brought forth the lie..."(Holy Quran-Ch.24:12). are a party from among you. Think it not to be an evil for you; nay, it is good for you. Every one of them shall have his share of what he has earned of the sin; and he among them who took the chief part therein shall have a grievous punishment."

"Why didn't the believing men and believing women, when they heard of it, think well of their own people and say, 'This is a manifest lie?'"

"Why did they not bring forth any witnesses to prove it? Since they have not brought the required witnesses, they are surely liars in the sight of Allah."

"Were it not for the grace of Allah and His mercy upon you in this world and in the Hereafter, a grievous chastisement would have befallen on you for what you have spread abroad."

"For what ye uttered with your tongues or spoke with your mouth of that which ye had no knowledge, you thought it to be a light matter; but in the sight of Allah, it was indeed a very precious thing."

"And, therefore, did you not say when you heard of it, 'It is not proper for us to talk about it.' Holy art Thou, O God. This is a grievous calumny!"

"Allah admonishes you never to return to the like thereof if you are believers."

"And Allah explains to you the commandments; and Allah is All-Knowing, Wise."

"Those who live immorally and spread among the believers will have a painful punishment in this world and the Hereafter. And Allah knows, and you know not."

(Holy Quran Chapter 24:11-20, reveled in the 5th year of *Hijrah*, migration from Makkah to Medina. Ayesha narrated:

"He had already seen me prior to the revelation of injunctions relevant to Purdah; he recognized me immediately, upon which he became flustered and said:

"Surely, to Allah we belong and to Him shall we return."[187]

I was awakened by his voice, and upon seeing him, I immediately veiled my face with my head cover. By God, he did not say a word to me, nor did I hear any words from him, except for the ones just mentioned. After this, he brought forward his camel and made it kneel close to me. Then he placed his foot upon its knees (so it would not stand up suddenly). I mounted the camel, and Safwan began to walk ahead, leading it by its halter, until we finally reached the place where the Muslim army had setup camp.

This is the account by those who were to be ruined; this slander was spoken by 'Abdullahbin Ubayy bin Sulul, chief of the hypocrites.

After this, we reached Medina, and it so happened that as soon as we arrived, I fell ill, and this illness lasted for one month. During this time, the statements of the slanderers were spoken widely and rumors were spread. However, until then, I had absolutely no notion of this incident. One thing I did notice, however, was that during my period of illness, the Holy Prophet (SAW) did not extend to me the usual affection and kindness that I was accustomed to, and this troubled me greatly. When the Holy Prophet (SAW) would visit me, he would only say, 'How are you feeling now?' Then he would return. This grieved me deeply. I remained unaware in this state, and

---

187 Sura:Al-Baqarah (Ch. 2: Verse 157 Holy Quran).

my illness rendered me very weak and frail. During these days, I learned of the scandal which was being propagated about me, by chance from a lady named Ummi Mistah who was distantly related to us as well. Furthermore, I learned that her son Mistah was also among those who had slandered me. When I heard these things, I forgot about my actual illness and it was as if another illness took hold of me. After this, when the Holy Prophet (SAW) came to visit me as usual, he asked, "How are you feeling now?"

I submitted, "O Messenger of Allah! If you permit, may I go to the home of my parents for a few days?"

The Holy Prophet (SAW) granted permission and I went to them. My purpose for doing this was to investigate, and I asked my mother various things. My mother said, "O Daughter! Worry not. It is common that when a person has more than one wife, and he loves one more than the others, other women spread scandal. Aysha stated:

I spontaneously said, "Holy is Allah! Are people actually saying these things about me?" Then I began to weep and my tears would not stop. I did not sleep all night. At dawn, I was still weeping.

On that day, the Holy Prophet (SAW) called 'Ali bin Talib and Usamah bin Zaid to seek their counsel because there had been quite a delay in revelations being sent down (and the Holy Prophet was very worried with respect to this matter). The Holy Prophet (SAW) asked both of them, "In the current state, when such things are being said, what shall I do? Shall I sever my relations with Ayesha?"

Usamah submitted, "O Messenger of Allah! Ayesha is your wife [i.e., as God the Exalted has chosen her to be your wife, then He has done so considering her to be worthy], and By God, We know nothing but goodness with respect to Ayesha."

However, taking the distress of the Holy Prophet (SAW) into consideration, Ali said, "O Messenger of Allah! The Exalted has not put you in difficulty and where there are plenty of women other than Ayesha. Nonetheless, [I know nothing of the actual incident] inquire of the household maid. Perhaps she knows something and may be able to tell you the actual truth."

Upon this, the Holy Prophet (SAW) called for his maid and inquired, "Have you ever seen anything in Ayesha as may be considered suspicious?"

Barirah, the household maid, responded, "I swear by that God who has sent you with the truth, I have never seen anything evil about her, except that on account of her young age, she is a bit careless. It often happens that she leaves the dough exposed and falls asleep, while the goats come and consume it.

On the same day, the Holy Prophet (SAW) delivered an address in the mosque and said, "I have been given great grief with respect to my family. Is there anyone from among you who can put an end to this? By God, I know nothing of my wife except piety and goodness. Moreover, I also consider the man who has been mentioned in this connection to be pious. He has never come to my home in my absence."

Upon hearing this address of the Holy Prophet (SAW), Sa'd bin Muadh, chief of the *Aus* tribe, stood up and submitted, "O messenger of Allah! I shall put an end to this. If this person is from our tribe, we consider him worthy of death and shall sever his head at once. If he is from our brethren [i.e., from the *Khazraj* tribe], even still we are prepared to do as you command."

Upon this, Sa'd bin 'Ub`adah, chief of the *Khazraj* tribe, stood up and though he was a righteous man at the time, he was overcome by ignorant indignation and said, "You have spoken a lie. By God! You shall not kill a man from our tribe, nor do you possess the power to do so. If such a person had been from among your tribe, you would not have said such a thing."

Upon this, Usaid bin Hudair, a chief of *Aus* who was the paternal cousin of Sa'd bin Muadh, stood up and addressed Sa'd bin 'Ubadah, saying, "Sa'd bin Muadh is not a liar. Rather, you are a liar and a hypocrite. For you argue on behalf of the hypocrites. This exchange of remarks incensed some from among the *Aus* and *Khazraj*, and an altercation almost broke out, but the Holy Prophet (SAW) who was still standing on the pulpit, admonished everyone and diffused the situation. Then, the Holy Prophet (SAW) descended the pulpit and left. My state was the same as usual in that my tears would not stop, nor could I sleep. I remained in such a state for two whole nights and one day. I felt as if my liver would burst into pieces.

I was sitting by my parents in this very state, weeping, when a lady from the *Ansar* sought permission and entered, and began to weep with me in a sympathetic manner. At this, the Messenger of Allah arrived and sat down next to me. This was the first day that he had sat down with me after the calumny. A month had elapsed but no divine revelation had been sent down in my case. The Holy Prophet (SAW) recited the *Kalimah,* praised God and then he addressed me saying, "O Ayesha! I have been informed such about you. If you are innocent, I trust that God shall affirm your innocence. If, however, you have committed a mistake, you should seek forgiveness from God and bow before him. Because when a person bows before God confessing his sin, Allah accepts his repentance and shows Mercy to him." When the Holy Prophet finished his address, I noticed that my tears had dried away completely and that there was absolutely no sign of them.

At that time, I looked to my father and mother and asked them to respond on my behalf. But they said, "By God! We do not know what to say in response."

At the time, I was a young girl and did not know much of the Qur'an, but being disappointed by my parents, I submitted to the Holy Prophet (SAW) myself, saying, "By God. I am aware that certain things which people have rumored about me have reached you, and you have been affected by these statements. Hence, if I advocate my innocence, you shall doubt me, but if I accept myself as being guilty despite being innocent, you shall believe me. By God, I find myself in the situation of the father of Joseph (ah) who said:

"So, comely patience is now called for. And it is Allah alone whose help is to be sought against what you assert [Ch. 12:19 of the Holy Qur'an]. That is to say patience is better for me and it is Allah alone whose help I seek against what these people assert."

Upon saying this, I turned to the other side, and at the time I had firm conviction that since I was innocent, Allah the Exalted would quickly manifest my innocence. However, I did not imagine that a Quranic revelation would be sent down to clear me of the charges and that God the Exalted would declare my innocence in his manifest word. I thought that perhaps the Messenger of Allah would be shown a vision, etc. by Allah the Exalted in this regard. However, by God, the Holy Prophet had not yet left this sitting, nor had any other person of the household left when he was overtaken by the state, which he would experience upon receiving divine revelation. Though it was a cold day, drops of perspiration began to fall from his countenance, and after some time, this state left him. The Holy Prophet (SAW) smiled and looked toward me saying, "O Ayesha! God has affirmed your innocence."

At this, my mother spontaneously said, "O Ayesha! Get up! Thank the Messenger of Allah."

At the time, since my heart was saturated with gratitude for God, I said, "Why should I thank the Holy Prophet? I am thankful to my Lord alone who has affirmed my innocence."

It was then that the verses of *Surah Al-Nur* were revealed, which begin with the following words:

"Verily, those who brought forth the lie…" (Holy Quran, Ch. 24:12).

When my innocence had been affirmed, my father Abu Bakr, who would grant regular support to Mistah bin Uthathah due to his poverty and kinship, swore that because Mistah had taken part in slandering Ayesha, he would no longer render him support. However, shortly thereafter, divine revelation was received that said such an action was most displeasing, upon which, Abu Bakr reinstated his allowance. Moreover, before I was absolved, the Holy Prophet (SAW) asked Zainab bint Jahash her opinion of me, and she responded, "O Messenger of Allah! I consider Ayesha to be a pious and God-fearing lady." This was said despite the fact that from among all the wives of the Holy Prophet (SAW), Zainab was the only one who competed with me and acted as my rival. However, due to her virtue, Allah the Exalted saved her from taking part in this calumny.[188]

I have added this lengthy narration of Hazrat Ayesha (ra) with the thought that firstly, as far as this issue is concerned, it is the most detailed and well composed of all narrations. The fact is that this narration brings together what was only stated in parts in narrations on the same topic, thereby creating a complete narration of the matter. In addition to this, such enlightening insight is derived from this narration on the domestic life of the Holy Prophet (SAW) that no historian can disregard it. Then, with regard to authenticity, this narration is of such an exceptionally high caliber that it leaves no room for uncertainty or doubt. Now, one should contemplate the magnitude of this conspiracy, hatched by the hypocrites. Namely, to doubt the narrative. The motive of such doubt was not only to attack the honor of a chaste, extremely righteous and pious lady. Rather, the greater objective of their doubt was to directly destroy the honor of the founder of Islam, and to dangerously shake the Islamic society. Such filthy and vile propaganda was spread by the hypocrites in such a manner that simple and loyal Muslims were caught in this snare of deception. The names of Hassan bin Thabit, the poet, Hamnah bint Jahash, the sister of Zainab bint Jahash, and Mistah bin Uthathah, have especially been recorded.[189] However, it is a testimony to her lofty character that Hazrat Ayesha forgave them all and did not harbor a grudge against them in her heart. As such, it is mentioned that after this occurrence, whenever Hassan bin Thabit would come to visit Hazrat Ayesha, she would receive him graciously. On one occasion, when he presented himself before Hazrat Ayesha, a Muslim named Masruq, who was present as well, became astonished and said, "What! Do you grant Hassan the permission of audience?"

---

188 Sahih ul-Bukhari, Kitabul-Maghazi, Babu Hadithil-Ifki, Hadith No. 4141
Sahih ul-Bukhari, Kitabut-Tafsir, Tafsriru Suratin Nun, Babu Lau Laidh Sami'tumuhu... Hadith No. 4750.
189 Sahihul-Bukhari, Kitabul-Maghazi, Babu Hadithil-Ifki, Hadith No. 4141.

Hazrat Ayesha responded, "Let it be. The poor man has lost his sight. Is this not misery enough? Then I cannot forget that Hassan would compose verses in support of the Holy Prophet (SAW) against his enemies." Hence, Hassan was granted permission, upon which he came in and sat down.

He spoke a verse in praise of Hazrat Ayesha:

"She is a pure and chaste woman who possesses wisdom and foresight, and her position is above and beyond doubt and uncertainty; she does not eat the flesh of upright and innocent women, i.e., she does not slander them, nor does she speak ill of them in their absence."

When Hazrat Ayesha (ra) heard this couplet, she related: "What about your own state? you did not prove to possess this quality, i.e., you took part in leveling an accusation against me though I was innocent.[190] Let us witness the Arabic scholarship, or prejudice, of Mr. Muir, who translates the above-mentioned couplet in an absolutely incorrect manner, in contradiction to the rules of Arabic grammar, and asserts that Hassan praised the slender body of Ayesha who in turn taunted him on his large figure, 'You should weep for such a level of wisdom and understanding.'"[191]

Mr. Muir has also committed other blatant mistakes in relating this incident. He writes that Safwan and Ayesha were unable to catch the army on route and then openly entered Medina before the gaze of all,[192] even though this is absolutely incorrect and categorically baseless. As previously quoted, narrations of several *Ahadith* and history both substantiate

---

190   Sahih ul-Bukhari, Kitabut-Tafsir, Tafsriru Suratin Nun, Babu Lau Laidh Sami'tumuhu... Hadith No. 4755.

191   The Life of Mahomet, by Sir William Muir, Chapter XV1 (Guilt or Innocence of Ayesha). Hassan reconciles with Ayesha by saying an ode in her praise, p. 315, footnote, published by Smith, Eder & Co. London (1878).

192   The Life of Mahomet, by Sir William Muir, Chapter XV1 (Misadventure of Ayesha). p. 311, published by Smith, Elder & Co. London (1878).

that Safwan and Hazrat Ayesha managed to catch up to the Muslim army on route in only a few hours.[193] Thankfully, however, in relation to the actual calumny itself, Mr. Muir accepts the innocence of Hazrat Ayesha. As such, he writes:

"Little remark is needed regarding the character of Ayesha and the alleged message from above to which it gave occasion. There are not materials sufficient for deciding upon the charges brought against her, and the question is immaterial."[194]

---

193 Sahih ul-Bukhari, Kitabul-Maghazi, Babu Hadithil-Ifki, Hadith No. 4141.
194 The Life of Mahomet, by Sir William Muir, Chapter XV1 (Guilt or Innocence of Ayesha).

Hazrat Ayesha's Relation with Co-wives

THE INTOLERABLE RELATIONSHIP for a woman is to be one of the several wives of a husband. Hazrat Ayesha had to live with as many as eight of the Prophet's wives but the company of the Holy Prophet (SAW) had ensured their relations were never clouded. Small differences did arise among them from time to time as such they are bound to happen when so many people live together, particularly if each is the wife of the same man. But they were always transitory and insignificant, and were quickly reconciled with spirit of cordiality and mutual respect. It is reported by authentic historians that the Holy Prophet's wife Juwayriyah, who was extremely pretty, was Ayesha's potential rival, but they also lived like good friends. Another wife, Zainab, was a cousin of the Holy Prophet and could claim greater nearness, but when the incident of *Ifak* (Slander) took place, she said to the Holy Prophet (SAW) that she had found nothing but good in Ayesha. When Zainab died, Ayesha said, "Have never seen a woman more religious, more pious, more truthful, more generous, or more ardent in seeking the good pleasure of God. She was, however, a little irritable, for which she used to be sorry."[195]

When Maimuna died, Ayesha extolled her virtues and said that she was pious and righteous if any difference arose. Hafsa, daughter of Hazrat Umar and Safiya, who was originally a Jew and had embraced Islam, would generally side with Ayesha.

Some chroniclers, in their eagerness to write about the smallest details of the Holy Prophet's life, have mentioned some of the differences

195 Muslim: Sahih.

among the co-wives, but most of them are false for these have been presented in a way that would require a reporter's presence at odd moments inside the apartments of the wives, and some are clearly made out to be merely stories derogatory to the other wives, particularly toward Ayesha when schisms arose in Islam and a new sect had been born, the creation of which had political overtones.

The greater proof of the cordial relations between the wives of the Holy Prophet (SAW) is the fact that the Holy Prophet's family's life was serene and undisturbed, barring one occasion when he had remained aloof from his wives for a month until a Quranic verse was revealed; he could engage himself in nightly prayers and pursue his prophetic mission with complete peace of mind. Bickering and dissensions rarely affected that peace.

Hazrat Ayesha had great affection for the Holy Prophet's daughter Fatima. Speaking about her, Ayesha said, "Besides the Prophet, I have never seen a better person."[196]

A *Tabii* (persons succeeding the compassions) had asked Ayesha who was the person dearest to the Prophet. Ayesha said, "It was Fatima". In her manners and deportment, she was nearest to the Prophet. Whenever she visited the Prophet, he would rise and kiss her forehead, and make her sit at his place. She would respond in the same manner whenever the Prophet visited her.[197]

She relates that, "One day, all the wives of the Prophet were sitting with him when Fatima came. Her gait was like that of the Prophet. He welcomed her profusely and made her sit close to him. The Prophet whispered something into her ears and she burst into tears. Seeing her distressed, the Prophet left. I asked her to tell us what the Prophet had told her. She replied that she would not tell the secrets of her father."

After the Prophet's death, I again asked her to tell me what the Prophet told her for the sake of my rights over hers. Fatima replied that she could tell me at that moment, unlike before. I started crying, for he had told me

---

196 Zarqani.
197 Tirmidhi: Al-Jam'i.

that he was soon to leave the world. I smiled when he said, "Would you not like it that you will be leader of the women of Paradise?"[198]

This event relates to the last year of Fatima's life. It proves beyond doubt that none had any grievances against the other relating to heritage and that no family dispute had clouded their hearts.

---

198 Muslim, Sahih: Book: The Excellence of the Companions.

Other Wives of The Holy Prophet (SAW)

———— ✿ ————

NON-MUSLIMS OFTEN MAKE an issue out of the fact that the Prophet had more than four wives at the same time because such goes against the commandment of the Holy Qur'an that says a Muslim should not have more than four wives at a time. However, we should look at the circumstances under which those marriages took place. If one does, one will find that it was an absolute necessity to have those marriages. First of all, the Prophet did not marry any other women while his first wife Khadijah was alive. It was after her demise that he married other women. Polygamy was common at that time and the commandment of God limiting the number of wives one can have, with certain conditions, had not yet been revealed. All the women he married were widows or divorcees, except Ayesha. None of the women who married the Messenger of God were forced into marriage. They married him with their own free will. Moreover, whenever he married a woman, it was for the abolishing of certain old traditions such as not marrying the wife of an adopted son or a widow with children. Furthermore, some of the women he married were quite old. So, the reason he married more than four wives is based on piety, and was for the religious needs of the time.

Hazrat Khadijah

THE HOLY PROPHET married Hazrat Khadijah when he was twenty-five years old and he did not take another wife until after she died.

Khadijah passed away before God's Messenger married Ayesha, so they did not live a joint life. Despite this, Ayesha envied Khadijah most among the wives of God's Messenger because she was the only consoler during those difficult years. Khadijah, the daughter of Khuwailid bin Asad bin Abdul and 'Uzza bin Qusayy, was an intelligent and rich business women. She was twice married before her marriage to the Holy Prophet. Her first marriage was with Abu Halah ibn Zurarah al-Tamimi. She bore two children from that marriage. They were named Hind and Harith. After the demise of her first husband, she married 'Atiq ibn 'A'yidah al-Makhzumi. From this marriage, she had a daughter who was named Hind, the same name of a child of hers from her first husband. After the demise of Atiq ibn A'yidah al-Makhzumi, Khadijha married the Holy Prophet. She was a well-respected, pious and rich lady, and due to her piety, was known as "Tahira" (true one).

Khadijah was a very clever businesswoman. She preferred to manage business herself. She was a widow and there were several men who sought to marry her. However, she refused to marry any of them. She was well aware of the truthful and excellent character of the Holy Prophet who from his early youth was known as truthful and trustworthy. Thus, both possessed unique qualities. At first, Khadijah acquired his services for taking care of her business. She was very much impressed with the character and other qualities of the Holy prophet. Her servant, Maisrah, who accompanied the Holy Prophet during the business trip, was also full of praise for the Holy Prophet. Soon, she proposed that the Holy

Prophet marry her. The Holy Prophet took advice from his relatives and then agreed to marry Khadijah. Abu Talib performed the *Nikah* of the Holy Prophet with Khadijah, with a dowry of 500 Dirham. The marriage took place in 595 A.D. She was 40 years old at the time of her marriage with Holy Prophet; the Holy Prophet was 25 years old.

Khadijah was the first one among men and women to accept Islam. All the children of the Holy Prophet except Ibrahim were born to Khadija. She gave birth to seven children; the sons were named Qasim Tahir and Tayyab, and the four daughters were named Zainab, Ruqiyya, Ummi Kulthum and Fatimah. All the children of Khadijah, before she married the Holy Prophet, accepted Islam. Khadijah died at the age of 65 years old and the Holy Prophet at that time was 50 years old. Thus, until the age of 50 years old, the Holy Prophet had one wife, Khadijah. She passed away in the month of Ramadan in 10 A.H. and was buried in the *Jannat-e-Mu'alla* graveyard. Khadijah was with the Holy Prophet during the siege of *Shi'b-e-Abi Talib* and, even at an old age, she endured the hardships of the siege for two to three years.

The Holy Prophet loved Khadijah so much that even after she passed away and he had several other wives, when anything reminded him of Khadijah he used to become full of emotion and kept her memory alive in various ways. Once Halah, a sister of Khadijah's, whose voice was very similar to Khadija's voice, asked the Holy Prophet for permission to go inside the house. When the Holy Prophet heard her voice, he immediately said it must be Halah and old memories of Khadijah overwhelmed him.

Khadijah was the Holy Prophet's first wife and the only consoler during the difficult years of his youth. During the fifteen years they shared before revelation, she was his loyal partner. In the chaotic environment of the first revelation, she was his greatest supporter. Until the end of her life, being a strong and unshakable woman, she was his helper. Her death coincided with the end of the difficult period. The Holy Prophet never forgot about his first wife who he was so close to, and who he spent his most troubled days with. Every chance he got, he turned a conversation toward Khadijah, even during critical times.

Once, he hesitated when he saw the necklace that his daughter Zainab sent to save his son-in-law Abu Al-As who was among the captives of the Battle of Badr. The Holy Prophet was moved because he remembered that it was a wedding gift to them from Khadijah. The sight of the necklace took the Holy Prophet into a reverie, and he remembered Khadijah as she was in those days. After a little while, he turned to the people around him and suggested them to set Zainab's husband free and give the necklace back to her.[199] Abu Al-As was set free for the sake of a memory of Khadija.

The situation did not change in later years. During the conquest of Mecca, while the Holy Prophet was walking with thousands of people to the city, people realized that he had changed his direction and visited the grave of his wife Khadija; also, that he prayed before her grave at great length. The people watched him curiously and again witnessed an example of his fidelity.

His love and fidelity continued until his death. When a gift was given to him, he first sent it to Khadija's relatives. He honored them and showed them respect, giving even the pillow on which he was sitting on to them. When someone asked why he did such, he replied:

"I Love the ones she loves too."[200]

He never allowed anything to be said against her and immediately interfered if someone said something negative about her. One day, when a conversation turned to Ayesha, someone coyly said:

"As if there is no one in this world but Khadijah!"

These words offended the Messenger of Allah and he turned to Ayesha and swiftly started to recount Khadija's qualities, one by one. Then he added that at the same, he had children who reminded him of Khadija.[201]

---

199 Abu Dawud, Jihad, 121 (2692); Ahmad ibn Hanbal, Musnad, 6:276.
200 Yamani, Ummu'l Muminin, 13.
201 Bukhari, Fadailu's Sahaba, 50 (3607).

Ayesha, who witnessed his excitement, watched with admiration how much Allah's Messenger still loved Khadijah. If he'd had such worthiness at his side, would she never need to worry in this world or the hereafter? It was a love worth striving for, so there had to be a way to gain it, which would be possible if the real reason behind his love was known. Thus, Ayesha asked:

"What is the reason for your concern for this woman who died years before and left you? God the Almighty has bestowed on you even more auspicious ones than her."

Her question explained what was going on in her mind; Ayesha wanted him to explain his love for Khadijah. It was impossible that someone as acute as herself would not know how he felt. Thus, it is likely that she was aiming to hear Khadijah's worth directly from the Messenger of Allah's tongue.

The messenger of Allah was again displeased with her words, and in a voice indicating his discontent, he asked:

"Was there someone like her? I swear to God that He never bestowed me one better than her! When people persisted in disbelief, she came and believed me. When people accused me of lying, she confirmed what I said. When people withheld their possessions from me, she brought whatever she had and gave it to me. And God granted me children with no one but her."[202]

Ayesha got the answer she expected. At the side of Allah's Messenger, everyone had a special place, and loving one of them did not mean that he did not love the others (meaning his other wives). Because of Ayesha's question, Khadijah became known to the entire Muslim society as a woman who should not have anything negative said about her.

---

202 Ahmad ibn Hanbal, Musnad, 6:117 (24908).

Ayesha decided to apologize to Allah's Messenger and ask for forgiveness. She promised never again to say anything against Khadijah.[203]

God the Almighty bestowed to Khadijah the merit of enjoying a love the others could never attain. She remained with the Messenger of Allah even after her death. Ayesha would express her feelings about Khadijah as follows:

"Although I did not share the same days with Khadijah, I did not envy any other wives of God's Messenger as I did Khadija. The Messenger of God mentioned her so often and spoke of her always with praise and admiration. Whenever he slaughtered a sheep, he would send some meat to Khadija's friends."[204]

After the death of Hazrat Khadijah, Sawda had the honor of becoming the Prophet's next wife. The woman who arranged the marriage mentioned the names of Ayesha and Sawda at the same time. However, while Sawda's marriage to the Holy Prophet took place ten years after the revelation, Ayesha's marriage to the Holy Prophet happened after a four-year delay.

Holy Prophet's wives and their family backgrounds.

Hazrat Khadija

- bint Khavelid, binAsad, bin Abdul Azee, bin Qasee, bin Kalab, bin Maraa, bin, Kaab, bin Loi
- Born 15 years prior to 'Ām-ul Feel; died 10 Nubuwah at age 65
- Year married: 25, post 'Ām-ul Feel; age at marriage: 40 year old; Prophet Muhammad's age at marriage: 25 years old; married for 25 years
- Number of Traditions attributed: none

---

203 Tabarani, Mujamu'l Kabir, 23:11.
204 Bukhari, Nikah, 97 (4914).

- Prior husband: Atuque, Hind
- Children from prior marriage: sons Hind and Haris, and daughter Hind
- Remarks: died after release from *Sha'ab-e Abi Talib*

Hazrat Sawdah

———— ✺ ————

THE HOLY PROPHET (SAW) married Hazrat Sawda in the tenth year of his Prophethood. The following is from Tabaaqat ibn Sa'd, narrating from al-Waaqidi, 8/52/-53: Ibn Kathir in al-Bidaayah wa'l-Nihaayah. 3/149.

Sawdah bint Zam'ah ibn Qais ibn 'Abd Shams, who was the widow of Sakran bin 'Amr, one of the servants of the Holy Prophet, was one of the early Muslims. She accepted Islam before her husband. According to the traditions, Sawda migrated to Abyssinia with her husband after being persecuted by the polytheists of Mecca. Sawdah was the first woman to immigrate to Abyssinia for the sake of her religion. Her husband died when the couple returned to Mecca. She had a son named Sakran ibn "Amr ibn 'Abd Shams from her first husband. After her husband's death, she lived with her father. At the same time, the Holy Prophet, after the demise of Khadijah himself, was taking care of his children. A relative of the Holy Prophet, Khaulah bint hakim, who was married to Uthman bin Maz'un, pointed out to the Holy Prophet that his children needed a mother. She purposed that he marry Ayesha who was the daughter of his dear friend Abu Bakr, or Sawdah who was a widow of his servant Sakran bin 'Amr. The Holy Prophet told Khaulah to talk with both families. Accordingly, Khaulah delivered the proposal firs to Abu Bakr and his wife Umm Ruman. Then she went to Sawdah bint Zam'ah and conveyed the message to her. Sawdah and her family agreed to the proposal. Thus, in the month of *Shawwal*, 3 B.H. (February/March, 619 A.D.) the *Nikah* of the Holy Prophet was performed with Sawda. Four hundred Dirhams were fixed as the *Haq Mahr* for her marriage ceremony which took place right away. Sawdah was a middle-aged woman at the time of her marriage with the Holy Prophet. According to one tradition, she was fifty years old at the time of her marriage to the Holy Prophet. Thus, she was very suited to taking care of the children, and immediately after the marriage she took over the care of the children and the household work. When Sawdah grew old, she gave up her share of the Holy Prophet's time in favor of Ayesha. She had the honor of performing *Hajj* in the company of the Holy Prophet. She passed away in 27 A.H. at the age of 75 years old.

The Holy Prophet, with the permission of his other wives, spent the last days of his life with Ayesha in her apartment. He passed away there, in her lap.

Hazrat Sawdah's family (ra)

- She was the (daughter)(Bint)of Zam'a, (bin, means son) Qais, bin Abd Shams, bin Abdood, bin Nasr, bin Malik, bin Hasl, bin Aamir
- Born 'Ām-ul Feel; died 19 Hijrah; age: 72 years old
- Year married: 10 Nubuwah; age at marriage: 50; Muhammad's age at marriage: 50 years old; married for 14 years
- Number of traditions attributed: 5
- Prior husband: Sukran bin Umro (ra)
- Children from prior marriage; son Abdur Rahman
- Remarks: migrated to Habsha with her 1st Muslim husband

Hazrat Ayesha

AYESHA WAS BORN to Abu Bakr and Umm Ruman. Ayesha was the only wife of the Holy Prophet who was a Muslim at birth. The rest of the wives of the Holy Prophet accepted Islam either by themselves or along with their parents. Ayesha relates that the Holy Prophet said to her, "You have been shown to me twice in my dream. I saw you pictured on a piece of silk and someone said to me, 'This is your wife.' When I uncovered the picture, I saw that it was yours. I said, 'if this is from Allah, it will be accomplished.'"[205]

Hazrat Ayesha (ra)

- Bint Abu-Bakr, bin Usman, bin Aamir, bin Umro, bin Kaab, bin Saad, bin Teem, bin Marah, bin Loi
- Born 4 Nubuwah; died 57 Hijrah at the age of 67 years old
- Year married: 1 Hijrah; age at marriage: 19-20 years old; the Prophet Muhammad's age at marriage: 53 years old; married for 9 years
- Number of traditions attributed: 2,210
- Prior husbands: none
- Remarks: most traditions narrated by women and scholars of faith

---

205 (Sahih Bukhari, Kitab Fada'il Ashabannabi, Bab tazwiinnabi Khadjata wa fadliha).

Hazrat Hafsah

———— ❧ ————

HAZRAT HAFSAH WAS the daughter of Hazrat Umar (the second Caliph of the *Caliphate-e-Rashdha)*. She was first married to Hazrat Khunais bin Hudhafah As–Sahmi who participated in the Battle of Badr. Upon returning to Medina from the battle of Badr, Hazrat Khunais became ill and died due to the illness. Thus, Hazrat Hafsah became a widow at a very young age. She was just 20 years old. Hazrat Umar started to look for a suitable match for her. Hazrat Umar first asked Hazrat Abu Bake to marry Hazrat Hafsah. However, Abu Bakr refused. Then, Hazrat Umar asked Hazrat Uthman to marry his daughter Hafsah. Hazrat Uthman also excused himself. Hazrat Umar felt sadness due to these refusals. He went to the Holy Prophet and explained the refusals of Hazrat Abu Bakr and Hazrat Uthman to marry his daughter. The Holy Prophet earlier mentioned to Hazrat Abu Bakr his intention to marry Hazrat Hafsah. This was the reason that Hazrat Abu Bakr refused to marry Hazrat Hafsah. The Holy Prophet himself sent the message to Hazrat Umar to merry Hazrat Hafsah. Hazrat Umar happily agreed to the proposal. Thus, the marriage of Hazrat Hafsah to the Holy Prophet took place in the month of *Sha'ban*, 3 A.H. (i.e., February, 625 A.H.). Hazrat Hafsah, being the daughter of Hazrat Umar, had high status among the wives of the Prophet. Hazrat Hafsah could read and write, skills she learned from Hazrat Shifa bint Abdullah. She possessed a copy of the Holy Qur'an too. She had the opportunity to perform *Hajj* in the company of the Holy Prophet. She passed away in 45 A.H. at the age of 63 years old. There are 60 *Ahadith* in the book of the *Ahadith*, which were related by Hazrat Hafsah.

Hazrat Hafsa (ra)

- Bint Umar (ra), bin Nafeel, bin Abdul Azeez, bin Abdullah bin Qart, bin Reyah, bin Zarah
- Born 5 years before Nubuwah; died 41 Hijrah, age: 59 years old
- Year married: 3 Hijrah; age at marriage: 22; Muhammad's age at marriage: 55 years old; married for 8 years
- Number of traditions attributed: 60
- Prior husband: Khanees bin Hazafa (ra)
- Children from prior marriage: none
- Remarks: known for impressive observance of Sala'at and fasting

Hazrat Zainab bint Khuzaimah (ra)

THE HOLY PROPHET (SAW) married Hazrat Zainab bint Khuzaimah during Ramadan, thirty-one months after the *Hijrah.* Tabaaqat ibn Sa'd 8/115.

Hazrat Zainab was first married to Hazrat Tufail. When Hazrat Tufail divorced her, she married Hazrat Ubaidah who was the brother of Hazrat Tufail. Hazrat Ubaidah was martyred during the Battle of Badr. She married a third time with Hazrat Abdullah bin Jahsh who was martyred in the Battle of Uhud. Thus, Hazrat Zainab lost her husband one after the other in two battles. This gave her a unique status. And because of such a status, the Holy Prophet sent a message that he wanted to marry her, and she accepted the proposal. She married the Holy Prophet in Safr, 4 A.H. (i.e., July 625) at the age of 30 years old. However, she passed away just a couple months after the marriage, in Rabi 'ul Akhir, 4 A.H. She was buried in the Jannatul Baqi graveyard. Due to her passion for serving the poor, she was often called the "Ummul Masakin."

Hazrat Zainab (ra)

- Bint Khazeema, bin Haris, bin Abdullah, bin Umro, bin Abd Munaf, bin Halal
- Born 13 years before Nubuwah; died 3 Hijrah at 30 years old
- Year married: 3 Hijrah; age at marriage: 30; Muhammad's age at marriage: 55 years old; married for 3 months
- Number of traditions attributed: none

- Prior husband: Tufail, Ubeeda, Abdullah (ra)
- Children from prior marriage: none
- Remarks: known as Umm-ul Masakeen

Hazrat Ummi Salamah (ra)

————— ✿ —————

SOME HISTORIANS NAME Hazrat Ummi Salamah "Umm Salamah Hind." A Muslim (in 918 A.H.) narrated that Umm Salamah said, "I had heard the Holy Prophet (SAW) say, 'There is no person who is faced with a calamity and says *inn lillaah wa inna ilayhi raajioon* (truly, to Allah we belong and truly to Him we shall return).'"

According to another report:

"When her previous husband Abu Salamah died, I said, 'Who is better than Abu Salamah, the companion of the Holy Prophet?' Then I got married to the Holy Prophet (SAW)."

In the early days of Islam, when the *Quraish* were persecuting Muslims in Mecca, Hazrat Ummi Salmah bint Abi Umayya, with her husband Abdullah ibn Abdul Asad and their son migrated to Medina. However, on their way to Medina, Ummi Salamah's tribe stopped them and refused to let Hazrat Ummi Salamah go with her husband. Thus, her husband left for Medina with his son and without her. She was truly saddened and for a year she sat in front of her house and cried, remembering her husband and son, two people she missed greatly. Ultimately, someone from her tribe took pity on her and convinced the tribe's people to let her go to her husband. So, she was untied with her family in Medina. Three more children were born to her, and then her husband was martyred at the Battle of Uhud. A few months after she became a widow, Hazrat Abu Bakr sent a message saying he wanted to marry her. However, she politely refused to marry him. Then, Hazrat Umar asked her to marry him. Again, she refused to marry. She had four children (Salamah, Umar, Zainab and Durra) and no assets or income to support them. Under these circumstances, the Holy Prophet sent her a message that asked her to marry him. Initially, she was reluctant. However, she later agreed to marry the Holy Prophet. This marriage became an excellent example for Muslims marrying widows with children.

With respect to age, Hazrat Ummi Salamah was the oldest of the wives of the Holy Prophet. This is probably the reason the Holy Prophet, in his daily routine of visiting his wives after the *Asr* prayer, used to visit Hazrat Ummi Salamah first and Hazrat Ayesha last; and then would go to the quarter of the wife whose turn was on that day.

Hazrat Ummi Salamah was always seeking blessing from the Holy Prophet. One such incident is mentioned in one of the traditions which is as follows, narrated by Hazrat Abu Musa:

Hazrat Bilal and I were with the Holy Prophet when he was encamping at Ji'ranah (a place between Mecca and Medina) during the battle of Ta'if.

A Bedouin came to the Holy Prophet and said, "Won't you fulfill what you have promised me?"

The Holy Prophet said, "Rejoice."

Then the Bedouin said, "You have said to me, 'rejoice' too many times."

Then the Holy Prophet turned to me and Bilal and said, "The Bedouin has refused the good tidings so you both accept them."

Bilal and I said, "We accept them."

Then the Holy Prophet asked for a bowl of water and washed his hands and face in it. Then he took a mouthful of water and spit it back into the bowl and said, "Drink of it and pour on your faces and chests, and be happy at the good tiding."[206] So they both did as instructed by the Holy Prophet. Hazrat Ummi Salmah, who was all seeing this from behind the curtain, called and said, "Keep some blessed water for your mother."

So, they left some water for her.

---

206 (Sahih Bukhari, Kitabul Maghazi, Ghazwah Ta'if).

Hazrat Ummi Salmah died at the age of eighty-four years old. She was the last to die among the wives of the Holy Prophet. She migrated to Abyssinia as well as Medina. She could read and thus played a major role in the education and moral training of Muslim women. There are 349 *Ahadith* in the books of the *Ahadith* which are related by Hazrat Ummi Salmah. She had the opportunity to travel with the Holy Prophet during the battles of Ahzab, Hudaybiya, Khaiber, Wadi al-Qura, Fadak, the Conquest of Mecca, Hunain, Aufas and Ta'if. In this regard, she had the opportunity to perform Hajj and was with the company of the Holy Prophet.

Hazrat Umm-e Salma Hind (ra)

- Bint Abi-Amia, bin Mugeera, bin Abdullah bin Umar, bin Makhzoom, bin Yukta, bin Marah
- Born 6 years before Nubuwah; died 60 Hijrah at 80 years old
- Year married: 4 Hijrah; age at marriage: 24; Muhammad's age at marriage: 57 years old; married for 7 years
- Number of traditions attributed: 378
- Prior husband: Abu Salma Abdullah (ra)
- Children from prior marriage: a daughter named Salma
- Remarks: 1st women to migrate to Medina; last to die among the wives of the Prophet

Hazrat Zainab bint Jahsh (ra)

— ❧ —

WHEN ALLAH REVEALED a verse in the Holy Qur'an, Hazrat Zainab bint Jahsh (ra) would boast about it to the other wives of the Holy Prophet (SAW), saying, "Your families arranged your marriages but Allah arranged my marriage from above the seven heavens." The following is narrated in the *Saheeh Bukhari, 7420:*

Hazrat Zainab bint Jahsh was a cousin of the Holy Prophet. Hazrat Zaid was a slave of Hazrat Khadijah who had given Hazrat Zaid to the Holy Prophet. The Holy Prophet freed him and raised him as a son. The Holy prophet thought that Hazrat Zainab would be a good match for Hazrat Zaid. Furthermore, the marriage of an ex-slave with a woman belonging to a noble family would set a good example of marriage based on qualities other than the nobility or wealth of a person. The family of Hazrat Zainab was shocked at the proposal and refused to marry Hazrat Zainab to Hazrat Zaid. At that time, this verse of the Holy Qur'an was revealed:

"And it behooves not a believing man or believing woman when Allah and His Messenger have decided that they should exercise their own choice in the matter concerning them. And whoso disobeys Allah and his Messenger surely strays away in manifest error" (Qur'an, Ch. 33:37).

Thus, the family of Hazrat Zainab agreed to marry their daughter to Hazrat Zaid. However, the marriage had problems and was not a happy marriage. Hazrat Zaid was patient for a long time but the situation did not change. Ultimately, Hazrat Zaid divorced Hazrat Zainab. In those days, it was a custom to free a slave and adopt him as a son. The adopted son was given the family name and he was eligible for inheritance as if they were actually their sons. Similarly, they considered marriage to an adopted son's wife, forbidden as it was to the wife of their blood-related son. However, an adopted son was not like a blood-related son in the sight of Allah.

When Hazrat Zaid divorced Hazrat Zainab, the Holy Prophet was commanded by Allah to marry Hazrat Zainab. The underlying reason for this marriage was to establish that an adopted son is not like a blood-related son. Because of the long-established tradition of accepting an adopted son as a blood-related son among Arabs, it was difficult for them to understand this new order, namely that the adopted son is not the same as a blood-related son.

Their reservation changed with the revelation of the following verse of the Holy Qur'an:

"And remember when you did say to him on whom Allah had bestowed favors and on whom you also had bestowed favors, 'keep your wife yourself, and fear Allah.' And you did conceal in your heart what Allah was going to bring to light and you were afraid of the people, whereas Allah is right that you should fear him. Then, Zaid finished doing what he wanted with her, so as to have no further need of her; in the Holy Qur'an, it is revealed, "We joined her in marriage to you so that there may be no hindrance for the believers with regard to the wives of their adopted sons when they have accomplished their want of them. And Allah's decree must be fulfilled" (Qur'an, chapter 33:38).

Accordingly, the Holy Prophet obeyed the commandment of Allah and married Hazrat Zainab. The marriage took place sometime before the Battle of Mustaliq, either in *Jamadi-ulThani* or *Rajab*, 5 Ah (i.e., 626 A.D.). Hazrat Zainab was a cousin of the Holy Prophet. Her brother Hazrat Abu Ahmad bin Jash acted as her guardian at the *Nikah* ceremony. The *Haq Mahr* (Dowry) was 400 Dirhams. On the second or third day of the wedding, the *Walima* (wedding ceremony) was held. Due to the special significance of this marriage, the *Walima* was rather elaborative. At the time of marriage, Hazrat Zainab was 37 years old. She was a very charitable woman and was an expert in sewing clothes. She used to sew clothes and distribute them among the poor. The Holy Prophet once said that she was the mother of the charitable. Once the Holy Prophet said to his wives:

> "[In the hereafter] The one [amongst you] who will meet me first is the one who has longest hands."[207]

Hazrat Ayesha states:

> "Upon hearing his saying of the Holy Prophet, all the wives of the Holy Prophet started measuring the length of their hands by placing their hands on a wall. Hazrat Sawdah had the longest hands. However, Hazrat Zainab was the one who passed away before the other wives of the Holy Prophet. Then it was realized that what was meant when the Holy Prophet spoke about the one with longest hands is that such a person is the one who is the most charitable."[208]

During the *Chilaphat*, Hazrat Umar sent a pile of gold to Hazrat Zainab, which was her share of the gold that fell into their hands as war booty when the Persians were defeated by Muslims. Hazrat Zainab told her maid to call the poor of Medina, and distributed the gold among them. When all the gold was distributed, Hazrat Zainab asked her maid to remove the cover from another pile. When she removed the cover, there were eighty Dinars. Hazrat Zainab accepted the Dinars as her share and thanked God Almighty.

---

207 Sahih Muslim, Kitab Al-Fada'il As-Sahabah, Bab fada'il Zainab Ummil Muminin.
208 Sahih Bukhari, Kitabul Zakat, Bab ayyu Sadqtu afdal.

Hazrat Zainab was a very broadminded, pious and honest woman. Although she had some personal differences with Hazrat Ayesha, when the Holy Prophet asked Hazrat Zainab about her observation of the incident of slander against Hazrat Ayesha by the hypocrites, she said that it was clear slander against Hazrat Ayesha.

Hazrat Zainab passed away in 20 A.H. at the age of 52 years old, in Medina. She traveled with the Holy Prophet during the Conquest of Mecca and battles of Hunain, Autas and Ta'if. She also had the honor of performing Hajj with the Holy Prophet.

Hazrat Zainab bint Jahsh (ra)

- Bint Hajash, bin Ramab, bin Yaamar, bin Sabra, bin Marah, bin Kabir, bin Ganam
- Born 16 years before Nubuwah; died 20 Hijrah; age: 49 years old
- Year married: 5 Hijrah; age at marriage: 36 years old; Muhammad's age at marriage: 57 years old; married for 6 years
- Number of traditions attributed: none
- Prior husband: Zaid (ra)
- Children from prior marriage: none
- Remarks: well-known for charity

Hazrat Juwayriyah (ra)

―――――― ⋄ ――――――

WHEN HAZRAT JUWAYRIAH (ra) became a prisoner of the Muslims during a battle, she went to the Holy Prophet and asked him to help her by buying her freedom. He offered to buy her freedom and then he purposed that he marry her; she accepted his invitation. Then, the Holy Prophet (SAW) married her and made her manumission her dowry. When people came to know that such happened, they set free their own prisoners as a way of honoring the in-laws of the Holy Prophet (SAW). Ibn Ishaaq narrated in *Seerat ibn Hisham*, 3/408-409, that, "No woman brought a greater blessing to her people than she did."

The tribe of *Banu Mustaliq* was preparing to attack the Muslims. When the Muslims came to know of said tribe's plan to attack them, they attacked first and defeated the enemy. Hazrat Juwayriyah bint al-Harith belonged to the tribe of *Banu Mustaliq* and was one of the prisoners captured in the Battle of Mustaliq. The prisoners were brought to Medina and were distributed among the Muslims. During the division of the prisoners, an *Ansar*, Hazrat Thabit bin Qais, was given custody of her. Her name was Barrah. Barah made an agreement with Hazrat Thabit bin Qais about her freedom, based on the principle of *Mukatbat*.[209] That is, if she paid him such an amount of ransom, she would become a free woman. She was worried that she would be used to collect a large amount of ransom from her father. She went to see the Holy Prophet and talked with him about her dilemma. She told the Holy Prophet that she was the daughter of a chief of *Banu Mustaliq* and needed assistance with the payment of her freedom money. The

---

209   As-Siratun Nabawiyyah Libne Hisham, vol. 3, p. 295.

Holy Prophet understood the problem and wanted to save her and her tribe from further difficulties. The Holy Prophet thought that the marriage with her would open the ways for spreading the message of Islam to her tribe's people. Therefore, he decided to pay the ransom for her freedom and to marry her. The Holy Prophet sent her the proposal for marriage which she wholeheartedly accepted. The Holy Prophet changed her name from Barrah to Juwayriyah. The marriage took place in Sha'ban in 5 A.H. (i.e., December of 626). At the time of her marriage, Hazrat Juwayriyah was 25 years old. After marrying Hazrat Juwayriyah, the Holy Prophet felt it against the status of a Prophet that his in-laws were his prisoners. Accordingly, the Holy Prophet freed hundreds of prisoners without collecting any ransom, and all the war booty collected from *Banu Mustaliq* was returned.

This action had a positive effect on the *Banu Mustaliq* tribe. Hazrat Ayesha used to say that Hazrat Juwayriyah turned out to be a very blessed person for her tribe. This openheartedness of the Holy Prophet won the hearts and minds of the people of the *Banu Mustaliq* tribe and they soon accepted Islam. Hazrat Juwayriyah had the honor of performing *Hajj* in the company of the Holy Prophet. Hazrat Juwayriyah was 70 years old when she passed away in *Rabi 'ul Awwal*, 59 A.H. According to one tradition, she passed away at the age of 75 years old in 56 A.H. There are seven *Ahadith* attributed to Hazrat Juwayriyah in the various books of the *Ahadith.*

According to one tradition, the father of Hazrat Juwayriyah came to the Holy Prophet to request the freedom of his daughter. He accepted Islam and then married his daughter willingly to the Holy Prophet. According to another tradition, when Harith, the father of Hazrat Juwayriyah, came to see the Holy Prophet, he could not be kept as a prisoner because he was the leader of a tribe. The Holy Prophet told him that Hazrat Juwayriyah should be asked for her opinion. If she wanted to get freedom and go home, they would let her go, said the Prophet. However, the Prophet also said that if she decided to stay, then she can do that as well. When Hazrat Juwayriyah was asked for her opinion on the matter, she preferred to become a Muslim and stay in the company of the Holy Prophet. Accordingly, the Holy Prophet freed her and then married her.

Hazrat Javeriah (ra)

- Bint Haris, bin Abi Zarar al-Khaziea al-Mustalkia
- Born 1 year before Nubuwah; died 56 Hijrah; age: 70 years old
- Year married: 5 Hijrah; age at marriage: 20 years old; Muhammad's age at marriage: 57 years old; married for 6 years
- Number of traditions attributed: 7
- Prior husband: Musafeh
- Children from prior marriage: none
- Remarks: was among those captured in the Battle of Mreseh

Hazrat Safiyyah (ra) bint Huyyay ibn Akhtab

As narrated by Imam Bukhari in Saheeh *Bukhari* 371, she was taken prisoner at the Battle of Khaibar, and came to the Holy Prophet (SAW) for help; he set her free and married her.

Hazrat Safiyyah was the daughter of Huyyay ibn Akhtab, the chief of the Banu Nadir tribe. She was brought to the Holy Prophet as a captive after the Battle of Khaibar, a battle that resulted in Muslim victory over Jews. At the time of the distribution of the prisoners of war, she was allotted to Hazrat Dihyah Kalbi. One of the Companions of the Holy Prophet mentioned to the Holy Prophet that Hazrat Safiyyah, who had been given to Hazrat Dihyah Kalbi and was a princess of Banu Nadir and Banu Quraiza, deserves none other than the Holy Prophet. Accordingly, the Holy Prophet sent the message to Hazrat Dihyah Kalbi regarding his decision to marry Hazrat Safiyyah. Hazrat Dihyah Kalbi sent Hazrat Safiyyah to the Holy Prophet. The Holy Prophet treated her with respect and told her that if she would like to stick to her religion, there would not be any pressure put on her to change her decision. However, she was told that if she accepted Islam, it would be a blessing for her. Hazrat Safiyyah accepted Islam as her religion. After this, the Holy Prophet freed her and gave her the option of either becoming his wife or going back to her family. Hazrat Safiyyah preferred to marry the Holy Prophet. Accordingly, the Holy Prophet married her and her freedom was considered as her *Haq Mahr* (Dowry). The marriage took place in *Safr*, 7 A.H. (i.e., June of 628). At the time of her marriage, Hazrat Safiyyah was 17 years old. When Hazrat Safiyyah agreed to marry the Holy prophet, the Companions of the Holy Prophet were keen to see whether or not she observed Purdah.

If she observed Purdah, that meant she was the Mother of the Faithful. The Holy Prophet made her observe Purdah, thus making people know that she had become the Mother of the Faithful. On the third day, after returning from Khaibar, when the Holy Prophet along with his Companions reached a place called Sahba, proper arrangements were made for the wedding ceremony. Hazrat Umm Sulaim, the mother of Hazrat Anas bin Malik, prepared Hazrat Safiyyah as a bride, and the wedding took place. The next day, the Holy Prophet told Hazrat Bilal to spread table cloth. Dates, cheese and butter were placed on the tablecloth, food which everyone ate together. This was served at the *Walima* (wedding ceremony). There was no bread or meat served at this function.

Being the daughter of a great chief, the only way she could avoid being a slave was to marry the Holy Prophet. Her father, Huyyay Ibn Akhtab, was a staunch enemy of the Holy Prophet and was determined to destroy Islam. However, Hazrat Safiyyah accepted Islam and became the wife of the Holy Prophet. Hazrat Safiyyah had difficulty adjusting as wife of the Holy Prophet because the other wives of the Holy Prophet belonged to the *Quraish* and other Arab tribes and they considered themselves better than Hazrat Safiyyah who came from a Jewish family. She was so annoyed with the attitude of the other wives of the Holy Prophet that one day she could not bear such anger any more. She complained to the Holy Prophet while her eyes were overflowing with tears. The Holy Prophet told her to tell his other wives who annoyed her that she is better than them, as the Holy Prophet is her husband. He also told her that Moses was her great granduncle and Aaron her great grandfather. This made her happy and after this talk with the Holy Prophet she never felt inferior to any of the wives of the Holy prophet.[210] Hazrat Safiyyah was a widow of Kinanah ibn al-Rabi', a Chief of Khaibar who was killed in the Siege of Khaibar when she was married to the Holy Prophet. The Holy Prophet saw that Hazrat Safiyyah had a mark on her face which appeared to be an impression of a hand. The Holy Prophet asked Hazrat Safiyyah about the mark on her face. Hazrat Safiyyah stated the following:

---

210 Jami' Tirmidhi, Abwabul Manaqib Fi Fadli Azwajin Nabiyyi.

"I saw the moon fall in my lap in a dream. I related the dream to my husband. No sooner had I related the dream when my husband gave a heavy slap on my face and said, 'You desire to marry the king of Arabia.'"[211] Hazrat Safiyyah passed away in the month of Ramadan, in 50 A.H. At the time of her demise, she was 60 years old. During the journey from Khaibar to Medina, she accompanied the Holy Prophet. She also had the opportunity to perform hajj with the Holy Prophet. There are ten *Ahadith* in the books of the *Ahadith* which have been related by Hazrat Safiyyah.

When the Holy Prophet became seriously ill, Hazrat Safiyyah, along with the other wives of the Holy Prophet, witnessed such. Hazrat Safiyyah said, "I wish that the Holy Prophet becomes completely healthy and I get his disease."

Hearing this, the other wives looked at each other. Then, the Holy Prophet said:

"By Allah, she is truthful."

Hazrat Safiyyah bint Huyyay, the Mother of the Faithful, relates:

"The Holy Prophet was in retreat in the mosque, and I went there to see him one evening. After finishing talking with me, he stood up to accompany me a part of the way [on my journey]. Two men passed us and when they saw the Holy Prophet they quickened their pace. The Holy Prophet called out to them, saying, 'Stop a moment. This is my wife Safiyyah bint Huyyay.' They expostulated:

'Holy is Allah, Messenger of Allah.'

---

211   Life of Muhammad, Hadrat Mirza Bashir ud din Mehmood Ahmad, p. 125.

The Holy Prophet observed, 'Satan courses through a man's mind like the circulation of the blood, and I apprehended, lest Satan might create suspicion in your minds.'

Or, he said something similar to it."[212]

Safiyyah (ra)

- Bint Haye, bin Akhtab, bin Shaaba, from among Sabt Haroon
- Born 4 Nubuwah; died 50 Hijrah at the age of 50 years old
- Year married: 7 Hijrah; age at marriage: 17 years old; Muhammad's age at marriage: 59 years old; married for 4 years
- Number of traditions attributed: 10
- Prior husband before the Prophet: Salam, Kanana
- Children from prior marriage: none
- Remarks: was among those captured in the Battle of Khayber

---

212 Sahih Bukhari, Kitabul Itikaf, Bab hal yakhrujul mu 'l' takif li hawaijih. P. 272/1, Sahih Muslim, p. 202/9.

Hazrat Ummi Habibah (ra), bint Abi Sufyan

———— ✿ ————

HAZRAT UMMI HABIBAH was the daughter of Abu Sufyan, who at one time was a staunch enemy of the Holy Prophet and had fought against the Muslims in many battles. Her actual name was Ramla bint Abu Sufyan. She accepted Islam along with her husband 'Ubaydullah ibn Jahsh. Ubaydullah ibn Jahsh was the brother of Hazrat Zainab, the wife of the Holy Prophet. Both had migrated to Abyssinia where their daughter Habibah was born. After the birth of Habibah, she became known as Ummi Habibah. In Abyssinia, her husband embraced Christianity. He tried to persuade her to do the same. However, she held onto Islam. She found herself in a terrible situation. She did not want to stay with her husband and could not go to her father who was an arch enemy of the Holy Prophet. She separated from her husband and lived with her daughter under miserable conditions. However, she remained a staunch Muslim. Allah rewarded her for her steadfastness in adhering to Islam.

The Holy Prophet sent a message to king Negus through 'Amr bin Umayyah al-Zumar; the message asked the king to let the immigrants return. He also asked the king to perform his *Nikah* with Hazrat Ummi Habibah. Upon receiving this message, the king started to make preparations for the marriage. One day, a maid of Negus, the king of Abyssinia, received a message from the king. The message asked if the Holy Prophet would like to marry Hazrat Ummi Habibah and asked her to appoint someone as her guardian. She appointed Hazrat Khalid ibn Sa'd ibn al-as as her guardian. It was due to the will of God that she was chosen to be the wife of the Holy Prophet. The marriage ceremony took place in Abyssinia even though the Holy Prophet was not present there. The king invited Hazrat

Ja'far and other Muslims present in Abyssinia for the *Nikah* ceremony and he himself delivered the *Khutbah Nikah*. Hazrat Khalid ibn SA'd made a speech in reply to the king's sermon. On behalf of the Holy Prophet, Negus offered a dowry of four hundred Dinars to Hazrat Ummi Habibah. It was a large sum of money which she badly needed at that time. A huge wedding feast was prepared on behalf of the Holy Prophet after the ceremony. The *Nikah* ceremony was held in the month of Muharram, 7 A.H. (i.e., May of 628).

In those days, it was difficult for Muslims to travel from Abyssinia to Medina. Therefore, Hazrat Ummi Habibah lived in Abyssinia for six years and when the situation changed and Muslims were able to return from Abyssinia to Medina, she went back to Medina and lived with the Holy Prophet. It was Negus who made the arrangements to send her to Medina by boat under the supervision of Shurahbil bin Hasana. When Hazrat Ummi Habibah arrived in Medina, after traveling from Abyssinia, she was thirty years old.

Hazrat Ummi Habibah saw the Holy Prophet as so honorable that she didn't mind sacrificing her life for the sake of the Holy Prophet. Once Abu Sufyan went to Medina to see the Holy Prophet, trying to get the time period of the Hudaybiya pact extended. At first, he went to the house of his daughter, Hazrat Ummi Habibah. There, when he was about to sit at the bed of the Holy Prophet, Hazrat Ummi Habibah immediately folded the bed. Abu Sufyan realized that something was wrong. So, he asked Hazrat Ummi Habibah, "Does the bed not deserve me or do I not deserve the bed?" Hazrat Ummi Habibah told him that the bed belongs to the Holy Prophet and that he (Abu Sufyan), being a disbeliever and an impure person, did not deserve to sit on the bed.

Hazrat Zainab bint Abi Salmah relates:

"I visited Hazrat Ummi Habibah, wife of the Holy Prophet, after her father Abu Sufyan died. She sent for a yellow perfume and rubbed it on one of her maids, and then rubbed it on both cheeks and said, 'I had no desire for perfume.'

I then heard the Holy Prophet say from the pulpit, 'It is not permissible for a woman who believes in Allah and the Last Day that she should mourn a dead person for months and three days, except in the case of her husband, when the period of mourning is four months and ten days.'"[213]

Hazrat Ayesha relates that when Hazrat Ummi Habibah was close to her last days, she called her (Ayesha) and said, "During our lives, once in a while it happened that I did or said things which were unpleasant to you. I apologize for that. Please forgive me." Ayesha prayed for her, namely that God Almighty ignore her shortcomings and forgive her. Then, Hazrat Ummi Habibah said, "You have made me happy. May God Almighty keep you also happy." Then Hazrat Ayesha called Hazrat Ummi Salmah and said the same which she had said to me.

Hazrat Ummi Habibah passed away in 44 A.H. in Medina. At the time of her death she was 67 years old. She had the honor of performing Hajj in the company of the Holy Prophet. She had related 65 *Ahadith*.

Hazrat Umme Habiba Ramlah (ra)

- Bint Abi Sufyan, bin Ania, bin Abd Shams, bin Abd Munaaf, bin Qasee
- Born 15 years before Nubuwah; died 44 Hijrah at the age of 72 years old
- Year married: 6 Hijrah; age at marriage: 36 years old; Muhammad's age at marriage: 58 years old; married for 5 years
- Number of traditions attributed: 65
- Prior husband: Abdullah bin Hajash
- Children from prior marriage: a daughter named Habiba
- Remarks: Najashi conducted Nikah; 400 Dinaar dowry.

---

213 Sahih Bukhari, Kitabul Jana'iz, Bab ahadadal mirata 'ala ghairi zaujiha.

Hazrat Mariah al-Qibtiyyah (ra)

HAZRAT MARIAH AL-QIBITIYYAH belonged to Egypt and had started serving in the place of Muqawaqis, the ruler of Egypt, at a very young age. The Holy Prophet wrote a letter to Muqawqis and sent it to him through his messenger Hatib bin Abi Balta'ah; the message was an invitation for Muqawaqis to accept Islam. Muqawaqis treated the letter with great respect. He put it in an ivory box and kept it in a safe place. He asked the messenger of the Holy Prophet to tell him in detail about the Holy Prophet. After the conversation, he said to the carrier of the message of the Holy Prophet, "I was expecting the appearance of a prophet. However, I was expecting the prophet to come from Syria. My people are Coptic Christians who, I think, will not accept the new messenger. I also hate to give up my kingdom for the sake of the Messenger." As a symbol of his great respect for the Holy Prophet, Muqawaqis sent back a letter, many precious presents such as a special kind of honey, one thousand *Mithqal* (Quality of the gold) of 20 pieces of a special kind of soft cloth, and two sisters, Mariah and Sirin, to the Holy Prophet. He also sent a sturdy gray donkey named "Duldul" and a donkey named "Afir." He wrote a letter to the Holy Prophet in which he stated that the girls who were being sent to the Holy Prophet were sisters and had high status among the Coptic Christians. The sisters arrived in Medina in 7 Ah (628 A.D.). On her way from Egypt to Medina, Hazrat Hatib bin Abi Balta'ah preached to the girls about Islam. Both girls accepted Islam before reaching Media. An old man by the name of Maboar, who was accompanying the two girls, did not accept Islam during the travel to Medina. However, after they arrived in Medina, after some time, he also accepted Islam. Upon arrival in Medina, both sisters along with the king's letter and the gifts were presented to the Holy Prophet. The Holy Prophet married Hazrat Mariah al-Qibitiyyah, and Hazrat Hassan bin Thabit married Sirin. Hazrat Ayesha relates that in the beginning, the Holy Prophet kept Hazrat Mariah in the house of Hartha bin al-Aman and then later on he moved her to another place in Medina which was known as Al-Aliya. To her last days, Hazrat Mariah lived there. In *Dhul Hijja, 8 A.H.* (i.e., March 630) a son was born to Hazrat Mariah, whom the Holy Prophet had named Ibrahim. The Holy Prophet was very happy with the birth of a son as all his earlier sons had died in infancy. Hazrat Ibrahim lived for 15 to 16 months and passed away in *Rabiul Awwal,* 10 A.H. The Holy Prophet, upon the infant's demise, stated:

"If he had lived, he would have been a truthful prophet."

Tradition related about this son of the Holy Prophet as follows:

Hazrat Ibn Abass relates that when Hazrat Ibrahim, the son of Holy Prophet died, the Holy Prophet led his funeral prayer and said:

"If my son Ibrahim had lived, he would have been a *Siddiq* (truthful) prophet, and his maternal grand-parents' family, who are Coptic Egyptians, would have been liberated from bondage."[214] Hazrat Mariah Passed away in 16 A.H., during the Caliphate of Hazrat 'Umar.

Hazrat Maria Qabtia (ra)

- From the Qabti tribe
- Born 3 Nubuwah; died 27 Hijrah at the age of 36 years old

---

214 Sunan ibn Majah, Kitabul Jana'iz Bab ma ja fissalate ala ibn rasulullah wadikr wafati, p. 237/1 Matba' Ilmiyyah 1313 H.

- Year married: 7 Hijrah; age at marriage: 20 years old; Muhammad's age at marriage: 59 years old; married for 4 years
- Number of traditions attributed: none
- Prior husband: none
- Children from prior marriage: none
- Remarks: mother of Ibrahim; was a gift from King Manqoos of Egypt

Hazrat Maimunah (ra)

HAZRAT MAIMUNAH, WHO was the daughter of Harith and hind, was fist married to Mas 'ud bin 'Umair Thaqfi. When Mas 'ud bin 'Umair divorced her, she married Abu Ruham bin 'Abdul 'Uzza. After the death of Ruham, she lived for some time as a widow. Hazrat Abbas, who was the brother-in-law of Hazrat Maimunah, was concerned about her marriage. He conveyed his concerns to the Holy Prophet. Thus, the Holy Prophet married Hazrat Maimunah after Hazrat Abbas suggested that he do so. Hazrat Abbas made the announcement of Hazrat Maimunah's *Nikah* with the Holy Prophet with a *Haq Mahr* of 400 Dirhams. The marriage took place in Dhul Qa'da, 7 Ah (i.e., March 629). At that time, she was 36 years old. Before her marriage to the Holy Prophet, her name was Barrah. The Holy Prophet changed her name to Maimunah just like he had changed Hazrat Juwayriyah's name. Hazrat Maimunah was the real sister of Hazrat Ummul Fadl, the wife of Hazrat Abbas who was the uncle of the Holy Prophet. Hazrat Maimunah was the last one to become the Mother of the Faithful and passed away in 51 A.H. At the time of her demise, she was 80 years old. Although her *Nikah* ceremony took place in Medina, her wedding took place at a place called Sarif. Hazrat Maimunah, before her death, picked Sarif for her burial. Accordingly, in 51 A.H., she was buried at Sarif, which is 7 miles from Mecca and close to Tan 'im. She had the honor of performing Hajj in the company of the Holy Prophet. There are 67 *Ahadith* narrated by her.

Hazrat Mamona (Barah) (ra)

- Bint Haris, bin Hazan, bin Bajir, bin Hazam, bin Robiah
- Born 15 years before Nubuwah; died 51 Hijrah at 80 years old
- Year married: 7 Hijrah; Age at marriage: 36 years old; Muhammad's age at marriage: 59 years old; married for 4 years
- Number of traditions attributed: 76
- Prior husbands: Masood, Abu Rahm
- Children from prior marriage: none
- Remarks: Zanab bin Khazeema: real sister from her mother's side

Hazrat Rehana

———— ⚬⚭ ————

HAZRAT REHANA WAS the daughter of Sham'oon. The history of Rehana coming to the service of the Holy Prophet has a great resemblance to that of Hazrat Safiyyah and Hazrat Juwayriyah. Rehana was the daughter of the chief of the Banu-Qurazia tribe. His name was Sham'oon bin Zaid. The Banu Quraiza tribe was mostly comprised of Jews and lived in the Suburbs of Medina.

"Hazrat Rehana was married to Hakam who was assassinated along with other Jews in the Battle of Banu Qurazia" (Tabqat, Vol. 8, p. 93).

After settling down and establishing an Islamic state, the Holy Prophet endeavored to promote good relations with the neighbors of his tiny Islamic state. As a result of this effort, a treaty was signed with the Banu-Quraiza tribe by Medinites. This treaty had two clauses:

> Firstly, that both parties would not wage war against each other, and secondly that in case of aggression from any foreign tribe, the two parties would defend and meet the aggression jointly. But in clear violation of the agreement, the Banu-Quraiza tribe kept going against Muslims. They extended secret operations to Meccans and anti-Islamic forces. Further, they instigated the anti-Islamic forces to attack since the Muslims were weak at that time. These nefarious activities could not remain secret and soon there was a battle between the Muslims of Medina and the Banu-Quraiza tribe. As a result, the Banu-Quraiza tribe lost this battle and their property, lands, riches, chattels and wealth were confiscated by the Muslims. According to the universally accepted

custom, the booty included bondmen and bondmaids. Hazrat Rehana was among such people.

"Hazrat Rehana's temporary stay was arranged in the house of Almunzer bint Qais" (Tabqat, Vol. 8, p. 93).

Rehana was brought before the Holy Prophet as a part of the booty. She was introduced as the daughter of the chief of the Banu-Quraiza tribe. The Holy Prophet addressed the prisoners of war and invited them to follow the path of Allah, i.e., Islam.

After the address of the Holy Prophet, Rehana stood up and said:

Ibn Sa'd and Hafiz Ibn-Hajar have narrated that she was married to the Holy Prophet after accepting Islam. In this regard, one event will shed more light on this. One day, the Holy Prophet was sitting in a social gathering, and he heard the sound of somebody's footsteps; instantly he said:

"Listen, this is the Alb who is coming to announce that Rehana has embraced Islam" (*Seerat Ibn Hisham*).

To the greatest surprise of the audience, the incomer was Tha 'alba and he announced what the Holy Prophet had already revealed. After Rehana embraced Islam, the Holy Prophet met her and offered, "If you like and agree, I can marry you and you may observe hijab (Hijab or Purdah: the tradition of Muslim women hiding their faces and bodies) as the rest of the wives are doing."

"The Dowry of Hazrat Rehana was according to the other wives of the Holy Prophet. Hazrat Rehana's marriage to the Holy Prophet took place in *Muharam* 6 Hijri" (Tabqat, vol. 8, p. 93).

The Holy Prophet loved Rehana very much and he would fulfill all her wants and needs. Her permanent residence was at Dar-ul-Qa'is bin Fahad. She was very attractive and good-figured; and was of a very pious and sound character. She preferred to always stay in veil and the Prophet visited her on assigned days. Hazrat Rehana died a few months before the Prophet's own demise and she was buried in *Jannat-ul-Baqee'* (Asabah, Vol. 2., p. 592).

All the Prophet's wives joined his household after the emigration. They became the mothers of the believers. The Holy Prophet talks about the good treatment of the family:

> "The best among you is the one who is best in the treatment of his family and I am better than all of you in the treatment of the family."[215]

It was the Holy Prophet's routine that he would visit his wives daily in their quarters and then go to the quarter of the wife who he was to stay with for the night. In the evening, all the wives would get together in the quarter of the wife the Holy Prophet was staying with for the night, and after socializing for some time, go back to their own houses. The Holy Prophet used to take good care of his wives and their sensibilities. However, their lives were very simple as was the life of the Holy Prophet. Most of them belonged to well-to-do families.

Hazrat Rihana (ra)

- Bint Shamoon, a Jewish tribe; Banu Qureza
- Born? _____; died 63 Hijrah; age?:____ years old
- Year married: 4 Hijrah; ____; Muhammad's age at marriage: 58 years old; married for 5 years

I have thus examined the wives of the Holy Prophet (SAW). Three of them died during the lifetime of the Holy Prophet (SAW), namely Khadijha Zainab, bint Khuzaimah and Rehana bint Shamoon.

---

215 Jami 'Tirmidhi, Abwabul Manaqib, Bad fadl as azwajunnabi.

Abstention from Wives

———— ✤ ————

THESE WIVES OF the Prophet were divided into two groups. One included Ayesha, Hafsa, Sawdah and Safiya, and the other group was comprised of Zainab and the other wives of the Prophet.

After the *Asr* (evening) prayers, the Prophet used to visit all of his wives for almost equal duration. On some days, however, he overstayed with Zainab and the others had to wait for him. After inquiring about such, Ayesha learned that Zainab had received some honey and she used to offer it every day to the Prophet (SAW). The Prophet was extremely fastidious about cleanliness and any bad odor was very repugnant to him. The smell of honey depends on the type of flowers visited by the honey bees producing honey.

Maghafir is a flower of Arabia which has a pungent smell. Ayesha, Hafsah and Saudah decided that when the Prophet came they would ask him if he had taken honey collected from Maghafir. When he was told about this, he developed an aversion for honey and declared that he would never take it again. Had this related to an ordinary person, it would have been of no significance and nobody would have noticed it. But, it related to the Apostle of God, who's every word and deed would pave the way for laying the foundations of laws. God, in his infinite Wisdom, warned the Holy Prophet:

"O Prophet! Why dost thou forbid thyself that which Allah has made lawful to thee? Thou seekest the pleasure of thy wives? And Allah is Most Forgiving, Merciful."[216] It is to this incident that the

---

216 Holy Qur'an, Ch. 66:2.3.

verse just cited is generally taken to be referring to. But it seems improbable that the Holy Prophet, merely to satisfy his wife or wives irritation, should have taken such drastic steps as to have permanently forbidden himself the use of something which was lawful, particularly of a thing in which, according to the Qur'an, there is cure for mankind. "There comes forth from their bellies a drink of varying hues. There in is healing for mankind. Surely that is a Sign for a people who reflect."[217] It appears that the narrator or narration of this incident suffered from some misunderstanding or mental confusion, particularly when, according to one tradition, the Holy Prophet took honey from the house of Zainab and Ayesha, and Hafsah contrived to draw him into making the aforesaid promise, while according to another tradition, it was at the house of Hafsah herself that he was served with honey and that the wives who objected were Ayesha, Zaniab and Safiyyah. Moreover, according to the Hadith, two, or at the most three, of the Holy Prophet's wives were concerned in the affair. But according to verse 2 and 6 of chapter 66 of the Holy Qur'an, all of them were connected with it, two of them taking a leading part. These facts show that the Surah refers to some incident of much greater significance than the taking of honey by the Holy Prophet at the house of one of his wives. In the commentary on this Surah, Bukhari (*Kitab al-Mazalim wa'l Ghasb*) quotes Ibn 'Abbas as relating that he was always on the look-out to ask Umar about the two wives to whom reference is made in the verse that says, "Now, if you two turn unto Allah, it will be better for you, and your hearts are already so inclined." One day, finding Umar alone, he sought to satisfy his curiosity. He hardly finished his question, says Ibn 'Abbas, when 'Umar said that they were 'Ayesha and Hafsah, and then proceeded to relate the story: "One day when my wife offered me her advice concerning some domestic affairs, I curtly told her that it was no business of hers to advise me, for in those

---

217 The Holy Qur'an. Ch. 16:70.

days we did not hold our women-folk in much respect. My wife sternly replied, 'Your daughter Hafsah takes so much liberty with the Prophet that she retorts back when he says something which she does not like, until he feels offended, and you do not allow me to speak to you even about our domestic affairs.' After this, I went to Hafsah and told her that she should not be misled by Ayesha in this matter as she was nearer to the Prophet's heart. Then I went to Ummi Salmah. I had hardly broached the matter with her when she curtly told me not to interfere in affairs concerning the Prophet and his wives. A short time after this, the Holy Prophet separated himself from his wives and decided not to go to the houses of any of them for some time. The news went around that the Holy Prophet had divorced his wives. I went to him and asked him if it was true that he had divorced his wives, to which he replied in the negative.

This incident shows that 'Hazrat Umar and Ibn 'Abbas were of the view that the relevant verses of the Surah referred to this temporary separation of the Holy Prophet from his wives. The fact that the preceding Surah mentions the subject of *Talaq*, which means the separation of a permanent character, lends weight to the inference that these verses relate to the Prophet's separation from his wives which, however, was of a temporary nature. Besides, as reported by Ayesha in the above-mentioned tradition, immediately after such separation, it was over. In chapter 33:29 of the Qur'an, Allah says, "O Prophet! Say to thy wives, 'If you desire the life of this world and its adornment, come then, I will provide for you and send you away in a handsome manner.'" In this verse, the Prophet's wives are given the choice between the Prophet's companionship with a life of poverty and austere simplicity or separation from him with a life of ease and comfort and all sorts of material benefits. The choice was given to all the wives of the Prophet. This fact shows that the incident referred to concerns all the wives and that two of them took a prominent part in the situation. And it is stated in one record that the incident occurred when the prophet's wives, led by Ayesha and Hafsah, demanded him, since the financial conditions of Muslims had greatly improved, to allow them to enjoy amenities of life and comfortable living. Thus, the words, "Thou seekest the pleasure of thy wives" would seem to signify something like this. "Since thou always desired to please thy wives and meet their wishes, they have become so emboldened by this loving attitude of thine as to lose sight of thy high position as great Prophet of God and to make excessive demands from thee."

In that period, the Holy Prophet disclosed a secret to Hafsah and she passed it on to Ayesha. The Holy Qur'an refers to it: "And when the Prophet confided a matter unto one of his wives and she divulged it, and Allah informed me of it, he made known to her part thereof, and avoided mentioning part of it. And when he informed her of it, she said, 'who has informed thee of it?' He [the Prophet] said, 'The All-knowing, the All-Aware God has informed me.'"[218] It is difficult to say to what particular incident this verse in fact refers to. The reference, which seems to be supported by the context, may concern the incident described by Ayesha herself, which is to this effect: when verse 33:29 of the Qur'an was revealed, giving the Holy Prophet's wives the choice between his companionship and separation from him in reply to their demand for a life of comfort and ease, the Prophet broached the matter to Ayesha (Bukhari, Kitab al Mazalim wa'l-Ghasb). The Holy Prophet appears to have taken that action because it was Ayesha who had led the demand along with Hafsah, and it is not unlikely that Ayesha should have passed on the Holy Prophet's secret communication to Hafsah. Whatever the actual facts of the case may be, the verse emphasizes the obligation of a person to whom a secret is confided in, not to spread it, particularly when the parties concerned are husband and wife and the secret relates to a private domestic affair; or for that matter, when the parties are a Prophet of God and one of his followers.

In the 5th verse of the Surah being examined, Allah says, "Now if you two turn unto Allah repentant, and your hearts are already so inclined, it

---

218   Ch. 66: Verse 4.

will be better for you. But if you back up one another against him, surely Allah is his helper and the Angel Gabriel and the righteous among the believers and all the angels are his helpers."

The words, "You two" seem to refer to Ayesha and Hafsah who led the demand for worldly comforts in their domestic lives. All the other wives of the Holy Prophet had, however, joined in the demand, though the leading part was taken by these two, and this perhaps means they were the daughters of Abu Baker and Umar respectively, the two most re-spected people among the Holy Prophet's companions. The phraseology of the verse indicates that the matter referred to in the verse was of a very serious nature, but taking honey from the house of one's wife evidently is not so serious an affair as to have led to the separation of the Holy Prophet from all his wives for about a month. Nor was the admonition to the Prophet's wives implied in the words. Allah is his helper and the Angel Gabriel and the righteous among the believers called for in such a case.

By the time the incident of seclusion occurred, even distant parts of Arabia had come under the sway of Islam, and tributes and spoils of war were filling the State treasury. After the conquest of Khaiber, the Prophet fixed a certain percentage of the produce of Khaiber as allowances for his wives, such falling short of their requirements. They were pressing for an increase in their portions, for many of them were daughters of chieftains or widows of well-to- do husbands and were not used to so much auster-ity which the Prophet adopted. He could not, however, abandon his aus-terity for their sake and this led to some estrangements. It was then that another revelation came. In the Holy Qur'an (Ch. 33:28-29) it says, "And he made you inherit their land and their houses and their wealth, and also a land on which you have not yet set foot. And Allah has power over all things." The allusion here seems to be either to the lands of Khaibar or to the eventual conquest of Persian and Roman Empires and of the countries beyond, upon which Muslims had not set their feet on yet.

"O! Say to thy wives, 'If you desire the life of this world and its adorn-ment, come then, I will provide for you and send you away in a handsome manner.'"

As the Holy Prophet's wives were to serve as a model in social behavior, it was in the fitness of things that they should have been required to set an example in self-denial. The use of money and the amenities of life were not completely forbidden to them, but they were certainly expected to set a very high standard of self-abnegation. It is to this high standard of the sacrifice of material benefits and of an affluent and easy living to which the verses above and the ones following refer to. Having companionship with the Holy Prophet demanded this sacrifice, and his wives were told to make a choice between comfortable life and his companionship.

The Holy Prophet first spoke about such to Ayesha and asked her to consult her parents before giving an answer. She asked what there was to be consulted about given she would definitely choose God and His Apostle. The Prophet was glad to hear that answer. As mentioned earlier, Ayesha requested the Prophet not to disclose her answer to his other wives. The Prophet said, "I have come as a teacher and not as a transgressor."[219]

---

219 Bukhari: Sahih. Chapter: Seclusion.

Hazrat Ayesha's Excellence and Superiority

ACCORDING ALLAH'S PLAN, we find that fate places an extraordinary role on some of the Messenger's wives. Ayesha's status, in particular, was special and acknowledged by the other wives. Ayesha was the only wife of the Holy Prophet who was Muslim by birth. The rest of the wives of the Holy Prophet had accepted Islam either by themselves or along with their parents.

It was because of Ayesha that the Qur'an revealed the punishment for slander, and the sentence for such was applied directly by the Holy Prophet (SAW). In various ways, too, Ayesha was different from the other wives. Because of Ayesha, the verse about *tayammum* (performing ablution with sand or earth) was revealed, and Muslims learned how to cleanse themselves in a place where there was no water. In Mecca, she was shown to the Prophet in a dream, and he was told directly by the Angel Gabriel that she would be his wife.

Ayesha was the only wife of the Holy Prophet (SAW) who was a virgin when marrying. His other wives were widows.

Ayesha was the only one of the Prophet's wives whose mother and father were emigrants. Another distinction of her family is that members of four generations of the same family, including her grandfather, father, brother and two nephews, believed in the Holy Prophet and became Companions.

Ayesha was the only wife of the Prophet who witnessed a revelation as it came to the Prophet. The Companions who wanted to bring a gift to the Holy Prophet preferred to give it on his day with Ayesha, believing he would be happier and more likely to accept it.

Ayesha was the only wife of the Prophet who saw Gabriel in human form, and Gabriel greeted her as well.

Ayesha's bridal due was higher than the other wives of the Prophet. Years later she explained this and accepted only Umm Habiba whose wedding was held in Ethiopia?

"Her marriage ceremony was done by a king."

After the day that Sawda gave her turn to Ayesha (to be with the prophet), the time that Ayesha spent with the Holy Prophet was double that of the other wives of the Prophet.

Ayesha had a different kind of relationship with the Holy Prophet who wanted to make her content. Sometimes she behaved coyly as a result of her favored position, and enjoyed how the Prophet of God tried to please her.

The Holy Prophet raced against her twice during his life. Ayesha was surely the best among the mothers of the believers; the Holy Prophet was content with her when he died.

Ayesha became distinguished in knowledge. She excelled not only among the common women-folk, other wives of the Holy Prophet and the wives of the Companions. But she also excelled more than most of the Companions with only a few exceptions.

Tirmizi records that Abu Musa Ash'ari said, "We Companions were never presented with a problem to which Ayesha did not present a satisfactory solution."

Attar bin Abi Riyah, who was a disciple of many Companions, said, "Ayesha was the best theologian, the most learned and the one having sound judgment."

Imam Zuhri, the leader of *Taba'een*, said, "Ayesha was the most learned. Even the important Companions used to consult her."

Abu Salma, son of Abdul Raman bin Auf, a leading *Tabai'l*, said, "There was no one better conversant than Ayesha with the Traditions of the Prophet; nor a better theologian or a person knowing better the chronological sequence of the descent of the Qur'an, nor one more knowledgeable of the details of obligatory duties."[220]

---

220 Ahmad Musnad.

Amir Muawiyah asked one of his courtiers, "Who is the most learned among the people? "Amir-ul Mominin, you are the most learned."

Amir Muawiyah said, "I put you to oath. Tell me correctly."

The courtier replied, "In that case it is Ayesha."[221]

Urwa bin Zubair said, "In the matter of lawful and unlawful [things] in knowledge, poetry and medicine, I saw no one better versed than Ummul Mominin Ayesha."[222]

Masrooq Tabaii said, "By God. Even the most exalted Companions used to consult Ayesha for details of obligatory duties."

Though the other wives also propagated Traditions of the Prophet, none touched the stature of Ayesha in this regard. *Imam* Zuhri says, "If the knowledge of all the men and the Mothers of the believers are gathered at one place, the knowledge of Ayesha would be greater."

Some Traditions have recorded that the Prophet once said, "Learn part of your religion from Ayesha."

No other wife, no other woman among the Companions narrated as many Hadith as Ayesha; the depth of her knowledge had a stronger influence than that of any other woman, including the other wives of the Holy Prophet (SAW). When those who were unable to decide on an issue came to ask her about the matter, they left her place without worry and with an answer to their issue.

When God's Messenger's sickness worsened, he wanted to spend his last fourteen days with Ayesha. He passed away in her room. Ayesha continued to live in the same room of her house after his death (the room the Prophet died in).

After his death, Ayesha became the best source of information about his behavior. Everyone, even the leading Companions, went to her about that topic, and all of them got answers.

People who considered her according to her innate superiorities respected her more and competed with each other to please her in order to receive her prayers on their behalf. Hazrat Umar, during his *Khilafat*,

---

221 Hakim in Mustadarak.
222 Ibid.

treated her more respectfully than the other mothers of the believers including his own daughter Hafsah, and reserved more for Ayesha than anyone else when he divided the spoils during his *Khilafat.*

Ayesha's Knowledge and Interpretation

———— ❦ ————

IN RELATION TO interpretation of the Qur'an and Traditions of the Prophet, theology, commands and injunctions, Ayesha's name can be mentioned along with Hazrat Umar Farooq, Ali Murtaza, Abdullah bin Masood and Abdullah bin Abbas.

The Qur'an

THE QUR'AN IN the present form had not yet been complied during the life-time of the Prophet. Some of the Companions, including Abu Bakr, recorded things for their own reading. Ayesha had her literate slave Abu Yunus record information. Ayesha learned the manner of its recitation, the inner meaning of its verses; she also learned to appreciate it. When finding a solution for every point and elucidation, she referred to the Qur'an first and then looked into the Traditions. Some Companions requested her to tell them about the manners of the Prophet. She said, "Do you not read the Qur'an? The ways of the Prophet were a reflection of the Qur'an."

They asked, "What was his practice in relation to prayers during the night?"

She asked, "Have you not read the *Surah Muzammil?*"

The major interpreter of the Qur'an was the Messenger of God. He was the only one who knew the divine purpose and recognized when to give this information to the people. Ayesha closely followed the explanations of God's Messenger related to the Qur'an and learned its obscure points directly from the true interpreter himself (the Prophet). She acquired the ability to understand the purpose of the Qur'an and to interpret general principles within the framework of Islam. She was not only a narrator who conveyed what she heard and saw. She was also an interpreter of the meaning of the Qur'an and Islam. Narration related to understanding the Qur'an generally passed through Abdullah ibn Abbas and Ayesha which proves Ayesha's importance as an interpreter of the Prophet's understating of the Holy Qur'an.

One day, Ayesha's nephew Urwa asked her about a verse from the Holy Qur'an which reads as follows:

"If you fear that you will not be able to observe their rights with exact fairness when you marry the orphan girls [in Ayesha's custody], you can marry from among other women who seem good to you two, or three, or four. However, if you fear that [in your marital obligations] you will not be able to observe justice among them, then content yourselves with only one, or the captives that your right hands possess. Doing so makes it more likely that you will not act rebelliously" (Nisa, 4:3).

Ayesha answered:

"O my nephew! The orphans mentioned in the verse are those under the care of their guardian and after some time, when they grow up and attract attention because of their beauty, the guardians may start to desire them and want to keep them without giving a bridal due, or by giving a very small one. The guardians were forbidden from their former behavior and directed to marry other women."

After Ayesha's explanation of the verse stated above, people questioned God's Messenger further. Then another verse came:

"And they seek of thee the decision of the Law concerning marriage with more women than one. Say, Allah gives you His decision concerning them. And that which is recited to you elsewhere in the Book concerns the orphan girls who you give not what is prescribed for them and who you desire to marry, and also concerns the weak among children. And He enjoins you a deal equitably with the orphans. And whatever good you do, surely Allah knows it well" (Ch. 4:3).

Traditions or Hadiths.

In the *Sahih Bukhari* (the book of Hadiths or Traditions compiled by Imam Bukhari) it is narrated that, "In those days, a female orphan would be desired if she was beautiful. She was engaged according to her bridal due and genealogy. But it did not happen that way if there was some deception in her beauty or wealth. In these circumstances, men had nothing to do with orphans and married other women. It was therefore ordered to give the exact amount of bridal due that orphans deserved, whether they were desired or abandoned" (Chapter: *Nikah*. Muslim Wedding Ceremony) (1, 38, 4777, 4838).

A few examples will illustrate how she interpreted the Qur'an.

There is a verse in the Qur'an regarding covering of the distance between the hillocks of *Safa* and *Marwa* as one of the rites of *Hajj*. It reads:

"Verily, *Safa* and *Marwa* are among the signposts of God. Whoever then performed the *Hajj* or the *Umra*, no blame will lie on him if he goes around the two posts" (Chapter 2, verse 159).

Urwa said, "Auntie! This would mean that there would be no harm if the distance between the two hillocks is not traversed."

Ayesha replied, "It is not the meaning. Had it been so, the verse would have been worded differently. The verse has to do with something concerning the *Ansar*."

Before their acceptance of Islam, *the Ansar* used to worship the idol *Manat*. After embracing Islam, hesitation in going around the hills and asking the Prophet why he was going around the hills was common. They also asked the Prophet about his order in relation to this practice. Then the verse came which says, "Go around the two posts. There is no harm in it." This meaning is confirmed by the practice of the Prophet and it has become an integral part of the rites of *Hajj*. In chapter 12, verse 11 of the Qur'an, Almighty Allah says:

"And when the Messenger despaired of the believers and the nonbelievers, they were convinced that they had been told only lies. Our help came to the Messengers, and then saved those whom we pleased. And our chastisement cannot be averted from the sinful people."

The high status of Ayesha as a commentator, narrator of *Hadith* and as one having great knowledge of Islamic Law is well established. Whenever the Companions of the Prophet faced a tough question they wanted to tackle, they usually consulted Ayesha. She is quoted as a source for many *Hadith*. She has narrated 2,210 *Hadith*, out of which 316 are mentioned in both *Sahih Al-Bukhari* and *Sahih Muslim*. The Holy prophet's personal life is the topic of many traditions quoted by her.

Hazrat 'Urwah bin Zubir relates that he has seen no one more knowledgeable than Hazrat Ayesha regarding the knowledge of the Holy Qur'an, patrimony *Halal* and *Haram*, *Fiqh*, poetry, medicine, *Hadith*, Arabs and genealogies.

It was not only Caliphs who came to Ayesha for information and insight; a great number of people visited her often, considering her advice as the safest way to learn. Ayesha was the source of knowledge for everyone. Those who were not able to visit her either sent messages through someone else or sent her letters.

Hazrat Umm Hani relates that the Holy Prophet said, "O Ayesha! Your mark should be knowledge and the Holy Qur'an."

Hazrat 'Amr bin al-'As relates that once he asked the Holy Prophet, "Whom do you love the most amongst the people?

He said, "Ayesha."

Zayd ibn Abu Sufyan, the governor of Basra and Kufa during Muawiya's Caliphate, wrote one day to ask whether a statement of Abdullah ibn Abbas was true. Abdullah ibn Abbas asserted that until an animal was scarified, the prohibitions of pilgrimage were applicable even to the person who did not go to pilgrimage himself, but sent his sacrificial animal there.

Ayesha wrote:

"This is not true. I prepared the ropes for sacrificial animals of God's Messenger and he tied them up with his own hands, and then sent them to Mina with my father. Until the time the animals were slaughtered, nothing that God permitted was forbidden to the Messenger of God!"[223]

Some Companions thought wearing perfume was forbidden while doing the *Hajj* rites, after cutting their hair and during the stoning in Mina. But Ayesha did not consider perfume a problem based on the behavior during the era of God's Messenger.[224] When they heard from Ayesha, Abdullah ibn Abbas and the others left behind their preference and did as Ayesha said.

Another day, ibn Abbas was incorrect about when to take off the pilgrimage garb, and when it reached her, she again revealed the truth through examples from God's Messenger's life.

The exchange of knowledge between them was so natural that Abdullah ibn Abbas, who had problems with his eyes toward the end of his life, asked Ayesha whether to apply the treatment that doctors had recommended he use, and did not start using it until he became unable to perform ablution and daily prayers.

One day, Abu Hurayra said:

"There is no fasting for someone who wakes up with the necessity of making *ghusl* [taking a bath] in the morning."

He had probably not been informed of the new judgment or depended on weak information. When Abu Bakr ibn Abdurrahman heard this, he told it to Abdullah ibn Harith. And the questioning continued because the people of that era considered nothing they heard as fact until they

223 Muslim, Hajj 39 (1190).
224 Bukhari Ghusl, 12, 13 (264-67).

got conformation on a particular thing. This sensitivity was especially observed on issues that appeared to be against general knowledge.

Abdullah ibn Harith told his father who also found the information strange. Finally, they went to Ayesha to relieve the confusion.

Umm Salma was with Ayesha, and both were asked about the matter. They responded:

"On the mornings when the Messenger of God woke up like that, he fasted those days."

The matter was clarified. The two went to the governor of Medina, Marwan ibn al-Hakam, to tell him. Because incorrect information that needed correction was circulating, Marwan said:

"It is your duty to tell Abu Hurayra what you told me. I demand it."

Leaving Marwan, the two went directly to Abu Hurayra who asked:

"Is this really true?"

They responded in the affirmative:

"Our two mothers know better."

From then on, he began to fast as he had learned from the wives of the Holy Prophet.[225]

Hazrat Ayesha narrated the following: "I know when you are pleased or angry with me." I said, 'How do you know?' He said, "When you are pleased with me, you swear like this: La wa rabbi Muhammad [No, by the Lord of Muhammad]. However, when you are angry with me, then you swear like this: La wa rabbi Ibrahim [No, by the Lord of Ibrahim].'

---

225 Muwtta, Siyam, 4 (639); Sunan, 4:214 (7785), Nasi, Sunann'l Kubra, 2:180.

"Then, I said 'yes, but by Allah. O Messenger of Allah, I leave out only your name. There is not a slightest change in my love for you.'"[226]

On another day, *Imam* Shurayh visited Ayesha and expressed his discomfort over what had been said:

"O mother of the believers. I heard Abu Hurayra narrating a Hadith from God's Messenger that, if it is true, means all of us will perish."

"Whoever perished had already perished. But tell me what the real reason for your worry is," Ayesha said.

"The Messenger of God said, 'Whoever desires to reunite with God and likes this idea, God wants to reunite with him, but whoever considers reuniting with God undesirable, God considers him undesirable too.' But who among us does not fear death and see it as undesirable?"

Ayesha then understood the reason for the transformation in *Imam* Shurayh and asked him to recite the following to relieve all believers:

"Yes, the Messenger of God said this, but it is not how you think. May God bestow mercy on Abu Hurayra; he narrated you the ending of the *Hadith* but not the beginning. The Messenger of God said, 'When God the Almighty wishes to reward one of His servants, He sends him an angel in the year that he is going to die and gives good news by supporting him for the Hereafter. In this way, when the angel of death comes to him, and says, 'O soul at rest [*nafs al-mutmainna*], let you set forth toward the mercy and good pleasure of God the Almighty. When he wills to punish one of His servants, He sends him a devil in the year that he is going to die and the devil misleads him. When the angel of death comes to him, and says, 'O evil-commanding soul [*nafis al ammara bis su*], come on, prepare for the wrath and displeasure of God.' At that moment, the servant shakes like a leaf and starts

---

226 Sahih Muslim, Kitab Fada'il Ayesha, Bab fada'il Ayesha.

to gulp. He never wants to reunite with God and God does not wish to reunite with him either. When death is faced and it stares without blinking, the soil starts to part and moves from the chest. The fingers become paralyzed and the hair on the skin stings like a prick. Whoever wants to meet with God, God wants to reunite with him."[227]

When an important Companion, Abu Saeed al-Khudri, was on his death-bed, he made his final preparations. He changed his old clothes for new ones, remembering the following statement from the Messenger of God:

"No doubt that the dead person will be reborn with the clothes he was wearing at the time of [his] death." [228]

He thought the Hadith meant the burial shroud, the clothing one is wrapped in when they die. But the opinions of others, including Ayesha, were different, and she said:

"May God bestow mercy upon Abu Saeed."

The duty of revealing the truth again fell on her shoulders. Ayesha had interpreted the Hadith differently because she had analyzed it generally and combined it with what she already knew. The clothing of this world did not have any value in the Hereafter, and being reborn was like one's first birth into the world. She explained:

"In this narration, the Messenger of God meant the deeds of a person when he died, because God's Messenger also said, 'On that day [the day of Resurrection], people will be reborn

---

227 Muslim, Dhikr, 17 (2685); Nasai, Janaiz, 10 (1834); Ahmad ibn Hanbal Musnad, 2:346 (8537). The information from two different narrations is combined.
228 Abu Dawud, Janaiz, 18 (3114); Hakim, Mustadrak, 1:490 (1260).

without clothes, naked like they were when they were born of their mothers."[229]

It is also true that Ayesha's brilliance did not only benefit those who lived during her time; her legacy continued to illuminate after her death. This will continue until the Last Day. She was sought by the Companions of the Holy Prophet and those who know the value of correct knowledge. Umar ibn Abdul-Aziz sometimes sent letters to Muhammad ibn Amr ibn Hazam and in these letters he wrote:

"Explore and search around yourself very well. If you find a narration of God's Messenger, a *Sunna* that remained after him or a statement belonging to Amra, tell me about it. During the times when the people of knowledge are leaving us one by one, I am afraid that some knowledge may be lost."[230]

Amra was a special student of Ayesha, and the aunt of Medina's governor, Abu Bakr ibn Muhammad.

---

229 Bayhaqi, Shuabu'l Iman, 1:318 (359). See also: Bukhari, Riqaq, 45 (6162); Muslim, Janna, 56 (2859).
230 Ibn Sa'd, Tabaqat, 8:480; Ibn Abdilbarr, Tamhid, 17:251; Ibn Hajar, Tahzib't Tahzib, 12:466 (2850).

Hazrat Ayesha and Transmission of Knowledge

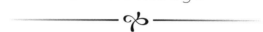

THERE IS NO doubt that Ayesha was a leader in knowledge among the Companions. From the beginning, she analyzed everything that happened, assimilated new information, clarified obscure issues by asking questions, and learned intimate details that others could not witness, by directly asking the Messenger of God.

God's Messenger was the center of her life, and she dedicated hers to his cause. Her conditions supported her work, for she shared his room. Day and night, Ayesha went to his well of fresh water and filled her bucket until it overflowed. She asked about everything, even intimate things that other people could not ask out of modesty, and received answers from the Messenger of God directly. She had the advantage of having a room which was adjacent to the Prophet's Mosque, and also followed the sermons the God's Messenger delivered. Whenever something stuck in her mind and bothered her, she resolved it by asking God's Messenger when he returned to the house of felicity. She never quit asking about something until she fully understood.[231]

Ayesha's inner nature made her enjoy questioning and contemplation. She was uncomfortable and never believed anything she saw or heard until she learned the reality behind them.

Describing her, Ibn Abu Malayka made the following statement:

---

231 Ahmad ibn Hanbal, Musnad, 6:75 (24507, 24511, 24514).

198

"When she was faced with something that she did not know, she was not able to stand without learning more."[232]

Respected scholars, such as Hakim, have said that one-fourth of the body of religious knowledge was transferred to us through Ayesha.

In her time, people came to her to solve their problems under her guidance; today she is still the source of much authentic information.

Expressing her superiority, Abu Musa al-Ashari said:

"As the Companions of God's Messenger, whenever we came across a complicated issue, we took it to Ayesha because she always had the information that could solve a difficulty."[233]

Ayesha's intelligence was so obvious that Ata Abu Rabah said:

"Ayesha was the most intelligent, scholarly person and the one who had the best thought and opinions among people."[234]

Imam Masruq expressed the following:

"I saw the leading Companions of God's Messenger asking questions to Ayesha on obligatory duties related to the division of inheritance."[235]

Another leading *Imam*, Muhammad ibn Shihab al-Zuhri, said:

"She was the most knowledgeable of people. For this reason, the most important Companion of God's Messenger learnt things by

---

232 Tafsiri baghawi, 1:374; Ayni, Umdatu'l Qari, 2:136.
233 Tirmidhi, Manaqib, 63 (3883).
234 Hakim, Mustadrak, 4:15 (6748), Dhahabi, Siyar, 2:185, 200.
235 Hakim Mustadrak, 4:12 (6736), Darimi, Sunan, 2:442 (2859).

asking her.[236] If the knowledge of Ayesha was put on the right scale, and the knowledge of all the women, including the other wives of God's Messenger, was put on the left scale, Ayesha's knowledge would dominate in its superiority."[237]

Abu Salma, the son of Abdurrahman ibn, said:

"I did not see anyone who knew the *Sunna* better than Ayesha or who was deeper than her in *fiqh* knowledge, or who was more acquainted with where each verse or declaration was revealed."[238]

Her nephew and special student, Qasim ibn Muhammad, under lined the depth of her knowledge of Islamic theology (*klam*) and eloquence:

"I did not meet anyone as eloquent as Ayesha, or anyone who was as cognizant of Islamic theology as her, among men or women, both before and after her [time on this Earth]."[239]

Her unique knowledge did not only attract the attention of scholars. Almost everyone agreed on her merit. One day, Caliph Muawiyya called Ziyad, a key name of the era, to his presence and asked:

"Who is the most knowledgeable among the people?"

"Certainly you are, O leader of believers."

But Muawiyya, who was aware that this response reflected flattery more than truth, insisted:

---

236 Sa'd, Tabaaqat: 374.
237 Hakim, Mustadrak, 2:12 (6734), Ibn Hajar, Isaba, 4:349.
238 Ibn SA'd Tabaqat.
239 Isbahani, Aghani, 20:331.

"For the sake of God, tell the truth."

"For God's sake, it is Ayesha."[240]

Her superiority in knowledge was so clear that in later years there would be entire works, such as *al-Ijba* by Zarhashi, written only about that one aspect of her personality. Her intellectual curiosity was unequaled; she never felt comfortable until she learned information from whoever possessed it. When God's Messenger told Fatima a secret before his death, Ayesha learned what it was after his passing. If she had not insisted on learning it, no one would ever have learned what the secret was.

Her inquisitive personality had not changed since the day she entered the house of felicity; she recognized early on that the door of knowledge would be opened by asking questions and thus asked the Messenger of God about every matter she thought of. Such was her defining characteristic. She judged what she heard or saw and was discriminating about adding to her knowledge. She compared and contrasted new information to what she already knew, and asked God's Messenger about any inconsistencies she found.

As a living witness of revelation, Ayesha arranged her copy of the Qur'an, placing chapters and verses according to Gabriel's recitation of the whole. This copy would become the standard in the times to come, and people from outlying parts of Islam's expanding borders wanted to learn the ordering of the Qur'an from her.

Ayesha's Quranic knowledge was beyond the comprehension of other Companions, although they were leaders in knowledge.

Abdullah ibn Abbas repeated the following verse of the Holy Qur'an (4:6):

"And give not to those who are weak of understanding, your property which Allah has made for you a means of support; but

---

240 Hakim, Mustadrak, 4:15 (6747).

feed them therewith and clothe them and speak to them words of kind advice."

In one commentary we find that, "The verse speaks of the property of orphans and that people should be very careful about spending their property and should treat it as their own." It may also signify that orphans are in one's custody. It is also possible that the expression has been used here to include all property whether belonging to the orphans or to their guardians.

He said that the above verse is abrogated by the revelation of the following verse:

"And let those fear Allah, who if they should leave behind them weak offspring, would be afraid on their account. Let them, therefore, fear Allah and let them say the right word" (Chapter 10 of the Qur'an).

In other words, the verse translates as such: "Surely those who consume the property of orphans wrongfully; certainly they will consume a fire in their bellies; and soon they will be roasting in a Blaze."

The verse contains a strong and highly forceful appeal in favor of the orphans.

In response, Ayesha indicated that whoever abused the wealth of orphans would be punished, but not those poor guardians who needed the wealth of orphans in order to take care of them. She said there was no contradiction between the two verses. The punishment is reserved for the transgressors who take the wealth of orphans although they do not deserve it.[241]

Ayesha's uniqueness in interpreting the Qur'an was due to her closeness to Allah's Messenger. Some Companions concluded that the midmost prayer expressed in the verse that says, "Be ever mindful and protective of the prescribed prayers and the middle prayer, and stand in

---

241 Bukhari, Buyu, 95 (2098), Wasaya, 23 (2614), Tafsir, 81 (4299).

the presence of God in utmost devotion and obedience (Baqra 2: 38), was the morning prayer, while other Companions such as Zayd ibn Thabit and Usma asserted it to be the noon prayer. But Ayesha said it was intended to be the *asr* (afternoon) prayer, her assertion being based on what the Messenger of Allah himself had said. She also noted her opinion on the copy of the Qur'an she kept, near the mentioned verse, deeming the mentioned verse to be the *asr* prayer.[242]

Her approach reflected the majority of the Companions' opinions, primarily that of Ali, Abdullah ibn Masud and Samurah ibn Jundub.[243] Something similar happened about the verse:

"To Allah belongs whatever is in the heavens and whatever is in the Earth; and whether you disclose what is in your minds or keep it hidden, Allah will call you to account for it" (Al-Baqra, 2:285).

Leading imams, such as Abdullah ibn Umar Abdullah ibn Abbas and Ali, asserted that this verse was abrogated by the verse, "Allah burdens not any soul beyond its capacity" (2:287) which was revealed after the assertion made by such leading imams.

But Ayesha said they were wrong:

"No one has ever asked me about the verse since I asked Allah's Messenger. He said, 'It is for those who have a high fever or illness, or any kind of disaster or wealth that he was afraid to lose after possessing it, which is bestowed on a servant by God. By the cause of those things, a servant can be purified from dust and rust.'"[244]

---

242 Muslim, Masajid, 207 (829).
243 Abu Dawud, Salat, 5 (409), Ahmad ibn Hanbal, Musnad, 5:205 (21840); Tirmidhi, Tafsir, 3 (2984, 2985).
244 Tirmidhi, 3 (2990-92).

Hadith or Traditions

THE SUBJECT OF *Hadith* is, in fact, an exposition of the life of the Prophet. The narration of *Hadith* required nearness to the Prophet. Barring four or five Companions, the number of *Hadith* narrated by Ayesha is larger than the number narrated by anyone else. The leading Companions like Abu Bakr, Umar Uthman and Ali hold a higher position than her considering their benefit from being a part of the company of the Prophet, their excellence of speech and their intellectual capacity and understanding, but they were all busy people preoccupied with important matters of State and most of the Companions were themselves aware of the precepts and practices of the Prophet and did not need to ask anyone about them. The work of collecting *Hadith* was started by the Tabaeens who were born twenty-five to thirty years after the leading Companions died. The narration of *Hadith* was done mostly by the younger Companions. There are seven of them who narrated more than a thousand Traditions. Their names and the number of *Hadith* reported by them are mentioned below:

1.	Abu Huraira	5,364
2.	Ibn Abbas	1,660
3.	Ibn Umar	2,630
4.	Jabir	1,540
5.	Anas	2,286
6.	Ayesha	2,210
8.	Abu Saeed Khudri	1,170

Some of them lived after Ayesha. They could mix with the people freely and visited all the important centers of the Islamic world unlike Ayesha who was observing Purdah. Her contribution to the creation of *Hadith* is the most out-standing and remarkable. Mere number is not, however, the only criterion when making the assertion I just made. The real test to determine the most impressive contributors to *Hadith* is one's capacity to understand and explain difficult and intricate points. Five of the above narrators are only narrators and not theologians. Only Abdullah bin abbas could match Ayesha in number of narrations side by side with knowledge of Islamic Jurisprudence, power of interpretation, thinking and capacity of deduction. Her distinction is that besides narrating the commands, injunctions and events; she also described the causes, reasons and prudence behind such things.

Ayesha's position among the *Mukthirun* was special because in most of those she narrated, she was the only one to narrate them. This was the natural result of her being with Allah's Messenger in places impossible for others to be. Such *Hadith* she narrated are termed *fard* (Individual) or *munfarid* (Individually). And it was not only her intimacy that allowed her to be so praised. Ayesha is the resource for information about the family life of Allah's Messenger, his private state, his night prayers and how he spent his time alone. From this perspective, it can be said that if Ayesha had not been there, much knowledge about the private life of Allah's Messenger would have been lost and the *Umma* (community) would have been deprived of a treasure trove of fascinating information.

If she attended every gathering where the Messenger of Allah was present, like the other *muksirun*, and had attended many journeys, and if she had not spent most of her time at her home, the *Hadith* that she narrated could be more numerous. The number of *Hadith* Ayesha narrated directly from Allah's Messenger is more than two thousand.

When making a healthy decision, the true reason should be known. Ayesha always learned the reason behind a judgment by witnessing what happened or directly asking the person judging about it. Allah's

Messenger recommended performing *ghusl* (full body ablution) on Fridays. While other Companions who narrated this said it in a general way, Ayesha's narration includes details that explain the reasoning behind the Prophet's recommendation. The Messenger wanted believers who were soaked with sweat from the morning's work to cleanse themselves of their dirt and wear perfume when they went to the congregational prayer that purified them spiritually. Ayesha's narration stated:

"On Fridays, people, particularly those who came from far away, were covered to dust and dirt, and were sweating heavily. When I was near the Prophet, such a man came to the mosque and the Prophet asked the man, 'Why don't you clean yourself for this day?'"

Another *Hadith* that Ayesha narrated started by saying:

"People were working at their businesses and came to the Friday Prayer in the same condition that they were in while working. At that time, I said to them, 'I wish you came after you perform whole-body ablution.'"[245]

During the feast of sacrifice (Eid al-Adha), Allah's Messenger said:

"No one among you should eat the meat of a sacrificed animal for more than three days."

While leading Companions such as Abdullah ibn Umar and Abu Saeed al-Khudri thought of what the Prophet said, quoted above, as an absolute judgment and a binding order that meant storing meat for more than three days wasn't permitted,[246] Ayesha had a different opinion. She said the Prophet's statement, cited above, was an encouragement not to store

245 Bukhari, Jumu'a, 13, 14 (860, 861).
246 Muslim, Eid-'ul-Adha, 26 (1970).

the meat of a sacrificed animal for more than three days so that one would instead give more to needy people. Storing the meat of a scarified animal by putting salt in it was a common practice in that day and she narrated this *Hadith* as follows: "We used to preserve the meat of scarified animals with salt and produce it before him [the Prophet] in Medina. The Prophet observed, 'Don't take it after three days.' It was not a definite order but he wished the people should feed others also." As it was possible to preserve the meat for more than three days, the meaning of the *Hadith* needed to be clarified. Rabia asked:

"Is it true that Allah's Messenger banned the meat of a sacrificed animal?"

Ayesha replied:

"No. In those days, the number of people in society who sacrificed animals was very few and they were asked to give some of the meat as charity to those who were not able to sacrifice an animal. We ate the front leg of a lamb even ten days after *Eid al-Adha*."[247] Further, she says, "Some people thought that the Messenger of Allah liked the shoulder meat of lamb, but the lamb's shoulder meat was not the portion that Allah's Messenger enjoyed most. In those days, meat was so scarce that when they had it, they rushed to offer it to Allah's Messenger. And the shoulder meat was the part that could be cooked easily and quickly."

The book of *Hadith* records that the Prophet used to send someone every year to see the produce of Khaiber, and to assess its worth. Ayesha, in narrating this *Hadith*, further says that he used to have the crop assessed in order to determine the *Zakat* before eating the fruits and distributing them. If anybody approached her to enquire about any *Hadith* and she was not herself the narrator of it, she would refer any such person to the

---

247   Tirmidhi, Eid-'ul-Adha, 14 (1511): Ibn Maja, At'ima, 30 (3313).

actual narrator of the *Hadith* being asked about. For instance, somebody asked her about drawing the hand over socks (in connection with ablution). She asked him to approach Ali who narrated the *Hadith* the person was asking about.

Though the principles of judging a particular *Hadith* had not been formulated yet, she had adopted some rules for evaluating the narrations of her contemporaries and they appear to be the following:

(1) The *Hadith* should not go against any verse in the Qur'an.

    (a) Abdullah bin Abbas and Abdullah bin Umar narrated that the Prophet said that when the inmates of the house bewail the death of any member of the family, the deceased is chastised. Ayesha refused to accept it. She said that the fact was that the relatives were lamenting his death.

The Prophet observed that, "These people are crying while the dead person is being chastised." Chastisement has nothing to do with mourning. The two are separate acts.

As an authority, Ayesha cited the Qur'an: "No person bears the burden of the sins of another." Among the doctors of Islamic Jurisprudence, *Imam* Shafi, *Imam* Muhammad and *Iman* Abu Hanifa agree with Ayesha.

    (b) A number of infidels were killed in the battle of Badr. The Prophet said at their burial ground, "Have ye too truly secured what your Lord hath promised you?" (Qur'an, chapter 7:44).

Some of the Companions said to the Prophet, "Are you addressing the dead?"

Ibn Umar says the Prophet replied that, "They hear better than you but cannot answer."

When Ayesha learned about it, she said the Prophet had not said this but had actually stated, "Now they know for certain that what I was telling them was true." 'O Prophet! Surely, thou can't make those dead pay heed' (Qur'an, chapter 27:80).

'And thou cannot make those who are dead in hearing [the believers have been called 'the living' because by accepting the truth, they receive a new life; and disbelievers are called 'the dead' because by rejecting the truth, they bring spiritual death upon themselves]' (Qur'an, chapter 35:23).

Some people told Ayesha that Abu Huraira relates that the Prophet had said, "Inauspiciousness lies in three things: in women, in houses, in horses."

Ayesha said that this was not correct and that Abu Huraira heard only a part of the Prophet's statement. Ayesha said the statement was actually as follows: "The Jew says that inauspiciousness lies in three things: in women, in horses and in houses."[248]

It is reported that Ibn Abbas relates that the Prophet had seen God twice. Masrooq Tabaii asked Ayesha about it. She replied, "You have said something which makes my hair stand on end. Whoever has said this, has lied." Then she recited the verse, "No vision can take Him in and he takes in all visions and He is the subtle, the All-informed" (Qur'an, chapter 6:104) and the verse, "Nobody can possibly speak to Him except through inspiration or from behind a veil." Muslim records say that the Prophet had said, "God is Light. How can I see Him?"

The Prophet ordered the civil servant responsible for collecting alms to estimate the amount of possible alms based on the amount of fruit some had been eating.

The completeness of Ayesha's narrations indicates factors such as Ayesha's witnessing incidents many times and asking about the matters that she did not witness or that contradicted her previous knowledge. In this way, Ayesha was very sensitive and was always searching. She followed up on any information that she heard, attempting to get confirmation on the information from its original source.

One day, two visitors told her of a *Hadith*:

---

248 Abu Daud: Sunnan.

"There is bad luck in three things: women, mount and house." And they asked her, "What do you think of that?" The words made Ayesha angry and her wrath was apparent from her behavior. Looking around, she said:

"I swear to the One who revealed the Qur'an to Abu Qasim that this matter is not like what Abu Hurayra said. While the Prophet of Allah was talking, Abu Hurayra entered. At that moment, the Prophet of Allah was stating:

"During the age of ignorance, people used to say, 'There is bad luck in three things: women, mount and house!" (Abu Daud: Sunnan).

Abu Hurayra heard the end of the *Hadith* but not the beginning. After explaining it, Ayesha recited the following verse: "There befalls not any calamity either in the Earth or in your own persons, but it is recorded in a Book before We bring it into being" (Qur'an, Al-Hadid: 57:22).

With the above quoted verse, Ayesha explained that there cannot be such misunderstanding in the presence of absolute ill and drew attention to the domain of human will.

During the age of ignorance, family structure changed and many different marriage models appeared in the society. The practice of Muta, temporary marriage, was very common.

A temporary marriage for a specified period of time was customary in the days of ignorance and continued until 7 A.H. when it was abolished; Ibn Abbas and some others thought that it had not been totally banned.

Islam's final judgment of *Muta* was revealed in the seventh year of *Hijrah*, during the conquest of Khaybar. The Prophet of Allah firmly told his society that *Muta* was forbidden. When some people witnessed this and told Ayesha, she flew into towering rage and recited the Quranic verse that says, "They guard their private parts except for their wives or those [bonds maids] whom their right hands possess (Qur'an, chapter 23:6-7).

Once Ayesha heard a ruling that said women should undo their hair braiding when they perform ritual, full-body ablution. Abdullah ibn Amr ibn As ("As" is a name) asserted such and she immediately said:

"I am surprised with Abdullah ibn Amr ibn As's statement. He orders women to undo their hair braiding while they are taking ritual, full-body ablution! Why doesn't he order them to save their heads too? Nonetheless, the Prophet of Allah and I used to perform ritual, full-body ablution in the same place, and I used to pour water onto my head only three times."[249]

Another day, Ayesha heard the *fatwa* of Abdullah ibn Umar who asserted that kissing one's spouse invalidated ablution. He was making a judgment according to general principles in a field in which he was not well-informed in. But Ayesha felt she must correct his statement. She explained how the Prophet of Allah himself had behaved:

"Allah's Prophet used to kiss some of his wives and go for daily prayers without performing ablution again."[250]

She also taught others about the Prophet's manner of speaking and how a *Hadith* should be reported. Someone asked about the speaking style of the Prophet, and Ayesha answered:

"He used to speak so slowly and distinctly that whoever wanted to count his words could do so easily."[251] At another time, while Ayesha was performing prayer, she heard someone outside narrating a *Hadith*. He passed on the statement of Allah's Prophet but was speaking very quickly and almost none of his sayings were understood.

---

249 Muslim, Hayd, 59 (331); Ibn Maja, Tahara, 108 (604).

250 When the person who reported the *Hadith* asked Ayesha whether it was her, she smiled and replied in the affirmative. See Abu Dawud, Tahara, 69 178, 179; Tirmidhi, Tahara, 63 (86).

251 Bukhari, Manaqib, 20 (3374).

Ayesha naturally was bothered by the narration of *Hadith* in this manner, near her room. She said, "A man came and narrated *Hadith* from the Prophet of Allah in front of my room in a way that I could hear, and then [he] disappeared instantly. I was busy with reciting my invocations and he finished the *Hadith* before I finished my invocations. If I had been able to catch him, I would have told him, 'The Prophet of Allah would have never put forward a *Hadith* like you did.'"[252]

---

252 Bukhari, Manaqib, 20 (3375).

The Collection of Hadith

———— ✿ ————

THE WORK OF collecting *Hadith* was started by the *Tabaeens* who were born twenty-five to thirty years after the leading Companions died. The narration of *Hadith* was done mostly by the younger Companions. There are seven of them who narrated more than a thousand Traditions. Their names and the number of *Hadith* reported by them are mentioned below:

1.	Abu Huraira	5,364.
2.	Ibn Abbas	1,660.
3.	Ibn Umar.	2,630.
4.	Jabir	1,540.
5.	Anas	2,286.
6.	Ayesha	2,210.
7.	Abu Saeed Khudri.	1,170.

Some of them had lived after Ayesha. They could mix with the people freely and had visited all the important centers of the Islamic world unlike Ayesha who was observing Purdah. If this is kept in mind, her contribution is the most outstanding and remarkable. Mere number is not, however, the only criterion for such a determination. The real test is one's capacity to understand and explain difficult and intricate points. Five of the above narrators are only narrators and not theologians. Only Abdullah bin Abbas could match Ayesha in the number of narrations side by side with knowledge of Islamic Jurisprudence, power of interpretation, thinking and capacity of deduction. Her distinction is that besides narrating the commands, injunctions and the events; she also described the causes, reasons and the prudence lying behind them.

Though the principles of judging a particular *Hadith* had not been formulated until then, she had adopted some rules for evaluating the narrations of her contemporaries.

Compilation of Ahadith Narrated by Ayesha

COMPILATIONS OF *AHADITH* narrated by the Companions started by the middle of the first century *Hijri*. When Umar bin Abdul Aziz became Caliph in 101 A.H., Abu Bakr bin Umar bin Hazmul Ansari was the *Qadi* of Medina. He owed his learning and excellence, to a large measure, to his aunt Umyat who had been trained and educated by Ayesha. Umar bin Abdul Aziz sent a royal order to *Qadi* Abu Bakr to collect all the *Ahadith* narrated by Ayesha and send them for compilation to him.

Reflection of Ayesha

———— ✼ ————

SOME DIFFERENCES IN the narration of *Hadith* by the Companions are due to their varying degrees of grasp and understanding. Since Ayesha was highly intelligent, the science of *Hadith* was greatly benefitted by her.

On the basis of narration by Abu Huraira, a story related that a woman had tied up her cat and did not feed it until it died of hunger and thirst. Then she was chastised for those actions. When Abu Huraira met Ayesha, she said, "Are you the person who has related this story?" He replied that he had heard it from the Holy Prophet. Ayesha said, "A believer in the sight of God is on too high a pedestal to be punished for a cat. Besides committing this sin, the woman was an infidel. Abu Huraira, when you relate something from the Prophet, ponder over what you are saying."

When Abu Saeed Khudri was on his death bed, he wore new clothes, saying that a Muslim is raised in the clothes he wears at the time of his death. When Ayesha heard him say that, she said, "May God have mercy on Abu Saeed. What the Prophet had meant by apparel was man's deeds. He had clearly said that, 'On the Day of Judgment, people will be raised naked without any clothing.'"

According to *Shariah*, a widowed woman has to live for four months and some days in the house of her deceased husband. A companion named Fatima used to relate that she had been permitted to leave the house before the end of this waiting period. She narrated as an authority before several Companions. Some accepted it and some rejected it. During the governorship of Marwan, a similar case arose in Medina and the woman cited the case of Fatima. When Ayesha came to know about it, she severely criticized Fatima, saying that she had done no good in publicizing her case. The Prophet had no doubt given her permission, but it was a special case as the house of the deceased husband was insecure and situated at an isolated place.[253]

Abu Huraira related that the Prophet had said, "Even if I get a lash in the way of God, I would prefer it than freeing a bastard slave."

When Ayesha heard of it, she said, "My God, have mercy on Abu Huraira. He neither heard the Tradition properly nor has related it properly. When the verses of the Qur'an [chapter 90:12-14] were revealed, he attempted not the steep ascent. And what should make thee comprehend what the steep ascent is? It is the freeing of a slave [from bondage]."

Tafsir of the above verses is, "Through the Holy Prophet, God opened up all the ways and means; by using him, man could make unlimited spiritual and material progress, but he refused to make the necessary sacrifices to achieve this object" (the abve is the English Translation and Commentary by Malik Glum Freed; published by The London Mosque, 1981).

Somebody said, "We poor people do not have any slaves, male or female. Some have Negresses for doing household work. Should they be allowed to have illegitimate sons who can be freed?"

The Prophet then said, "Even if I get a lash in the way of God, I would prefer it than permitting this evil thing: to get an issue for being freed."

Umar and several Companions said that Prayers (*Salat*) should not be observed after the morning and afternoon prescribed Prayers. Ayesha said, "May God have mercy on Umar. He misunderstood things. The Prophet had said that one should not do the *Salat* at the time of sunset and sun rise [Bukhari: Sahih, Times of Prayers]."

Theologians have explained that these are the timings of worshipping the sun by some people and therefore they should avoid such times. Viewed in this light, Ayesha's version is more correct and creditable, for she has grasped the real significance. Umar also understood the real significance but as a precaution he widened the time, i.e., after the prescribed morning and afternoon Prayer (*Asr*), hoping there would be no possibility of offering Prayers at the times of sunrise and sunset.

---

253 Bukhari & Muslim: Sahih, the book of divorce.

Abu Huraira said that if one does not say the *Witr* Prayers, it is as if he had said no prayers. Ayesha commented that they all heard the Prophet saying, "Whosoever observes the five daily Prayers after ablution and performs keeling and prostration well without any deficiency, has taken a guarantee from God that he would not be punished; whosoever does not enter into this covenant, it is up to God to forgive him or punish him. His deliverance is thus not certain. Neglect of obligatory duties will entail punishment but not of what are *Sunnah*. Witr is only *Sunnah*."

Memory of Ayesha

A GOOD MEMORY is a necessary pre-requisite for narrating *Hadith*. Ayesha's memory was prodigious and much of her criticism of others' narrations is because of this.

When Sa'd bin Abi Waqqas died, Ayesha wished that his bier should be brought to the mosque so that she could participate in the funeral prayers. Some people objected to it. She said how quickly people forget that the Prophet of Allah had said the funeral prayers of Suhail bin Baidha inside the mosque.

Abdullah bin Umar was asked how many times the Prophet had done Umrah. He answered that the Prophet had performed it four times and one was in the month of *Rajab*. Urwa called on the Prophet to tell her this. She said from behind the curtain, "God have mercy on Abu Abdul Rahman [*Kunyat* of Ibn Umar]. I had accompanied the Prophet in all his *Umrah* and none were performed during *Rajab*."[254]

Ibn Umar told people that the days in a month are twenty-nine. This was mentioned to Ayesha who said that the Prophet had said that sometimes a month lasts twenty-nine days.

---

254 Bukhari: Sahih, The Book of Umrah.

Ayesha's Ability and Distinction

———— ✐ ————

SAHIH MUSLIM RECORDS that the Prophet said, "I am leaving two supreme things amidst you. One is the Book of God and the other is my family." Though the Book of God is self-sufficient and presents no difficulty when trying to understand it, the presence of persons who can understand and explain its hidden meaning and underlying purpose are required. Who could be better exponents than the members of the family of the Prophet? Among them, Ayesha occupies a high position because of the intelligence and talent bestowed by God on her, her training under the care of the prophet and his appreciation of her qualities. Who could be a better interpreter of the Book of God, exponent of the ways of the Prophet and teacher of Islamic laws? Others saw the Prophet in congregations; she saw him in assemblies as well as in private. The Prophet had himself said, "Ayesha had superiority over other women as *Tharid* [Arabic dish which is considered delicious] had over other dishes." In a dream, the Prophet was shown that Ayesha would be his wife; the Qur'an was not revealed in the house of any of his wives except that of Ayesha; Gabriel had conveyed his salutations at the thresh-hold; she saw Gabriel with her eyes; the all-pervading voice of the angelic world testified to her purity and chastity; the bearer of the revelations gave glad tidings of her being the favorite wife of the Prophet in the hereafter. Hakim records in *Mustadrak* and ibn Sa'd in Tabaqat, that Ayesha said, "I am not taking pride but I am mentioning it as a fact that God bestowed upon me nine things which he did not confer on any one else in the world. Angels presented my figure before the prophet in a dream. There was no other maiden amongst

220

the wives of the Prophet. The Qur'an was revealed even when he was occupied in bed. I was his favorite. Some Quranic verses descended in relation to me; I saw Gabriel with my own eyes and the Prophet died in my lap."

Muslim Canonical Jurisprudence and Theology

— ❧ —

From the academic point of view, the Book and the *Sunnah* are the Foundation of the Faith, and Jurisprudence and theology are the deductions of the Faith.

In the time of the Prophet, he was himself the source of knowledge and he gave verdicts. In the time of Abu Bakr, if any new matter or problem arose they would collect the learned Companion for consultation, and if anyone knew a *Hadith* relevant to the point, he would cite it; otherwise, judgment was given on the basis of analogy. The consultation body operated until the first half of Uthman's reign. When sedition broke out, many people migrated to Mecca, Taif, Damascus and Bsra. Ali made Kufa his capital. Many of the learned men also migrated. While such helped the expansion of knowledge, the stature of the collective body was lost. After the leading Companions had gone, Ibn Umar, Abdullahbin Abbas, Abu Huraira and Ayesha were the chief successors for deciding matters about which positive orders were not available. They had different approaches. Abdullah bin Umar and Abu Huraira kept silent if no pertinent verse of the Qur'an or *Hadith* decree of the preceding caliphs was known to them. Abdullah bin Abass used to give findings on the basis of analogy. Ayesha would try to find authority from the Qur'an, then refer to *Hadith*. Ayesha's novel was based on her previous knowledge of the Qur'an. If the Qur'an or *Hadith* were silent on a matter, she resorted to intellectual reasoning.

Fiqh depends on comprehending the reasoning and justification for judgments. Called "real cause" in jurisprudence, it explains the principal aim in religious judgment. When there is no clear statement, a ruling could only be made by reasoning, and Ayesha's knowledge was advanced compared to her peers.

As explained before, Ayesha asked the Prophet of Allah for the reasoning behind many matters when she was unable to comprehend their lawful causes and received answers to such questions directly from him. She corrected misunderstandings with examples from the Prophet's own life.

Ayesha, who expressed that a divorced or widowed pregnant woman could marry someone else when she gave birth, concluded that the waiting period for such a woman ended at the birth of the baby. She based this on an incident she witnessed: when the Prophet of Allah allowed Subaya al-Aslamiyya, who gave birth after the death of her husband, to marry someone else.[255]

Explaining why the obligatory part of the sunset Prayer is three cycles, Ayesha said, "Because it is *Witr* of day!" She knew why the morning Prayer is two *rak'ah*, and considered it akin to reciting the Qur'an, expressing that the quality, not the quantity, was essential.[256] Ayesha, who warned people not to get stuck on the physical aspects of pilgrimage, stated actions such as the circling and going back and forth between *Safa* and *Marwa*, and stoning the devil, such being causes to remember God according to Ayesha.[257] She also explained that visiting Muhassab Valley, which was called Abtah, was not required in Pilgrimage, and expressed that since the aforementioned Valley was on the closest route during that time, that route was the preferred one.[258]

Ayesha questioned the Prophet of Allah as to whether the Hatim, a crescent-shaped place adjacent to the, (ka'ba)would be considered part of the *Ka'ba*, and asked, "Why isn't it included in the *Ka'ba*?"

The Prophet of Allah replied:

255
256 Ahmad ibn Hanbal, Musnad, 6:241 (26084).
257 Abu Dawud, Manasiq, 51 (1888); Tirmidhi, Sawm, 64 (902).
258 Bukhari, Hajj, 146 (1676).

"Certainly during those days, your people were in financial difficulties. Thinking of their own means of support did not let them do that."

She asked:

"Why is the door of *Ka'ba* so high?"

He replied:

"Your people did so in order to allow those people who wanted to enter [to do so], and [to] prevent those people who did not want [to]."

She asked:

"O Prophet of Allah. Don't you think you should reconstruct it on the foundation of Prophet Abraham?"

The Prophet of Allah replied:

"If your people had not recently been saved from paganism, I would have done it."

Such a brilliant mind as hers would conclude many results from these expressions. She did not insist obstinately on a matter that people would not be able to accept before the right time and place; she also found it sensible to postpone some issues for later days, or years, or even centuries. Ayesha was one of the few people who understood the essential point that judgments may change according to the time and conditions. For example, she believed that the ruling encouraging women to attend congregational Prayer at the mosque had changed in later years. She said the conditions had changed and the purity of the time during the Prophet's life was not well kept.

Thus, the Judgment should be rethought according to current conditions, and a fresh conclusion should be reached.[259]

Ayesha's knowledge of *Fiqh* originated directly from the Qur'an and the *Sunna*, as did her knowledge in the fields of *Tafsir* and *Hadith*. She concluded results by reshaping information from those resources, and expressed her opinion when it was time. When a matter was brought before her, she first resorted to the Qur'an and *Sunna*, and searched for a similar or comparable judgment. On matters where she could not find any support, Ayesha would interpret it according to logic. When she was asked whether the meat of animals that fire worshippers slaughtered could be eaten, Ayesha reminded them of the Quranic prohibition on eating the meat of an animal that was not slaughtered in God's name.[260]

Ayesha differed from others too, by interpreting the length of the obligatory waiting period for divorced woman differently than it is stated in the Qur'an. If the divorced woman wants to marry another man, she must wait to make sure she is not pregnant. Ayesha interpreted this length as the end of three menstrual cycles, not at their beginning, and told others to act accordingly. Abu Bakr ibn Abdurrahman said, "I did not see any *fiqh* scholars other than her who interpreted and explained this issue like that."[261]

Some Companions considered a separation as a divorce; Ayesha asserted there had been no divorce. Her support for the assertion came from her own experience. To those who wondered about her reasoning, she said:

"The Prophet of Allah gave us the choice to leave or stay and we preferred to stay with him. He never considered this as divorce."[262]

---

259 Bukhari, Sifatu's Salat, 79, (831).
260 See Qur'an. Baqra, 2:174, Qurtubi, al-Jami, 2:224.
261 Malik, Muwatta, Talaq, 1198.
262 Bukhari, Talaq, 4 (4962, 4963).

One day, Sa'd ibn Hisham n said:

> "I wanted to ask you about celibacy. What do you say about lead-
> ing a celibate life?"

Ayesha replied:

> "Do not do it! Did not you hear God Almighty say, 'And, indeed, we
> sent Messengers before thee [like every other man] and we gave
> them wives and children, and it is not possible for a Messenger to
> bring a sign, save by the command of Allah. For every term, there
> is a Divine decree. Keep away from celibacy'"[263] (Qur'an, chapter
> 13:38, Al-Ra'd).

Many scholars appreciated her knowledge of *Fiqh* as well. Scholars like
Abu Salama ibn Abdurrahman[264] expressed that they never saw someone more knowledgeable than Ayesha. While people like Abu Umar
ibn Abdul Barr thought Ayesha was a unique product of her era,[265]
others like Qasim ibn Muhammad said she had become like a self-
governing *fatwa* (legal pronouncement) office during the Caliphates
of Abu Bakr, Umar and Uthman.[266] In those days, people from Basra
to Damascus, from Kufa to Egypt, were surging in crowds to Medina
to ask Ayesha questions about religion. Some people, who were unable to ask questions directly to Ayesha, wrote letters to her and sent
her gifts. Ayesha's special student, Ayesha bint Talha, wrote replies to
such letters.[267]

---

263 Tirmidhi, Nikah, 2: Ahmad ibn Hanbal, Musnad, 6:97 (24702).
264 Ibn Sa'd Tabaqat, 2:375.
265 Zarkashi, al-Iijaba, 9.
266 Ibn Sa'd, Tabaqqt, 2:375.
267 Ahmad ibn Hanbal, Musnad, 6:93 (24667), 95 (2467), Bukhari, Adabu'l Mufrad,
1:382 (1118).

Vision of God

There was controversy about the vision of God. Some Companions, after Ascension (*Miraj*), such as Abdullah ibn Abbas, held the opinion that the Messenger of Allah had seen God. They asserted some proofs and cited from the Qur'an: "Indeed he saw Him on the clear horizon" (Qur'an, chapter 81:24). Another verse they used is as follows: "And certainly he saw Him a second time, near the farthest Lote-tree of the utmost boundary" (Qur'an, chapter 53:14-15). Abdullah ibn Abbas further said:

"God all mighty, who raised Prophet Ibrahim to the rank of *Khalilullah* (*Khalilullah* means "one to whom God talked to;" Prophet Ibrahim: friend of God by making His relationship to him unique, and who elevated Prophet Moses to the rank of *Kalimullah*) by honoring him with His speech. Surely, exalted Prophet Muhammad (SAW) received the blessing of seeing Him."[268]

Ayesha, Abu Dharr, Abdullah ibn Mas 'ud and Ubayy ibn Ka'b did not agree with him. All of them said that the *Hadith* about the Ascension should be considered perspective. Hearing this, Abdullah ibn Abbas consulted Ayesha and asked her:

"O my dear mother, did Prophet Muhammad see his Lord?"

Ayesha answered:

"When I heard your words, I felt as if my blood froze. There are three points. First, whosoever tells you Muhammad saw his Lord does not tell the truth: 'Eyes comprehend Him not, but He comprehends all eyes. He is the Subtle (*Latif*), the Aware' (Qur'an, chapter 6:104) and, 'And it is not for a man or mortal that God should speak to him, unless it be by revelation or behind a veil...'

268   See the Tafsir of Ibn Kathir and Tabari (Qur'an, chapter 53:14-15).

(Qur'an, chapter 42:52). . Second whoever says Muhammad concealed some parts of revelation, you should know that this person is lying, because God the Almighty clearly orders His Messenger to, 'Convey and make known in the clearest way, all that has been sent down to you from your Lord...' (Qur'an, chapter 5:68). However, he saw Gabriel in his true form twice."[269] Ayesha clearly explained that no one besides God knows the Unseen. God alone is omniscient, knower of the visible and the invisible. Ayesha said, "Say, 'None in the heavens and the Earth except Allah; and they do not know when they will be raised up'" (Qur'an, chapter 27:65-66). It is, however, true that God, in His infinite wisdom, gives knowledge to His Prophets of some secrets or future events.

Classification of Sunnah

In jurisprudence, distinction is made between the acts of the Prophet which were religious in character and those which were purely personal or were done in the exigencies of particular situations. All of his acts and practices are called *Sunnah* which is divided into religious matters, which were done to acquire merit as a part of religion, and were habitual or personal if done in particular situations. The religious ones are again divided into a *Mawakkad*, those done regularly, and a *Mastahaba*, those not done regularly. It is not incumbent on the community to follow the practices though those seeking greater nearness make it a point to follow them as well. Among the Companions, Ibn Umar did not believe in this distinction and followed each and every practice of the Prophet irrespective of its character. But Ayesha and ibn Abbas upheld this distinction and therefore in a large number of small points there is divergence of opinion between the two groups.

---

269 Bukhari, Badu'l Khalq, 7 (3062); Tabrani, Mujamu'l Kabir, 12:90 (12565). Ahmad ibn Hanbal, 6:241 (26082).

Ayesha's Personal Knowledge

THERE ARE MANY matters in which the Companions gave their opinions on, on the basis of their interpretation or deduction of something, and Ayesha rejected them on the basis of her observations:

(1) Ibn Umar gave a verdict that in taking a bath a woman should open the plaits (braids) of the hair of the head and wash them thoroughly. When Ayesha heard this verdict, she observed, "Why does not Ibn Umar say that women should shave off their head? I used to bathe before the Prophet and often I did not open the plaits of my hair, and poured water over them."

(2) Ibn Umar used to say that kissing nullifies ablution. Ayesha said that the Prophet did not perform ablutions again after kissing.

(3) She heard that Abu Huraira said that if a donkey, dog or woman crosses in front of a man saying Prayers, the Prayers are nullified. Ayesha got angry and said, "You have equated us women with donkeys and dogs. I used to lay before the Prophet while he was Praying [as there wasn't much space in the room] and he would push me with his hand when he was to do the prostration and I would pull up my legs and would spread them again when he stood up. Sometimes I would go across the Prayer mat."

(4) Abu Darda said in one of his sermons that if the sun has risen and one has not said the *Witr* Prayers, it should not be said thereafter. Ayesha said that this is not correct. She had seen the Prophet saying *Witr* Prayers after sunrise.

(5) Some people said that the Prophet had been enshrouded in a sheet brought from Yemen. Ayesha said that only this much was correct: that a sheet from Yemen had been brought. But it was not used.

(6) Abu Huraira said in his sermon that if during the days of fasting bathing in the morning is necessary, he should not fast that day. People came to Ayesha and Umm Salma to seek confirmation of Abu Huraira's statement. They said this was not a pre-condition for keeping fast, as demonstrated by the Prophet. Abu Huraira then withdrew his verdict.

(7) It was the general view that during the course of *Hajj*, everything became permissible after the stoning of the devils, except going to one's wife or using scent. Ayesha said that there was no harm in using scent, for she had herself scented the clothes of the Prophet.

(8) Ibn Abbas had given a verdict that if one does not perform the *Hajj* but sends an animal for sacrifice, then all the prohibitions attached to *Hajj* would operate until the animal was sacrificed. Ayesha refuted this view and said that the Prophet had himself sent animals for sacrifice but had not abandoned the permissible things which are used during the *Hajj*.

(9) Ibn Umar used to say that after having donned the *Ihram* in the morning, he would not like to use scent that night and would prefer to rub tar coal. Ayesha was asked about it. She refuted this view and said that she remembered perfectly well that the Prophet used scent the preceding night.

Ayesha's Other Skills

THE PUPILS OF Ayesha stated that she had considerable proficiency in history, literature, oratory and poetry, besides some knowledge of medicine. Hishambin Urwa says he had not found any one excelling Ayesha in knowledge of the Qur'an, obligatory duties, the lawful and unlawful poetry [here, lawful and unlawful mean moral and immoral], the history of Arabs and genealogy.

Ayesha's Poetry and Oratory

POETRY WAS THE gift of the Arabs; they expressed themselves in the language of poetry. Ayesha was born in an era when her father, Abu Bakr, was able to recite poetry for days without stopping. During that time, the most valued commodity in the market was poetry; they noted history in poetry, explained through poetry and livened up their gatherings with poetry. According to Ayesha, poetry came in two forms: good and beautiful poetry, and bad and ugly poetry. She recommended that people, "Leave the bad and ugly and be in search of goodness and beauty."[270] She heard this directly from the Prophet of God.

One day, poets asked Ayesha:

"Has the Messenger of God ever recited a poem?"

She answered that God's Messenger had recited a poem written by Abdullah ibn Rawaha and she did not neglect to give examples from the poem.[271] Ayesha had a photographic memory. She never forgot what she heard and could always recall such at the right time and in the right place. Years later, she passed on what she heard from the Meccans about the route they had experienced in the Battle of Badr. She told believers about the hatred the Meccans felt against Islam.[272] Ayesha had the sincere feelings of an old woman, and years later she was saved from the darkness of the pagan world and entrusted herself to the warm climate of the Prophet's Mosque.[273] Ayesha

---

270 Bukhari, Adabu'l Mufrad, 1:299 (865).
271 Bukhari, Adabu'l Mufrad, 1:300 (867).
272 Bukhari, Manaqibu'l Ansar, 45 (3921).
273 Bukhari, Slat, 57 (439); Manaqibu'l Ansar, 26 (3835).

presented some of the poems to the Messenger of God. And it was again Ayesha who passed on the poems, full of nostalgia, that had belonged to Abu Bilal and Fuhayra, whom she had visited after the *emigration*.[274]

One day, Ayesha recited two couplets from a poet written during the time of Ignorance by Abu Kabir Al-Huzali, near the Messenger of God. In the poem *Abu Kabir*, *Al*-Huzali wrote of his son and his legendary bravery. Then Ayesha said:

"If Abu Kabir Al-Huzali had seen you, he would have surely deemed you worthy of being the subject for his poem."

Upon Ayesha's arrival, the Messenger of God stood up and kissed her forehead, saying:

"May God Almighty reward you with the most beautiful and beneficial prize, O Ayesha. May God please you as you have pleased me."[275]

Ayesha related that a person named Sa'd had recited a poem on the day of the Battle of the Trench. In response to unbelievers who maligned Islam and the Muslims, the Messenger of God asked Abdullah Ibn Rawaha, Ka'b ibn Malik and Hassan ibn Thabit to defend Islam.

Ayesha was the one who passed these poems on.[276] She also shared poems that the Muslim women of Medina recited during weddings.[277]

Surely Ayesha's poems were not restricted to these. She was a woman with a treasure trove of poetry stored in her memory. She shared them when it was time, and was able to use the beauty of poetry to declare the values she believed in.[278]

---

274 Bukhari, Fadailu'l Medina, 12 (1889); Manaqibu'l Ansar, 46 (3926); Marda, 8, 22 (5654, 5657).

275 Bayhaqi, Sunan, 7: (15204).

276 Muslim, Fadailu's Sahaba 156 (2489, 2490).

277 Bayhaqi, Sunan, 7:289 (14466).

278 For more detailed examples about the poems Ayesha recited, see: Bayhaqi, Sunan, 7:289 (14466); Tabri, Tarikh 3:7, 47; 10:3; Ibn Kathir, al-Bidya, 7, 244; Tabrani, al-Mujamu's Saghir, 1:214 (343)' al-Mujamu'l Aswat, 3:360 (3401).

She said:

"Feed your children poetry so that their tongues shall be sweet."

She thought it was vital to teach poetry to children to help them speak more fluently and cultivate the skill of expressing themselves well.[279]

It is a fact that poetry has both a beautiful and an ugly face. The important thing for believers is to use language in good and beneficial ways. Ayesha explained that language could be used to hurt people, like biting a snake:

"The most sinful person is he who ridicules a tribe or a group of people in his poetry without any distinction."[280]

This was also the advice of the Prophet because Abdullah ibn Umar narrated from the Prophet that, "Poetry resides in speech; the beauty of it is like the beauty of speech. The ugliness of it is like the ugliness of speech too."[281]

When Abu Bakr passed away, Ayesha heard that some people were lobbying against her father and she became more upset. Evidently, the myth was told deliberately by the hypocrites. The truth needed to be told to warn people who would listen to her. She made a speech to make clear the position of the late Caliph once more, with details that some may overlook.

She finished her remarks and awaited the people's opinion.

She asked:

"For the sake of God, please tell me, is there anything that you found odd or untrue in what I have told you?"

---

279   Ibni Abdirabbih, al-Ikdu'l Farid, 5:239.
280   Bukhari, Adab'l Mufrad, 1:302 (874).
281   Bukhari, Adabu'l Mufrad, 1:299 (865).

The reply arose from the fair people gathering there:

"No, we swear to God that everything you said was true!"[282]

When Ayesha received the news that Uthman had been assassinated, she asked whether the news was true. Then she said:

"May God the Almighty bestow His mercy upon him and forgive him. Nevertheless, he was saved from the troubles of this world. Since in the past you raised no objection to those who opposed and resisted him and you submitted to them, today you should support justice more and you should work more to augment Islam's strength by exalting it. Even after so much benevolence from God, who bestowed on you blessings upon blessings in your religion, you still greedily desired this world and left behind the idea of helping His religion. You know very well that destroying something is much easier than constructing it. Do not forget that at the moment you expect thanks for your ingratitude; the blessings that you earned will vanish."[283]

On another day, Uthman ibn Hunaf asked her:

"O my dear mother. What is the reason for your visit here? Is it a duty that the Messenger of God promised to you or is it your own interpretation?"

She replied:

"On the contrary, I came here out of my own volition when I heard that Uthman was murdered. By killing Uthman, you violated three

---

282 Ibn Abdirabbih, al-Ikdu'l Farid, 2:206; Kalkashandi, Subbu'lAsha, 1:248; Nuwayri'l Arab, 7:230.
283 Abu Hayyan, Imta, 511; Ibn Tayfur, Balaghatu'n Nisa, 5; Buti, Ayesha, 81.

prohibitions and conducted three forbidden actions at the same time. You ignored the sacredness of this area, violated the honor of the Caliphate and defied the holy months. Although he had fulfilled your wishes, you caused him trouble upon trouble and killed him, thus purifying him like a white cloth cleaned spotlessly. Your tyranny made him suffer and I am angry with you because of what you did to him. Did you think that this is too much, that I became angry with you for wielding a sword against Uthman?"[284]

Although Ayesha was a small woman, she had a resonant voice. She lessened the tension of the crowd by speaking louder. Ayesha used her considerable powers of expression often during the Incident of the Camel to achieve peace. In one of her sermons', marvelous in its language, she said:

"As surely as I have the rights of motherhood over you, I have the right to advise you."

She explained her intention to be peace. She spoke of the blessings that God Almighty had bestowed on her because of God's Messenger and her father's efforts to ensure justice during his Caliphate.
She addressed them with gratitude:

"As you know, only the ones who rebel against God accuse me. The Messenger of God passed away while he was on my bosom. I am one of his wives in heaven. My Lord prepared me especially for him by protecting and securing me from negativity. You know that I really believed and the Hypocrites tried to cause discord among you. Because of me, God Almighty bestowed on you the ease of taking ablution with clean dust. You know that my father was one of the two people whose third was God. He was the fourth Muslim. He received the title of "The Loyal." The Messenger of

---

284 Ibn Kathir, Al-Bidaya, 7:232.

God was content with him while he was passing away, and he surely gave strength to the Caliphate. When the unity of Islam was shaken, it was he who gathered the two sides together and strengthened them. But the *fitnah* (discord) fire had been set and some became unbelievers after having believed."

These sermons left a deep impression on the listeners. The people of Basra were split into two and a significant number of them gave up making a stand against her. Those who listened to the sermon, later said they had never before heard such clear and eloquent speech. They also said they gave up obeying Uthman ibn Hunaf who had been leading them.[285]

Her literary skills, elegance of composition and dialogue was admired by her students. One of her pupils, Musa bin Tulha, said he had not come across any one more eloquent than Ayesha. And his view is shared by Ahnaf bin Qais *Tabaii* who stated that he had not seen any one excelling Ayesha in elegance of expression, depth of thought, or fluency and grace in language.[286] Eloquence and oratory was a natural talent of the Arab men and women. Many women were brilliant orators, equal to men, and their speeches have been preserved and compiled by Ahman bin Tahir in his book, *Balaghat-un-Nisa*. It includes speeches of Ayesha. *Tabari* has reproduced her speeches made in the field where the Battle of Camel occurred.

Ahraf bin Qais says that he heard the speeches of all the Caliphs but the excellence and the elevation he noticed in the speeches of Ayesha surpassed the others. Amir Muawiyya said he had not met any orator more eloquent, more fluent and sharp-witted than Ayesha.[287] She could raise and modulate her voice to make it grand and commanding.

---

285 Ibn Asakir, Tarikhu Dimasshq, 30; 390, Muttaqi, Kanzu'l Ummal, 12:224, 225. (35638).
286 Hakim: Mustadrak, Tirmidhi: Manaqib.
287 Zarqani: Muhabib, vol. 3. Page 267.

Ayesha's Experience in Medicine

———— ❦ ————

SHE GAINED KNOWLEDGE of medicine from the physicians visiting the Prophet. Ayesha's expertise in medicine cannot be compared to the scientific medicine of modern times of course. Cures to an illness were mostly found by using different mixtures from herbs, plants and animals. Usually, a master-apprentice relationship was necessary for the transfer of this science to future generations. Those who had knowledge of this science handed over knowledge and expertise to the next generation and so on.

But Ayesha was unusual in that she was neither formally educated in medicine or an apprentice. The most well-known doctor of Ayesha's era was Harith ibn Kalda, called "the doctor of the Arab people." [288] Ayesha was a master of the Arabic language. She knew what to say and how to say it. When she spoke, she commanded the attention of others. Her power of description was strong and she showed sensitivity in choosing words to use. Women were known for being able to cure young children. Looking at the general state of society, we see that there was sharing of duties between men and women. While men fought on the battleground, women undertook the duty of treating the wounded. Because Ayesha was present during many battles, it is not so difficult to understand how such experiences affected a keen intellect like herself.

Ayesha, with quickness and curiosity, never forgot what she heard or saw, and was not at ease until her questions were answered. Ayesha investigated everything that happened around her.

The home of the Prophet was a multipurpose school. Not only did she follow knowledge, but knowledge came to her naturally; this was how she

---

288

learned about medicine. Her information attracted the attention of others, and people came to ask her about many things. Of course there were some, even among her relatives, who found her knowledge of medicine strange and asked how she had obtained it. Ursa ibn Zubayr, the son of her older sister Asma, one day went to Ayesha and asked:

"O my dear mother. I am never amazed about your intelligence, depth of knowledge, comprehension or memory because I said to myself, 'She is the wife of God's Messenger and also the daughter of Abu Bakr', and considered it normal. I never found your knowledge of poetry or history strange, and accepted it by saying, 'She is the daughter of Abu Bakr, the most learned of people and scholar of the *Quraish*.' But I do not understand your knowledge of medicine at all. Please tell me: how did you learn it and where did you get the education for it [from]."

Ayesha rested her hand on his shoulders and said:

"O my Urwa. During the very last days of God's Messenger, he became sick so often and there were groups of doctors all around, both Arabs and Persians, who came to him to provide different kinds of treatments. Applying the treatments was my duty and I practiced them on God's Messenger. This is the source of my knowledge." [289]

From her own statements, Ayesha learned treatment methods from a range of sources and applied them. Many wanted to benefit from her experience and referred to her as the authority for healing. But it is also possible that this issue remained secondary because during this period of social unrest, the necessity of seeking and applying Ayesha's religious knowledge was primary. On one occasion we see Urwa lamenting the fact that Ayesha was questioned so often about the religious sciences

---

289 Ahmad ibn Hanbal, Musnad, 6:67 (2, 4425); Hakim, Mustadrak, 4:218 (7426).

that there was not time for medical sciences; that there was no time for medical science and untold volumes of information on medicine had been lost with her death. [290]

History and genealogy she learned from her father Abu Bakr who was regarded as an authority in genealogy. Many of the customs prevailing in the days of Ignorance and the condition of the society of that time we learn only from the narrations of Ayesha. For example, we learn about the different ways of marriage, the system of divorce, the songs sung at marriages, the days on which fasts were held, the rites of *Hajj*, etc. from Ayesha's narrations. The *Ahadith*, narrated by others, generally have few sentences, but many of those narrated by Ayesha cover several pages, for she has described the background and context as well and the cause and necessity thereof. She has given detailed descriptions of the battles of Badr, Uhad and The Trenches, as well as some details of the expedition of *Bani Quraiza*. She also described the prayers at moments of fear and insecurity in the expedition of *Dhat-ur-Ruqa*, the pledge of women at the Fall of Mecca and the necessary details of the Farewell Pilgrimage. Many of the details of the life of the Holy Prophet have been furnished by her such as the manner of descent of the Qur'an, the details of *Hijra*, the Prophet's death, his daily Prayers, his household engagements, his personal habits and deportment, and the hardest day of his life. She also described the succession of Abu Bakr, the demands of the views of the Prophet and his daughter Fatima, the grievance of Ali and the pledging of fealty.

---

290 Dhahabi, Siyar, 2:183.

Ayesha's Students

ONE *AHADITH* NARRATED that Ayesha had a special talent for passing her information along to others. With no child of her own to raise and educate, she was the mother of all. She found orphans and needy people and fought to educate useful members of society. She not only provided their material needs. She also aimed to turn into a store of knowledge.

In those days, Medina was like the heart of the Muslim world in terms of knowledge. The foremost scholar of Medina was Ayesha who was visited so frequently by all who sought information. And when she went to Mecca to perform the pilgrimage, a tent was set up between the *Hira* and *Sabir* mountains, and people visited her there and returned to where they came from, enlightened.[291]

Ayesha, who used all her days in this world to learn and teach, taught many students in various areas, primarily in the field of *Hadith*. Because of her, thousands of authentic *Ahadith* are available to every single Muslim until the Last Day.

Her door was open to everyone, whether free men or slaves, from intimates to distant relatives, with the condition that each must observe the essentials of religion. They came to her presence and listened to her lessons with great attention, and they left with the intention to pass such information along to others.

Concerning religious matters, Ayesha followed a path that anyone could pursue, and answered questions in a way that was easy to understand. When she saw that someone was shy to ask a question, she encouraged them and made it easier for them to ask and learn about the

---

291 Ahmad ibn Hanbal, Musnad, 6:40 (24107); Ibn Sa'd, Tabaqat, 5:595, 8:68.

things they were hiding inside.[292] Ayesha started a wave of knowledge that would reach more people and would become more valuable in future generations.

The environment of the Prophet of Allah was felt within her teachings. To her regular visitors, Ayesha passed on the maters that she had witnessed in conversations between the Prophet of Allah and his Companions, and she related the conversions in the style that he himself had used when telling a story. She avoided hastiness, and adopted a specific attitude toward those who thought they could acquire everything immediately in their first lesson taught by her. She told them that Allah's Prophet had not behaved in such a way.[293]

Ayesha's school of knowledge was frequented by Umar and his son Abdullah ibn Umar, Abu Hurayra, Abu Musa al-Ashari, Abdullah ibn Abbas, Abdullah ibn Zubayr. Even well-known Companions such as Amr ibn As, Zayd ibn Khalid al Juhani, Rabia ibn Amr al-Jurayshi, Saib ibn Yazid and Harith ibn Abdullah learned from Ayesha. The scholars of the next generation competed with each other to benefit from this spring (increase) in people visiting Ayesha to learn. It is said that the number of these scholars who attended her lectures and listened to her teachings is around one hundred and fifty. Urwa ibn Zubayr, Qasim ibn Muhammad, ibn Yazid Alqama ibn Qays Mujahid, Iqrima, Shabi, Zirr ibn Hubaysh, Masruq ibn al-Ajda, Ubayd ibn Umayr, Saeed ibn al-Musayyib, Aswad ibn Yazid, Tavus ibn Kaysan, Muhammad ibn Sirin, Abdullah ibn Harith ibn, Ata ibn Abi Rabah, Suleiman ibn Yasser, Ali ibn Hussain, Yahya ibn Ya'mar and ibn Abi Malaika were among such people.

Abu Amr, Zakwan, Nafi Abu Yunus, ibn Farruh Abu Mudilla, Abu Lubaba Marwan Abu Yahya and Abu Yusuf were freed slaves (*mawali*) and were also among those who were Ayesha's students.[294]

Ayesha's school of knowledge consisted not only of men. In the gathering, there were important women such as her sister Umm Kulthum

292 Ibn Maja, Tahara, 111 (610); Ahmad ibn Hanbal, Musnad, 6:97, 265 (24699, 26332).

293 Bukhari, Manaqib, 20 (3375).

294 Ahmad ibn Hanbal, Musnad, 6:32 (24845). 258; Tirmidhi, Daawat, 129 (3598).

bint Abu Bakr, Amra bint Abdurrahman, Amra bint Ayesha bint Tallha, Asma bint Abdurrahman, Muaza al-Adawiya, Ayesha, Jasra bint Dajaja Hafsah bint Abdurrahman ibn Abu Bakr, Safiya bint Shayba, Barira Sayiba, Marjana and Hasan al-Basri's mother Hayra. The total number of women who attended her lectures is around fifty.

Being a student of hers was a special virtue. The people closest to her were envied but without malice. Her nephew Urawa's position attracted the attention of almost everyone.[295]

---

295 Ibn Hajar, Tahzibu't Tahzib, 12:463.

Urwa Ibn Zubayr

—— ❧ ——

URWAIBN ZUBAYR WAS born in the twenty-third year of the Islamic calendar, during the last year of Umar's *Khilafat.* He sought knowledge from the start of his childhood. We see in him the desire of becoming a store of knowledge which people could benefit from.

He and three friends he met were talking about the future; they were adjacent to *Ka'bah.* Although Musab ibn Zubayr, Abdullah ibn Zubayr and Abdullah ibn Umar each had different wishes, Urwaibn Zubayr requested the following:

"O my Lord, bestow on me knowledge that people will benefit from after my death."[296]

Perhaps as a result of his prayer, a short time later he became one of Medina's scholars, respected by the elderly despite his youth. He stayed close to Ayesha, hardly ever leaving her alone, trying to get more information from her. Kabisa ibn Zuayb said:

"Surely Urwa was the one among us who best knew Ayesha's *Hadith* knowledge because he was the only one among us who entered the presence of Ayesha without any difficulty."[297]

---

296 Abu Nuaym, Hilyatu'l Awliya, 1:309; 2:176; ibn Asakir, Tarikhu Dimashq, 40:267.
297 Ibn Hajar, Tahzibu't Tahzib, 7:165; 12:463.

Ibn Shihab al-Zuhri, himself a leader in *Hadith* science, expressed Urwa's knowledge by depicting him as an ocean whose bottom was unreachable.[298]

Urwa himself said:

"During Ayesha's last four of five years, I thought to myself, 'If our mother Ayesha passes away, there is no *Hadith* in her knowledge treasure trove that I do not know.'"[299]

One day, Urwa ibn Zubayr and his son Muhammad went to visit Walid Ibn Abdul Malik. While they were in a barn, the startled horses got out of control. Muhammad died there in the turmoil. Urwa himself received a blow to his leg which later had to be removed because the injury turned into gangrene. Although he did not consent to doing so at first, he had to eventually consent after the suggestion of Caliph Walid. The fortitude that he showed while his leg was amputated before his eyes without anesthetic is impressive. When the surgery was complete, he read the verse, "We had some difficulties in this journey of ours." There was no one holding him and he eventually fainted. When he regained his senses, he wiped the sweat from his brow and asked those who were there to give him his amputated leg.

Holding his hand, he said, "I swear to God, Who exalted me by walking with you, I neither gave into a sin with you nor stepped into it."[300]

Then the people around him heard him praying:

"O my Lord! I had four limbs, two hands and two legs. You took one of them and left the other three to me; surely, as always, praise be upon you! I had four sons. You took one of them and left the other three to me; surely as always, praise be upon you! Aren't the ones who become everlasting the ones you take?"[301]

---

298 Ibn Sa'd Tabaqat, 5:181.
299 Ibn Hajar, Tahzibu't Tahzib, 7:165.
300 Ibn Asakir, Tarikhu Dimashq, 61:410.
301 Abu Nuaym, Hilyatu'l Awliya, 2:179.

Urwa had inherited the perfect manners of Ayesha in worship, as well as generosity and benevolence. It was he who transferred her worshiping habits to future generations. He spent his nights reciting the Qur'an, finishing one quarter of it in one night, and kept long vigils at prayer. Even after his leg was amputated, Urwa never shortened the time he spent worshiping. Only one night was he not to able to spend his night in prayer and recitation: the night his leg was removed. But he performed the worship the following night. He never wanted to lose his place in his spiritual life. He advised his family to pray all the time: "When any of you see something worldly that you like, you should go home and advise the family to perform Prayers; you should incline toward worshipping because God Almighty advises his Prophet, 'Do not strain your eyes toward what We have given some groups among them to enjoy the splendor of the present, worldly life, so that We may test them thereby.' The provision of you, Lord, is better and more lasting!" (Qur'an, Ta-Ha 20:132).

Speaking about Urwa, Urwa's son Hisham said, "My father used to fast his whole life and he was fasting on the day that he died."[302] Urwa inherited Ayesha's generosity too. In the season when the dates were ripening, he picked them from trees, spread them on his wall and invited people to his garden to take some. People came from all-around to visit his house and none left empty handed. Whenever he entered his garden, he said, "Masha Allah" (How beautifully God made). Then he recited the verse that reads, "What Allah wills [will come to past]! There is no strength, save in Allah!" (Qur'an, Kahf 18, 18:40). [303] The following statements expressing his depth are very meaningful:

"When you see someone doing a good deed, know that there are brothers of the good deed near that person too. Similarly, if you witness someone doing a bad deed, know that there are brothers of the bad deed near that person as well. Thus, if a good

---

302 Ibn Sa'd, Tabaqat, 5:180.
303 Abu Nuaym, Hilyatu'l Awliya, 2:180.

deed is the forerunner of another good deed, a bad deed is a sign of more bad deeds." Urwa died in the ninety-fourth year of the Muslim calendar. Since there were many other scholars who started their eternal journey in the same year, that year started to be called "The year of Fiqh scholars" (sanatul fuqaha).[304]

---

304 Ibn Sa'd, Tabaqat, 5:181.

Qasim Ibn Muhammad

―――――――――― ∾ ――――――――――

SINCE HIS FATHER had become a martyr, Qasim ibn Muhammad grew up near Ayesha and acquired all his knowledge in her presence. She took care of him, placed him under her own protection since early childhood and concerned herself with his education. Ayesha even cut his hair and dressed him up for festivals herself. But the most important inheritance that Ayesha left to him was surely knowledge. It is said that Qasim, together with Urwa and Amra, was one of the three people who had learned the extensive *Hadith* knowledge of Ayesha.[305] At the same time, he was humble. He disliked being regarded as important and did not think himself superior to others. One day, someone asked him whether or not he was more knowledgeable than the famous scholar Salim.

Qasim ibn Muhammad thought neither of exalting Salim with false modesty or of stroking his own ego by bragging. In response to the man's insistence, Qasim told the man to speak to Salim.[306] Like Urwa, Qasim lived without asking for anything from other people and never inclined even slightly toward any behavior that might damage his morality and gravity. One day, Umar ibn Ubaydullah sent him one thousand drachmas but Qasim returned them all. Some people insisted that he should keep just one hundred of them but his attitude did not change.

---

305 Ibn Hajar, Tahzibu't Tahzib, 8:300.
306 Ibid.

248

The *Khalifa* of the time, Umar ibn Abdul Aziz, treated Qasim with great respect and regard throughout his life. He even wanted to recommend Qasim as a *Khalifa* candidate after himself and did not hesitate to say this openly.[307] When Qasim saw people speculating about different interpretations of destiny, he warned them:

"You too should behave carefully on the points that God avoided expounding on." He interpreted the conflicts of the people who had lived before him, primarily the Companions', as God's great mercy for the following generation.[308]

When he lost his vision at the age of seventy years old, he called his son to be near him; when his death was imminent, he told his son his will: "Use the clothes that I performed Prayer in, including my shirt, *izar* and *rida*,[309] as my burial shroud."

"Oh, my dear father. Why don't we prepare a two-piece shroud for you?" His answer was like that of Abu Bakr who he considered a role model:

"O my dear son. Abu Bakr left this world with three pieces of cloth. Do not forget that those who live need new clothes more."[310]

Amra Bint Abdurrahman

Amra bint Abdurrahman was the sister of As'ad ibn Zurara of the *Bani Najjar*, one of the leaders of *Ansar*; Amra bint Abdurrahman was also the granddaughter of Sa'd ibn Zurara. She was a relative of God's Messenger, on his mother's side.

---

307 Dhahabi, Tazkiratu'l Huffaz, 1:97.

308 Ibn Sa'd, Tabaqat, 5:188, 189.

309 An *izar* is a wrapper covering the body below the waist and a *rida* is a cloak covering the upper body.

310 Ibn Sa'd Tabaqat, 3:204.

Ayesha, who took Amra and siblings under her protection, turned this family into distinguished scholars. She felt responsible for spreading the knowledge that she had accumulated during the era of God's Messenger among the children whose talents she noticed. Like her siblings, Amra appreciated Ayesha's consideration and took her place in history as the leading scholar of her time. The well-known Ibn al-Madini said, "Amra was among the most reliable scholars who were cognizant of Ayesha's *Hadith* knowledge."[311] And Amra bint Abdurrahman had the incredible vision to comprehend the knowledge of Ayesha.

Ibn Hibaan said, "She was the most knowledgeable of people about Ayesha's *Hadith* knowledge."

Sufyan Sarwi called her, "The most well-informed person who comprehended Ayesha's *Hadith* knowledge."[312]

The people of Amra's time liked her very much. Everyone who was interested in Ayesha was also interested in Amra and showed their love with gifts. But she sent the gifts to the needy, just as she had learned from Ayesha. And she never sent gift-senders home empty-handed either.[313]

The duty of correcting interpretation errors, after Ayesha, fell on Amra's shoulders. She corrected judgments and tried to explain the truth together with its reasoning.[314]

One day, Qasim ibn Muhammad said to *Imam* Zuhri:

"I see you are very desirous for learning. Do you want me to show you a bowl full of knowledge?"

"Yes," *Imam* Zuhru responded.

"You should go directly to Amra bint Abdurrahman because she was educated by Ayesha," Qasim ibn Muhammad said.

311   Ibn Hajar, Tahzibu't Tahzib, 12:466.
312   Ibn Hibban, Siqat, 5:288 (4881).
313   Bukhari Adabu'l Mufrad, 1:382 (1118).
314   Malik, Muwatta, Hudud, 11 (153).

Zuhri, who went to Amra bint Abdurrahman following Qasim ibn Muhammad's recommendation, later said:

"I realized that she was like an ocean where it was impossible to reach the bottom."[315]

In the age that Amra lived in, there were surely many people seeking knowledge but she was beyond that type of person. When she opened her eyes to the world, Ayesha was next to her; from early childhood, she was surrounded by Ayesha's treasure trove of information. Amra was one of the few who followed the path of Ayesha in searching for knowledge and applying it to her life, primarily in the *Hadith* and *Fiqh* sciences. She narrated *Hadith* from Rafi ibn Hadij, Ubayd ibn Rifa'a, Marwan ibn al-Haritha and Umm Salma; she even narrated *Hadith* from Ayesha.

During an age when the well-informed continually sought information, people visited her often. She turned her home into a madrasa, a place of teaching and learning, and educated many students. Among the students she taught were Haritha ibn Abi Rijal, Ruzayq ibn Hakim, Sa'd ibn Saeed, Sulayman ibn Yasar, Abdullah ibn Abu Bakr ibn Muhammad ibn Amr, Abdirabbih Ibn Saeed, Urwa ibn Zubayr, Amr ibn Dinar, Malik ibn Abi Rijal, Muhammad ibn Abu Bakr ibn Muhammad ibn Amr, Muhammad ibn Abdurrahman, Muhammad ibn Muslim, ibn Shihab al-Zuhri, Yahya ibn Saeed, Yahya ibn Abdullah, Abu Bakr ibn Muhammad, Raita al-Muzani and Fatima bint Munzir.

She passed away in the ninety-eighth year of the Muslim calendar. Her death caused great sadness to spread among scholars, and people looked for the information she had left behind. The Caliph of Umayyad, Umar ibn Abdul-Aziz, who had showed a special deference to Amra while she lived and consulted her on the matters that confused him, said:

---

315 Dhahabi, Tazkiratu'l Huffaz, 1:112; A'lam, 4:508; 5:247.

"No one who knows Ayesha's *Hadith* knowledge remained among us after Amra's death."

He assigned a team of people to search for any information, *Hadith* or application that she had passed on to future generations.[316]

---

316 Ibn Sa'd, Tabqaat 8:480; Dhahabi, Siyar, 4:507, 508.

Muaza al-Adawiyah

———— ༺ ————

MUAZA AL-ADAWIYAH, KNOWN by her nickname Umm Sahba, was the widow of Sila ibn Ashyam who had been murdered on a battleground near Qibla with his son Sahba Muaza. Umm Sahba inherited the good manners and knowledge of Ayesha and had such strength of character that upon hearing about the death of her husband and son, she told the women who came to her to offer their condolences:

"If you are coming to congratulate me, you are welcome. But if you have some other intention, it would be better not to come."

This great woman, who promised to spend her life in worship, kept vigil every night, particularly after the martyrdom of her husband. She was known as one of the most pious people of that time. Muaza, who attracted attention because of her depth of faith and worship, one day told those around her:

"I swear to God that my love for this world is not about making myself prosperous or about enjoyment of happiness. I swear to God, I love this world only because I want to get closer to my God. In this way, I hope that Almighty God will let me meet with my son and Abu Sahba in heaven."[317]

---

317 Ibnu'l Jawzi, Sifatu's Safwa, 4:23.

She performed prayers from night until morning, and when she felt sleepy or lazy she roamed around a little to give herself some vigor, and said to herself:

"O my *nafs* [soul]! Here, sleep is right in front of you. Submit to it. You should know that you will sleep in your grave at great length. But there is one difference: this sleep will either make you yearn in regret or be happy in mercy."[318]

When her time approached and the signs of death started to be seen on her face, those nearby witnessed that she wept in great sorrow and then smiled. They asked:

"Why did you cry and why are you smiling?"

"I thought that my illness would draw me away from fasting, prayers and remembrance of God; I never saw beauty like theirs in this world, so I smiled. I do not think that I will be here for even one more prayer."

As she had foretold, Muaza al-Adawiyah died that day, in the Muslim year eighty-three, before it was time for another prayer.[319]

---

318 Ibid, 4:22.
319 Ibid.

Ayesha's Married Life

AYESHA'S MARRIED LIFE was one in accordance with the precepts of the Qur'an. "And of his Signs is that He has created wives for you from among yourself, that you may find peace of mind in them; and He has put love and tenderness between you. In that, surely there are Signs for a people who reflect" (Qur'an, chapter 30:22).

It is not useful to show the merits or deficiencies of the Muslim wives or to show the status of women in Islam generally. It is important to show how the Holy Prophet (SAW) behaved toward his wives. In one of his traditions he says, "The best among you are those who treat their wives well and I am kindest toward my wives."[320] This kind of statement shows the cordiality and love that existed in his relationship with Ayesha, which was never disturbed except for a solitary incident. Sincerity and affection, tenderness and love, prevailed in that relationship which is greatly enhanced if the privation, hunger and poverty the family had to suffer is kept in mind.

Amir bin Al-'As once asked the Holy Prophet who was dearest to him in the world. The Prophet replied, "It is Ayesha." Amir bin 'As asked again about men and the Holy Prophet replied, "It is her father." Hazrat Umar had advised his daughter Hafsa not to be jealous of Ayesha. The Holy Prophet used to pray, "O God! I try to treat my wives equally in all material matters, but forgive me for what is beyond my control [i.e., my love for Ayesha]."

Generally, it is thought that the preference for Ayesha was due to her great beauty and charm, but this is not correct. Zainab, Juwayriyah and

---

320 Bukhari: Sahih, vol. 11, chapter: Behavior.

Safiya were also young and beautiful and much has been written about their external charm in the book of Traditions, while there is only one reference, perhaps two, about the beauty of Ayesha. In this regard, we find one Tradition repeated by Ayesha and narrated by Abu Huraira: "A woman can be selected for marriage on four grounds: her wealth, beauty, pedigree and piety. You should choose a pious woman."

The favorite could be the one who could serve the cause of religion the greatest. Ayesha distinguished herself among all the wives, regarding her understanding of religious precepts and her interpretation and intellectual grasp of the Shariah and assimilation, and her remembrance of legal commands and injunctions. The Books of Traditions record that the Holy Prophet (SAW) had said, "Among men, there have been many perfect persons, but among women, only two, Mary, daughter of Imran, and Ayesha, wife of Pharaoh, achieved perfection, and Ayesha has superiority over other women as *Tharid* [a dish] has over other dishes." Umm Salma ranked next in moral excellence and she was also very dear to the Holy Prophet (SAW), even though she was of advanced age. His first wife Khadija died at the age of sixty-five years old, but love and regard for her had so long persisted that even Ayesha used to grow jealous. The Holy Prophet (SAW) was visibly annoyed when she made any unkindly mention of Khadija.

Ayesha's Love for Her Husband

———— ✂ ————

HAZRAT AYESHA HAD such devotion and ardent love for her husband that she used to grow sad if anyone else claimed they had the same degree of affection for someone or something. She woke up one night and did not find her husband in bed. She stated she was reaching for him in the darkness and found him in prostration before the all mighty God. On another occasion, she thought he might have gone to another wife, and started looking for him only to find him busy in prayers. She was penitent and uttered, "May my parents be sacrificed for you. What have I been thinking and in what celestial state are you in?" On yet another occasion, she woke up after midnight to discover that her husband was not with her. She searched for him and didn't find him anywhere. She went to the graveyard where the Holy Prophet was busy in supplication. She quietly retraced her steps and mentioned it to the Prophet in the morning. The Prophet said, "Yes, I had seen something in black moving. Was it you?"

Once on a journey, both Ayesha and Hafsa accompanied the Holy Prophet (SAW). Every evening he went to the litter of Ayesha and talked with her until they stopped the caravan for the night. One day, Hafsa suggested to Ayesha that she change their camels. When the Holy Prophet (SAW) went to Ayesha's litter, he found Hafsa inside. The Prophet scolded her and went inside. Ayesha was waiting for him. When the caravan halted, Ayesha put her feet on the grass and said, "O God! I cannot say anything but send a scorpion or snake to bite me! What degree of feminine anguish is reflected by this!"

Once, the Holy Prophet (SAW) decided not to visit any of his wives for a whole month. Every wife, touched to the heart, was morose. Against his wish, they could not visit him. Ayesha was counting every day of the month. When the month was over, he visited Ayesha first. Among his wives were women of different statuses. Some belonged to rich and well-to-do families. They found the privations and austerity too hard to bear. Then the Quranic verse was revealed, to the effect that whoever wanted luxury and comfort could separate and whoever wanted the honor and dignity of being the Holy Prophet's wife could remain with him. None desired separation and those who wanted the honor and dignity of being the Holy Prophet's wife could remain with him. Ayesha was the first to make this decision. She begged her husband not to mention it to others. This was again a reflection of a feminine trait. In this period of anxiety came the verse that the Prophet could retain any of his wives and leave the others. However, he did not leave anyone of them. Ayesha reminded him that had the authority been given to her, she would have given the command to everyone else.

When the Prophet heard about the death of Jafar in the Battle of Muta, he became very sad. In Islam, a loud lamentation over anyone's death is not permitted. The Prophet asked the man, who brought the news of death to advise the women to stop her lamentationn. He reported back that they were not listening. Ayesha was observing from behind a door. She was growing very perturbed that the man was neither carrying out the directions nor leaving the Prophet.

The life of the Holy Prophet was an example for all of mankind. In order to show how one should gain the good will and affection of one's wife, he used to occasionally meet his wives with unusual delight and joy. Ayesha had brought up a girl of *Ansar* and when she was married, she supervised the simple ceremony. The Holy Prophet came from outside and asked why there was no singing.[321] On an *Eid* day, Negroes were demonstrating their wrestling prowess with the aid of spears. Ayesha wanted to see the performance. The Holy Prophet (SAW) stood in front and Ayesha observed the scene from behind him as long as she wanted to.

---

321 Musnad: vol. vi, p. 269; Bukhari: Marriages.

Once, she was talking very boldly with the Holy Prophet (SAW). Abu Bakr happened to stop by and he grew so angry at her daughter's behavior that he wanted to beat her, but the Prophet prevented him from doing so. After Abu Bakr left, he remarked, "See how I save you?"[322] The Prophet once brought a slave girl and asked Ayesha if she knew her. Ayesha answered in the negative. The Holy Prophet said, "The girl sings beautifully. Would you like to hear her?" The girl sang for her. At times, the Prophet would recite a story to her. Once, he told her the anecdotes of Khurafa, a man of the *Azra* clan who was picked up by Jinn who showed him some marvelous things which he narrated to the people after his return.

The Holy Prophet (SAW) could not take all his wives with him on his journeys. Many were randomly selected. She whose name was selected would go with him. Ayesha accompanied him on several of his journeys. She accompanied him in the expedition of *Bani Al-Mustaliq* and two singular distinctions were conferred by God on her. One is related to instruction for smearing hands and face with dust if water is not available for ablution and the other is related to upholding the chastity of innocent women. According to the *Musnad of Ahmad ibn Hanbal*, she also accompanied the Holy Prophet in the journey to *Hudaybiya* and was among the several wives who had gone on the farewell pilgrimage.

The Holy Prophet (SAW) was fond of riding and archery and would induce his Companions to practice these sports. On one of these expeditions, he asked all of his followers to go ahead. When they were left alone, he asked Ayesha to compete with him in a race; Ayesha agreed and she won the race. On a similar occasion, the Holy Prophet (SAW) was the winner and he remarked that he had avenged his earlier defeat.

Love is something that cannot be easily analyzed. Its depth cannot be measured either. Blandishment and coquetry are part of feminine traits. Conversations between the Holy Prophet and Ayesha should not be assessed as that of a Prophet and his follower, but as that between a husband and wife, for after all, they were human beings.

---

322 Abu Daud Sunnan; chapter: Manners.

Ayesha says she was surprised when the verse that says a wife can forego her *Mahr* was revealed. But, when the verse that says the Prophet could retain any of his wives as he liked and abandon the others was revealed, she said to the Prophet, "I see that God quickly fulfils your every desire." [323] This was not intended to raise any objection but was only an exhibition of loving coquetry.

Ayesha was not keen of sharing her time with the Prophet of Allah (SAW) with others and wanted to spend all the time she spent with him alone. However, he was a Prophet; everyone's Prophet. He wanted to reach all people, however inaccessible they were, and aimed to open doors that had not been opened before. Ayesha understood that people lined up to sacrifice their lives for the sake of his mission. They were devoted to him and their devotion made Ayesha anxious. Her anxiety persisted until the following verse was revealed:

"You can leave the turn of visiting any of them [his wives] you please, and take whoever you please. There is no blame on you if you give precedence to one who you left before" (Qur'an, chapter 33:52).

After the revelation of the verse, she turned to the Prophet of Allah (SAW) and said:

"As I see it, your God always bestows on you what your heart wants."

Her heart was a reflection of love and had the expression of intimacy. She wanted to be with him all the time but conditions did not allow it and again it was he who made the sacrifice. Each wife of the Prophet of Allah (SAW) took her husband, one day, away from her. The Prophet of Allah made a schedule for his wives and divided his days equally among them. While she had enjoyed the opportunity to be with him fairly often, eventually her turn came only every nine days.

---

323 Bukhari: Sahih-Commentary on Abzak.

The Prophet of Allah (SAW) did not change his attitude after these verses were revealed. Even if he had a preference that deviated from the planned schedule, he always got permission from his wives to do whatever such preferences called for. Ayesha specifically focused on this point when she reiterated the attitude of the Prophet of Allah.

The Prophet of Allah (SAW) continued to ask for permission regarding the schedule, even after the verse in chapter 33:52 was revealed. Ayesha, on her day with the Prophet, wanted to spend all her time with him and was sensitive to anything that interfered with their togetherness. One night, she woke up and realized that the Prophet of Allah (SAW) was not with her. Since there was no light, she was not able to see nearby. She was worried that he had left her to visit one of his other wives. She fumbled around with agitation. Then her hand touched one of his feet; she was relieved to discover that he was prostrating. She calmed down and took a deep breath. The Prophet of Allah (SAW) had not left her; he was in tears praying to God on the other side of the room. Ayesha was touched and as she listened, she heard his sincere supplications:

"O Lord, I seek refuge in Your pleasure from Your wrath, and in Your forgiveness from Your punishment; I also seek refuge in Yourself from You. I cannot praise You as You praise Yourself."

Ayesha was ashamed of her worries and turned to the Prophet of Allah (SAW). She then said:

"May my parents be sacrificed for you. How did I think about you when you were busy with this?"[324]

Ayesha was faced with the same situation another day. When the Prophet of Allah (SAW) was going to Medina cemetery, he left his sandals near it

---

324 Muslim Salat, 221 (485, 486, 512); Tirmidhi, Daawat, 76 (3493), Abu Dawud, Slat, 152 (879).

and hung his clothes nearby, as if he would be getting up and leaving immediately. Normally he got permission from his wives, even to get up for night prayers, considering other people's rights over him as essential.[325]

He was acting differently then and Ayesha did not understand why, and so she became suspicious. He started to rest on his bed. After some time passed, the Prophet of Allah (SAW) slowly got up from his bed. He walked quietly on his tiptoes to avoid awakening Ayesha. But Ayesha was not sleeping; she was watching him with curiosity. The Prophet of Allah (SAW) put his sandals and clothes on carefully, then opened the door and left. Ayesha was upset that he was leaving.

She rose instantly and covered her face with her veil. Then she started to follow him. He went to Medina cemetery (*Jannatul Baqi'*) and raised his palms to the heavens and started to pray with longing. When his arms grew tried, he lowered them, and then a little while later, raised them again to continue praying.

Then he left the cemetery and started to return home. Ayesh started to walk too, in order to hide herself. When the Prophet of Allah (SAW) walked faster, so did she. When he walked even faster, Ayesha ran.

She arrived home before God's Messenger, but she was out of breath. She laid down immediately, trying to pretend she had never left the room.

When the Prophet of Allah (SAW) came in soon after, he noticed her agitation and asked, "What happened to you, O Ayesha?"

She replied, "Nothing."

As the Prophet of Allah, he knew better. So he asked:

"Are you going to explain yourself or do you want God the All-Knowing and the Gracious to tell me about it?"

Her heart pounded. Turning to the Prophet of Allah (SAW), she said:

"O Messenger of God, may my parents be sacrificed for you."

---

325 Bayhaqi, Sbuabu'l Iman, 3:383 (3837).

It was an indirect way of confessing her guilt. He asked:

"Were you the indistinct figure I saw in front of me while I was walking?"

"Yes," she confessed.[326]

These incidents showed her that the Prophet of Allah (SAW) was beyond reproach and that she had nothing to fear.

Her love for him ran so deep that she could not allow anything negative to be said about him. One day someone said:

"May God grant death[327] to you."

Immediately after Ayesha heard this, she stood up and said:

"Who would dare to wish for the death of God's Messenger? On the contrary, may God bring both death and curses on you."

The Prophet of Allah (SAW) understood her sensitivity and appreciated the generous motive behind her words. But as the Prophet, he needed to consider everyone as a potential believer. A Potential believer's unkindness should not be repaid with unkindness. So, he turned to Ayesha and said:

"Be calm, O Ayesha! God the Almighty is the most Gentle (*Rafiq*) and he loves us to be kind in all matters. He does not bestow his blessings to those who act without kindness."[328]

---

326 Muslim, Janaiz 102 (974); Nasai, Janaiz, 103 (2037); Ibsartu'n Nisa, 4 (3963-3964).
327 Instead of saying "Salam" (greetings, peace) be upon you, certain adversaries of Islam deliberately greeted the Prophet by saying "saam" (death) be upon you.
328 Bukhari, Adab, 38, 95683.

Ayesha was not able to say no if someone asked her for something. Though she fretted inwardly about being away from the Prophet, she could not have acted differently.

When the Prophet of Allah (SAW) prepared for a military expedition, he drew many of his wives to determine who would accompany him on such expeditions. One time, Hafsah and Ayesha were drawn. They made much progress on the first day of the journey. When night fell and they took a break, the Prophet of Allah (SAW) sat and began to chat with Ayesha. Hafsah took this to mean that the first night would not be hers, but Ayesha's.

After some time had passed, Hafsah approached Ayesha and suggested:

"You mount my camel and I will mount yours, and let's see what the Messenger of God will do."

It seemed like a fine joke; Ayesha was sure that the Messenger of God would choose her camel and thus she would have bragging rights. Therefore, she replied in the affirmative.

When the army began to depart, the Messenger of Allah went to Ayesha's camel though Hafsah was inside the palanquin, not Ayesha. Thus Ayesha, who had received proof of her worth to God's Messenger, was actually deprived of traveling with him.

She said yes to the game but it was not easy to tolerate the result of the game. The Prophet of Allah chose her but she was not with him; she felt miserable and did not know what to do. Digging her feet into the grass, she felt sorry for herself and unburdened herself from God:

"O My Lord, send a scorpion or a snake to bite me! Your Messenger is going and I am not able to say anything to him."

In Ayesha's eyes, her husband was more handsome than Prophet Joseph who women had seen and who accidentally cut their fingers.   [In the

Chepter 12th: verse 51 of the the Holy Qur'an it is stated that [And the king (of Egypt) said, 'Bring him to me.' But when the messenger (yousuf) came to him, he said, 'Go back to thy lord and "ask him how fare the women who cut their hands; for my lord well knows their crafty design.'and Ayesha believed that if the women saw Prophet Muhammad, peace and blessing be upon him, they would have stabbed themselves in the chest instead.

Inside their warm home full of mutual love, there was not even the smallest problem that could damage their relationship. Every passing day increased their love by two and every incident served to feed their affection for one another. Neither did Ayesha abuse his love nor did the Prophet of Allah (SAW) feel the need to take certain measures into his own hands. This was the Prophet's general state regarding his affections for his other wives, for they were similar to Ayesha. He understood their wishes before they expressed them, and fulfilled their requests as he always had for others. Ayesha said:

"The Messenger of God neither hit a woman nor a servant; he hit no one with his hand."

Her love for him continued even after his death. The mother of believers, who sustained the humble lifestyle she had shared with the Prophet after his death, reached against anyone who brought endowments into her home, and kept herself far from worldly blessings. Those who viewed her as the mother of the believers were competing to do good deeds too, and so she gave away what was given to her as gifts to the needy. Most of the time she kept nothing for herself. At first, Ayesha wanted to return the gifts when they were given. But a phrase she heard from the Messenger of God made her unable to do so. Thus, she was obliged to accept whatever was offered to her.

One day, Abdullah ibn Amir's emissary brought clothing and food to Ayesha. She turned to him and said:

"O dear son! I accept nothing from anyone."

She returned the gifts to him. Even though he was only the envoy, he was sad. Their intention was merely to do good because when they gave something to Ayesha, they felt as if they had given to the Messenger of God. They respected her as their own mother and wanted to meet her needs, but it was necessary to respect her choice. The envoy felt a bit desperate as Abdullah walked home, worrying about what he would say happened.

At the same time, Ayesha was reconsidering what she had done. Immersed in deep thought, she wondered whether she had acted in opposition to the Messenger of God, and rashly. She said to those around her:

"Call him back!"

When they reached him, the envoy was shocked. He returned to Ayesha's home with anxiety, wondering what she was going to say.

Ayesha's former anger disappeared as if blown away by a sea breeze. In the gentlest manner, she said:

"I remembered something that the Messenger of God told me. He said, 'O Ayesha. If someone gives you something without you asking [for it], never return it; always take it. For it is a blessing God has offered to you!'"[329]

The meaning of the *Hadith* was clear and the envoy left with a smile.

Once, Ayesha had severe pain in her head. The Prophet of Allah (SAW) was also suffering from a severe headache which later developed into his fatal illness. He said to Ayesha, "If you were to die before me, I would have bathed you with my own hands, wrapped you in your shroud and buried you and prayed for you."

Ayesha said, "You are wishing for my death. If that were to occur, you would bring a new bride in my place in this very apartment!" The Prophet (SAW) smiled.[330]

---

329 Ahmad Ibn Hanbal, Musnad, 6:77(24524).
330 Bukhari: Sahih. Chapter: Illness, p. 46. Ahmad Musnad, VI, p. 228.

A prisoner was brought to the Prophet and was kept in Ayesha's custody; Ayesha was talking to other ladies. Then the prisoner escaped. When the Prophet came and found the prisoner missing, he said to Ayesha, "Your hand will be cut off." He went out and told the Companions about the prisoner's escape. The prisoner was then captured. When the Prophet entered his apartment, he found Ayesha looking at one hand and then at the other. He asked Ayesha what she was doing. She replied that she was trying to determine which hand would be cut. The Prophet was deeply moved and raised his hands in prayer for her.

One day, she asked her husband, "O Prophet of Allah. If there were two pastures, one untouched and the other browsed, which would you prefer, the first?" Ayesha had tactfully referred to the fact that amongst his wives, she alone was a maiden.[331]

The incident of slander against Ayesha took place and God attested to Ayesha's innocence in His revelation; her mother advised her to touch the feet of her husband. She curtly relied, "I do not worship anyone except my God who has attested [to] my innocence and ashamed the slanderers."

The Prophet once said, "O Ayesha! I know when you are pleased with me; also when you are angry with me. When you are angry, you swear by the God of Abraham and when you are happy, you swear by the God of Muhammad."

Ayesh replied, "O Prophet. The difference does not go beyond the tongue." As long as the service of the husband is concerned, there are several traditions narrated by *Imam* Bukhari. Though there was a maid servant, Ayesha used to do most of the household chores herself. She would grind the grain, knead the dough and cook the food. She would make the bed and store water for ablution, wash the clothes and the tooth stick, comb the hair of the Prophet and rub scent on his clothes.[332] She would also entertain the guests.

---

331 Bukhari: Sahih. Chapter: Marriage, p. 26.
332 Bukhari: Sahih: Ahmad Musnad, Vol. Vi. P. 68, Tirmizi Shimail.

Ayesha was obedient of her husband, and she fully complied with the wishes of her husband. During the period of her marriage life, she never disobeyed her husband and whenever she felt that something was not liked by him, she gave it up. A Companion wanted to give the wedding dinner but he didn't have the means to do so. The Holy Prophet (SAW) sent word to Ayesha to send a basket of grain. She complied with his wishes and did not retain anything for their evening meal.[333]

During the lifetime of their husbands, many women are obedient, but the real test arises after the death of their husbands: to do what their husbands liked and to abstain from what they disliked. Even after the death of the Prophet, Ayehsa meticulously followed all his commands and instructions. He had preached generosity. She retained this trait for the rest of her life. He had said that for women, *Hajj* is their *Jihad.* She made it a point to perform *Hajj* every year. Once, somebody sent some cash and clothes to her. She returned them but she accepted them later, saying that she had remembered some saying of the Prophet. She had kept fast on the day of *Arafa in intense* year. Somebody suggested that she break the fast. She went on sprinkling water on her head but did not break the fast, saying that fasting on the day of *Arafa* washes away one year of sins.[334]

A woman asked her if there was any harm in the use of henna. She replied that the Prophet liked its color but not its smell: "It is not prohibited; if you like, you can use it."

---

333 Ahmad: Musnad, Bol. VI. P. 758.
334 Ahmad: Musnad. Vol. VI. P. 128.

The Holy Prophet's Love for Hazrat Ayesha (ra)

———— ✣ ————

AYESHA LOVED THE Holy Prophet very much. But, the Holy Prophet, who set an example for society on every issue, also loved Ayesha deeply. As he did in every arena, the Holy Prophet (SAW) lived with excellence in terms of family relations.

He said:

"The best among you is he who behaves best toward his family. I am your leader in this."[335] The basis for being such a person is mutual love. The Holy Prophet (SAW) helped Ayesha understand his love for her and made it clear to others. Of course, the Prophet represented justice, but love cannot be constrained by human will. His love for Ayesha was a reflection of human nature. He never discriminated against any wife, equally cared for each one's provisions and behaved with kindness to them. Yet, he could not help how he felt. Because of this, after spending a day with any wife, the Holy Prophet (SAW) turned to God and prayed to Him to erase any deficiency that may have risen from his differing emotions:

"O my Lord! This is the share that I can do; do not judge me by the share that You can do which I am not able to do."[336]

---

335 Tirmidhi, Manaqib, 64 (3895); Ibn Maja, Nikah 50 (1977).
336 Tirmidhi, Nikah, 41 (1140); Abu Dawud, Nikah, 39 (2134).

This prayer was about Ayesha. The Prophet of Allah (SAW) had a rare intimacy with her compared to his other relationships. The Prophet of Allah (SAW), the most sensitive of people, wanted to be perfectly just, but took refuge in the most Merciful God from any injustice that might occur. A revelation that God sent shed light on this matter:

"[O husbands!] And you cannot keep perfect balance between wives however much you may desire it. But incline not wholly to one, so that you leave the other like a thing suspended. And if you are reconciled and act righteously, surely Allah is All-Forgiving and Merciful" (Qur'an, chapter 4:130).

Some Companions began calling Ayesha the "darling of God's Messenger." When something about Ayesha was said in the presence of Ammar ibn Yasir, he got angry and shouted:

"How could you talk about the darling of God's Messenger like that and hurt her?"[337] Ammar commanded the person who had said the negative remark to get out of his sight. The love that the Prophet and Ayesha had for each other was so obvious that the Companions preferred to give gifts to the Prophet on days that he was with Ayesha, since the smile on his face was more special on those days.[338]

It was a situation well understood, and in order to avoid problems, everyone warned and tried to help one another. One day, Umar advised his daughter Hafsah:

"O my dear daughter! I hope the state of your companion does not mislead you if she is more graceful and dearer to God's Messenger than you."[339]

---

337 Tirmidhi, Manaqib, 63 (3888); Hakim, Mustadrak, 3:444 (5684).
338 Bukhari, Hiba, 6, 7 (2435-2441).
339 Muslim, Talaq, 30 (1479); Tirmidhi, Tafsiru'l Qur'an, 387 (4629).

Umar was trying to impart to his daughter the special status of Ayesha, and was helping her early on to avoid her trying to compete with Ayesha.

A Persian neighbor of theirs cooked very delicious soup and one day he invited the Prophet of Allah (SAW) over for a meal. The Holy Prophet (SAW) never thought of accepting the invitation and wanted to take Ayesha who was suffering greatly from hunger. Refferring to Ayesha, the Holy Prophet (SAW) asked:

"Are you inviting her too?"

The man replied in the negative. Perhaps he had only a small amount of soup to share, or perhaps he did not understand that the Prophet wanted him to invite Ayesha. So, the Prophet responded to the invitation in the negative.

After a while, the man returned and repeated his invitation. The Holy Prophet gestured to Ayesha and asked:

"Are you inviting her too?"

Again the man said no, and again the Prophet said no to the invitation.

Finally, the man came for the third time and repeated his invitation once more. This time, the man understood that the Prophet of God did not want to attend without Ayesha. So, the man responded in the affirmative when the Prophet asked if Ayesha was invited for the meal too, and the Prophet of God and Ayesha went to the Persian man's house together.[340]

The love between Ayesha and the Holy Prophet (SAW) was so clear that people sent Ayesha to him to make him forget conflicts and make him happy again. One day, Safiya took Ayesha aside and said:

"O Ayesha. Can you make the Messenger of God pleased? If you can, I will give you my day."

---

340 Muslim, Ashriba, 139 (2037); Ahmad ibn Hanbal, Musnad, 3:123 (12265).

Ayesha replied in the affirmative and then went and sat down near the Holy Prophet (SAW). Knowing this day was not hers and that he never changed the schedule which determined which wife he would stay with, he found the arrival of Ayesha strange and told her to go to her room.

Since he had started the conversation, she continued it by saying:

"O Messenger of God. This is a blessing which is bestowed from God to the ones He wants."

She gained the undivided attention of the Holy Prophet (SAW). Ayesha explained to the Prophet of Allah a detailed account of the talk she'd had with Safiya, sharing the grief the latter had felt. It was an attempt at peace and Ayesha's sensitivity delighted the Prophet of Allah. The sensitivity he felt inside was reflected on his face.[341]

Once, on a trip together, Ayesha's camel lost its way and departed from the others, becoming lost in a place called Kharra. The Holy Prophet (SAW) became anxious and immediately everyone started to look for Ayesha. With the worry of losing the one closest to him while under his care, he shouted, "Wa arusah," an expression of sadness used by someone who has lost his wife.

Another time, a well-known Companion, Amr ibn al-As, asked the Holy Prophet:

"Whom do you love most among people?"

He had hoped to find out his own significance in the eyes of the Holy Prophet (SAW) and expected to hear himself named. But the Holy Prophet (SAW), without hesitation, replied:

"Ayesha."

---

341 Bukhari, Hiba, 14: Shahadat, 30 (2542).

Amr ibn al-As continued, expecting to hear his own name mentioned, asking:

"Then mong men?"

Then the Prophet replied:

"Ayesha's father."

Amr ibn al-As discerned that he was not the Prophet's top priority and that asking him more questions was risky. Considering the possibility that he could be last on the list of people the Prophet loved the most, Amr ibn al-As gave up asking any questions like this again.[342]

These events witnessed by everyone were embedded in their memories; every preference of the Holy Prophet (SAW) made people love him even more. When he went to an expedition and stayed away from his wives for a month, he would first go to Ayesha's home. [343]

Similarly, the Holy Prophet (SAW) asked for Ayesha's opinion first during the incident of *talryir*.[344]

When the Muslims of Medinah began to extricate all of the public of Meddinah from the poverty that they had been suffering from for years, some of his wives (he had four at that time) asked him, "Couldn't we live a bit better like other Muslims do?"

The Holy Prophet (SAW) reacted to their question by going into retreat. He excused himself, saying, "I cannot afford what they want." The Holy Prophet (SAW) was preparing them to be exemplars for all present and future Muslim women. He was especially worried that they might enjoy the reward for their good deeds in this world and thereby be among those referred to in the following verse:

---

342 Bukhari, Fadailu's Sahaba, 5 (3462).
343 Bukhari, Nikah, 83 (4895).
344 Bukhari, Mazalim, 26, (2336).

"And on the day when those who disbelieve will be brought before the Fire, it will be said to them, 'You exhausted your good things in the life of the world, and you fully enjoyed them. Now this day you shall be required with ignominious punishment because you were arrogant in the Earth without justification and because you acted rebelliously'" (Qur'an, chapter 46:21).

Thus, these special women were put to a great test. The Prophet of Allah (SAW) allowed them to choose his poor home or the world's luxury. If they chose the world, he would give them what he could afford and then dissolve his marriage with them. If they chose God and His Messenger, they had to be content with their lives. This was the peculiarity of his family. Since this family was unique, its members had to be unique. Thus, the Prophet first called Ayesha and said, "I want to discuss something with you. It's best if you talk with your parents before making a decision."
Then he recited the following verses:

"O Prophet! Say to thy wives, 'If you desire the life of this world and its adornment, come then, I will provide for you and send you away in a handsome manner; But if you desire Allah and his Messenger and the home of the hereafter, then truly Allah has prepared, for those of you who do good, a great reward'" (Qur'an, chapter 33:29-30)

Ayesha's decision was exactly what would be expected from the truthful daughter of the truthful father: "O Messenger of God, do I need to talk with my parents? By God, I choose God and His Messenger."[345]
Ayesha narrated in one of her traditions that:

"The Messenger received the same answer from all his wives. No one expressed a different opinion. They all said what I had said."

---

345 Bukhari, Mazalim, (2336); Tafsiru's Sura. 276 (4507); Talaq, 22 (1475).

Fatima explained a secret that the Holy Prophet (SAW) had told her before he passed away; she explained it only to Ayesha.[346]

All these incidents made society more careful when it came to Ayesha. His preference stayed the same until the day he died. On the day his fatal illness started, he asked:

"Where am I now? Who will I be with tomorrow?" And he expressed his wish to be with Ayesha during his sickness. It was the last proof of his intimacy with Ayesha which she described in this way:

"He died on the day when the turn was mine. God took his soul when his head was on my bosom."[347]

It was with all this in mind that Anas ibn Malik said that the first great love in Islam was the love of God's Messenger for Ayesha. When *Imam* Masruq narrated a *Hadith* transmitted by Ayesha, he would say:

"This was narrated to me by the beloved, one of the most beloved servants of God, and by the woman whose chastity was approved by the heavenly revelation, and who was the truthful daughter of the most truthful one."[348]

---

346 Bukhari, Manaqib, 22 (3426).
347 Bukhari, Janaiz, 94 (1323).
348 Bayhaqi, Sunan, 2:458; Ibn Sa'd, Tabaqat, 8; Ibnu'l – Athir, Usdu'l Gbaba, 1 (1384).

The Real Reason for the Holy Prophet's Love for Ayesha

IN ORDER TO evaluate and analyze, one cannot help but wonder about the reason for the Holy Prophet's (SAW's) love for Ayesha which was so great compared to his love for his other wives. First of all, the Holy prophet (SAW) often reminded his other wives that Ayesha was his closest friend's, Abu Bakr's, daughter.[349] Without a doubt, Ayesha was an attractive woman. Her mother (Umm-i- Ruman) once consoled her when she was grieved, saying:

> "Wait a little while! God will give you ease. I swear to God that there is no woman who is as beautiful as you and who is loved by her husband as you are, and has such good relations with her fellow wives, and who no one aims to defame. A woman in your situation is normally slandered often!"[350]

It was like the warning Umarhad had given to his daughter Hafsa about never competing with Ayesha or making her sad. It was the result of the same sensitivity toward Ayesha who had a special place at the side of God's Messenger.[351]

When the narrations are analyzed generally, the cause of the Holy Prophet's overflowing love for Ayesha seems to be her faith. Ayesha led

---

349 Muslim Fadailu'l Sahaba, 83, (2442); Nasai, Ishratu'n Nisa, 3 (3944); Ahmad ibn Hanbal, Musnad, 6:88 (24619); Bayhaqi, Sunan, 7:299 (14526).
350 Bukhari, Shahadat, 15.
351 Bukhari, Mazalim, 25 (2336).

her family in brilliance and knowledge and was the distinguished teacher of the members of the Holy Prophet's family.

While many witnessed the public behavior of the Holy Prophet (SAW), Ayesha saw his behavior in both public and private. She became the most important interpreter of the Qur'an and the main teacher of *Ahadith*, becoming the foremost transmitter of Islam. The Holy Prophet (SAW) advised Muslims to learn the details of religion from her. In a *Hadith* Ayesha narrated, the Holy Prophet (SAW) said:

"A woman is married for three things: her wealth, her beauty and her religion. Yet, you should prefer the religion aspect so that you could attain serenity."[352]

The Holy Prophet (SAW) first practiced and then advised what people ought to do in any given situation.

Several other wives of his were also known for their beauty. So clearly his particular affection for Ayesha cannot be explained only by saying she was beautiful. The beauty of his other wives is narrated in Ayesha's Traditions. For example, when Ayesha saw Juwayriyah during the War of Bani Mustaliq, her beauty grabbed her attention and Ayesha became anxious. Ayesha said:

"She was a very beautiful and nice person with an attractive posture. She came and asked the Messenger of God to determine a ransom for her emancipation. I swear that when I first saw her, I had a gnawing suspicion, and I was concerned from the moment she walked up to God's Messenger."[353]

Ayesha also felt a similar concern when she first saw Safiya. Safiya, who came to Medina after the conquest of Khaybar and who stayed as a guest in the house of Haritha ibn An-Numan, quickly attracted the attention

---

352 Ahmad ibn Hanbal, Musnad, 6:152 (25232).
353 Hakim, Mustadrak, 4:28 (6781); Ibn Sa'd Tabqat, 8:116, 117.

of the women of the helpers and they rushed to see her. Covering her face with her scarf, Ayesha was among them. Sometime after she left the house, the Messenger of Allah left too. While the Holy Prophet (SAW) planned to marry Safiya, and thus please a large number of people with whom he had fought until that day, he did not want to hurt his wives. He came close to Ayesha and asked:

"How did you find her, O Ayesha?"

He then realized that she was not pleased with the situation. Safiya had lived among people who had made the Companions and the Holy Prophet (SAW) suffer until that day. Now, she would be expected to live with a person from Khyber, where people with whom they had fought for many years lived; she was expected to live with one who would become the focus of atrocity. She replied:

"I see a Jewesh."

In order to avoid similar problems from the past arising in the future, it became necessary to think and behave differently. Whatever the thoughts and attitudes of a group may be, it was not correct to judge individuals according to the thoughts and attitudes of others. Just as there are good and virtuous people in society, there are also people who have been deprived of good values. Even if they did not display good values, ultimately they were the children of Adam. It was necessary to make a clean break from the prejudices of the past. Goodness begets goodness and goodness ultimately softens the hardest heart. Every incident was an opportunity to make progress among the Companions and the mothers of the believers. Turning to Ayesha in a compassionate manner, the Holy Prophet (SAW) said:

"O Ayesha. Do not talk like that. She became a Muslim and her conversion was wonderful."[354]

---

354 Ibn Sa'd, Tabaqat, 8:126, Dhahabi, Siyar, 2:227.

Ayesha was special in all respects. It was as if she was created to accomplish this mission in the house of the Holy Prophet (SAW). She saw Gabriel twice and received greetings from him through the Holy Prophet (SAW). Revelation was revealed when the Holy Prophet (SAW) was alone or when he was with Ayesha in her room.[355] Considering the status of the Holy Prophet (SAW) and the fact that he was directed by revelations from God, it is possible that the basis for their love was the Divine. We can't deny her role in the time of the Holy Prophet and in the time after his death. Ayesha was so invaluable to the Holy Prophet (SAW) that he once said:

"There are many men who attained spiritual perfection. However, no woman, save Imran's daughter Mary, and Pharaoh's wife, and the Prophet's wife, Ayesha, reached that point. Comparing Ayesha's virtue to other women is like the superiority of meat *tharid* to other meals."[356]

---

355 Bukhari, Fadailu's Sahaba, 30.
356 Bukhari, Ahadithu'l Anbiya, 33 (3230). Tharid is a special dish of Arab cuisine and the Prophet liked it very much.

Ayesha as an Intermediary Between the Holy Prophet and Women

—— ❧ ——

AYESHA LIVED PLAINLY in every situation. Her responsibility stemmed from the time she married the Holy Prophet (SAW). This serious responsibility she carried on her shoulders had to hold different repercussions if she were to fail to uphold such responsibilities. She became a representative for women when she entered the Holy Prophet's home, acting as an intermediary between the Holy Prophet (SAW) and all women. Ayesha's situation made her a vital confidant, especially for female Companions.

The women of that era in Arab society had been second class citizens; it was the result of many centuries of traditions. Ayesha's sensitivity to women including herself attempts to impart meaningful information to her close friends in her home, and most of her time with women was spent providing solutions to these age-old traditions.

The Holy Prophet (SAW) sometimes witnessed her efforts. In fact, when he arrived home, Ayesha's friends would try to run away, but the Holy Prophet (SAW) would call them back. Not wanting to disturb them, he would leave, leaving the women together.[357]

Ayesha sometimes kept toys in her house to allow the little ones to amuse themselves. One day, the Holy Prophet (SAW) saw a two-winged horse and asked:

"What is this, O Ayesha?"

---

357 Bukhari, Adab, 81 (5779).

She replied without hesitation:

"This is a Horse."

The Holy Prophet (SAW) asked:

"Does a orse have wings?"

Ayesha answered:

"Didn't Solomon's horses have wings too?"

Ayesha's answer showed that she considered the Qur'an even in mere children's games and entertainment.

The Holy Prophet (SAW) responded to Ayesha's wity reply with a smile.[358]

Since she joined the house of felicity, Ayesha was at the center of the duty to eliminate the ignorant pre-Islamic habits of their ancestors, formed during the age of Ignorance (*Jahiliyya*). Her closeness to the Holy Prophet (SAW), her knowledge of the Qur'an and her amiable attitude toward the troubles of women both before and after her marriage was an advantage to women.

In the age of Ignorance, women were generally treated with contempt; they were barely considered human. Though many were converting to Islam, the old attitudes of the society were not entirely erased overnight. Many women had neither rights nor value and remained in a state worse than slavery.

However, women had an influential representative at the side of the Holy Prophet (SAW). Ayesha was like a consultant for women; confessing their secret problems to her, they returned home with solutions. They had been reluctant to share intimate details. It is narrated by Ayesha that, "One woman came to Ayesha with great sorrow and

---

358 Abu Dawud, Adab, 62 (4932); Bayhaqi, Sunan, 10:219 (20771).

said, 'My husband neither divorces me nor leaves me on my own; nor has marital relations with me.'"

The woman wept, unable to suppress the tide of emotions erupting inside her soul. She explained the heartbreaking conditions that she had lived in for many years. She was nothing more than a toy under her husband's control. Further details of this woman's circumstances are as follows. First, her husband said that he was divorcing her, but before the waiting period ended, returned to her, claiming to have changed his mind. From that point on, he persisted in going back and forth, playing with her emotions. His real intention seemed to be to prevent his wife, who he wanted to divorce, from being married to someone else.

When the Holy Prophet (SAW) came home, Ayesha informed him of the situations. He felt uneasy. It seemed like a marriage of tyranny. However, no Quranic verse was revealed saying what to do in such a situation. Thus, he decided to wait. In the meantime, Gabriel appeared and revealed the verse that warned the believers that marriage is a serious matter:

"Divorce must be pronounced twice and then [a woman] must be retained in honor or released in kindness" (Qur'an, chapter 2:30).

It then became clear that a second statement of divorce meant that the husband and wife separated. This matter was more serious than suspected, for a man was by this point forbidden from returning to a wife that he had divorced three times, even if he felt regret. The only exception to these rules was if the wife married and divorced another man. Only then could she be married once again.

This was a difficult test. After this revelation, everyone put an end to arbitrary divorce practices and such tyranny was not tolerated.[359]

Another day, Khawlah bint Tha'labah visited Ayesha. She was miserable. Her years of suffering and hardship was apparent from her appearance. She explained her troubles one by one. Her husband had divorced

---

359 Abu Dawud, Talaq, 9 (2194); Ibn Maja, Talaq 13 (2039).

her according to a pre-Islamic custom. A husband would say to his wife, "You are henceforth as my mother's back to me," thus forbidding himself from marital relations with her. A woman in this condition was not allowed to re-marry. The only one who could solve her problem was the Holy Prophet (SAW). One time when he came home, Khawlah turned to him and said:

"O Messenger of God. He exhausted my youth; I gave him whatever I had. When I got older and was unable to give birth, he divorced me by saying, 'be as my mother's back to me.'" It was a difficult situation. She said that her children had grown up and she lived alone with her husband. So, if her husband left her, she would be left alone without anyone to protect her. She added that her husband would have agreed to re-accept her as his wife, but according to custom he was not able to do so. Holding her arms up, she prayed about what was weighing on her heart:

"O my Lord! I am complaining to you about my situation!"

The merciful Holy Prophet's heart ached. But her oppression would not last forever; even as Khawlah prayed, God revealed, to clarify the matter. Gabriel explained fully the situation of Khawlah and solved similar problems for all women. The verses explained that these wrong practices belonged to the pre-Islamic era of Ignorance and were entirely renounced. The verses also explained what women in this situation should do and what the punishment for anyone who persisted in this kind of behavior was:

"Allah has, indeed, heard the talk of her who pleads with thee concerning her husband and complains unto Allah. And Allah has heard the two of you conversing together. Verily, Allah is All-Hearing, All-Seeing."

"Those among you who put away their wives by calling them mothers-they do not thereby become their mothers; their mothers are only those who gave them birth. They certainly utter words that are manifestly evil and untrue; but, surely, Allah is the Effacer of sins, Most Forgiving.

Those who put away their wives by calling them mothers, and who then would go back on what they said, must free a slave before they touch one another. This is what you are admonished with. And Allah is Well-Aware of what you do.

But he who does not find a slave, he must fast for two successive months before they touch one another. And he who is not able to do so shall feed sixty poor people. This is enjoined on you so that you may have faith in Allah and His Messenger. And these are the limits prescribed by Allah; and for the disbelievers is a painful punishment" (Qur'an, chapter 58:2-4).

Tafsir (detailed explanation):

This chapter of the Qur'an opens with a sharp denunciation of the evil custom of Arabs and citing the case of Khaulah, a Muslim lady, lays down an ordinance. Khaulah, wife of Aus bin Samit and daughter of Tha'labah, had become separated from her husband because the latter called her "mother." The exact words used by him are as follows: "Thou are to me as the back of my mother." Thus, according to an old Arab custom, all conjugal relations had ceased between her and her husband after he said this. The unfortunate woman could neither demand divorce in order to contract a second marriage or enjoy conjugal rights, and thus remained a suspended woman who was uncared for. She complained to the Holy Prophet, mentioning the awkward situation in which she was placed in, and sought his advice and help in the matter. The Holy Prophet pleaded his inability to do anything for her as it was his want that he would not give a decision in a matter such as this one unless he was guided by revelation. The revelation came and the custom explained above, from the pre-Islamic era, was declared unlawful.

On another occasion, Thabit ibn Qays's wife Habiba bint Sahl visited Ayesha, saying that she wanted to divorce her husband and asking for

Ayesha's help. Habiba was the daughter of Abdullah ibn Ubayy ibn Salul, the leader of hypocrites; she married Thabit ibn Qays after the death of her husband Hanzalah in the Battle of Uhud. She was distinguished both in beauty and manners and was treated with great care by her family. Although Thabit was well-known for his speaking abilities, he was short and unattractive. Most likely, Habiba felt social pressure to divorce her husband. When the Messenger of God came, Habiba explained:

"O Messenger of God. I am not criticizing my husband for his religion or his character. Yet I am afraid of forsaking my belief after having accepted Islam. I want to divorce my husband."

Habiba's explanation was very decisive. The Holy Prophet asked her:

"Are you going to give his garden back to him?"

Without any hesitation, she replied:

"Yes."

After that, the Holy Prophet called Thabit and asked him about the marriage. Thabit had no solution either. Apparently, the unrest had grown and the wound had festered and had become incurable. The marriage could not be sustained under these circumstances.

Although divorce was known to be the permissible act that God hates the most, there was no other solution. The Holy Prophet said:

"Take the garden and divorce her."[360]

Considered within the context of the time, the incident meant an important expansion in the rights of women: a woman exercised her will and chose to divorce her husband.

---

360 Ibn Maja, Talaq, 22 (2056); Muwatta, Talaq, 11(1174).

When it was seen that such matters were resolved with authority, the number of people knocking on the door of the Holy Prophet for reasons similar to the one just cited above increased.

Khawlah bint Hakim, the wife of Uthman ibn Madun, who was among the first believers of Islam, found her way to Ayesha's door. She was distraught. The Holy Prophet knew Khawlah; years before, she arranged the marriage between himself and Ayesha.

When the Holy Prophet went home and saw her in such a state, he turned to Ayesha and asked:

"O Ayesha, what made her become this way? What has happened to her?"

Ayesha explained the following about Khawlah's husband Uthman ibn Madun:

"O Messenger of God. It is as if she is unmarried; in fact, she is a married woman without a husband. For her husband spends his days in fasting and his nights in prayer. Therefore, she is unable to control herself and as you can see, she is ruined."

Uthmanibn Madun had devoted himself entirely to worship and thus had neglected his family's rights over him. Though, like a shepherd, he was responsible for the people under his control and he had neglected his wife. But these sad circumstances became a cause for a revelation of truth from God.

The Holy Prophet then sent a message to Uthman ibn Mudun. He came to God's Prophet soon afterward. The Holy Prophet said:

"O Uthman. We are not ordered to live as monks. Am I not enough for you as an example? Or do you break off from my Sunna?"

Uthman ibn Madun was confused. His aim in performing so much worship had been for a religious life and he thought that what he did was for the hereafter. Uthman replied:

"No, Messenger of God. On the contrary, I am trying to practice your Sunna, letter by letter."

But of course, there could be no doubt that the Messenger of God knew exactly what the Sunna was. After he heard Uthman's words, the Holy Prophet gave the following advice:

"I am the one who, at the highest level, fears God and observes the boundaries of God's religion among you. Yet I pray and sleep, fast and break my fast, and at the same time, I am married to women. Be afraid of God, O Uthman, because your family members have rights over you. Your visitors have rights over you. Your own self has rights over you. Therefore, you should fast some days but not on others. And you should pray at a certain part of the night, but also sleep at certain parts [of the night]."[361]

In some traditions, it is narrated that there were female Companions too, who never slept during the night; they attracted the others and were talked about in the society. Khawlah was one of them. When she went to Ayesha, Khawlah mentioned her habits and Ayesha shared them with the Holy Prophet. When he heard that she prayed all night, his reaction was negative. Such habits could not be sustained indefinitely and small but constant worship was more pleasing to God.

"What? Does she not sleep at night?" He asked again, as if he did not want to believe what he had heard. Then he said:

"Oh, why do you burden yourself with more than you can bare? Do not forget: you become tired and exhausted; it is only God who never needs rest."[362]

---

361 Ahmad ibn Hanbal, Musnad 6:226 (25935); ibn Habban, Sahih, 1:185, 2:19.
362 Bukhari, Tahajjud, 18 (11000).

One day, a young girl went to Ayesha with great sorrow and said that her father wanted her to marry his cousin even though she did not want to.

In those days, girls were not permitted to state their opinions regarding those they were expected to marry; their feelings were considered irrelevant. The final decision always belonged to the father and what he said was final. But another wrong custom would be changed by the Holy Prophet. This was what the girl hoped for.

Ayesha listened to her and as she had said to many others, said:

"Wait here until the Messenger of God returns." Ayesha was going to inform the Holy Prophet of the situation and, through this young girl, a general problem stemming from the era of Ignorance was going to be clarified.

When the Holy Prophet came, Ayesha explained the girl's situation to him immediately. The Holy Prophet sent a message to the girl's father, calling him to his home. When the Prophet invited someone, it was virtually not a choice for the one invited not to respond to his request. The Holy Prophet asked the father about the issue. What the girl had related turned out to be accurate and the Holy Prophet gave advice to the father. When he spoke to him, it was as if he was speaking to the society at large. From the Prophet, the father began to understand what he had done wrong and announced that he would not force his daughter to marry against her wishes, and the matter was settled pleasantly. For the first time, a young girl's wish had been treated seriously. At least that's what everyone expected, that the two would not marry. However, the situation ended differently. When the Holy Prophet turned to the girl and told her the decision was her own, the girl, contrary to what was expected, said:

"O messenger of God. I do accept the marriage that my father arranged. By asking you to intervene, I was trying to show women that fathers did not have any right to force their daughters into marriage."[363]

The above quoted examples do not show the only women who went to Ayesha to share their problems with the Holy Prophet through her; there were many who went to Ayesha and ultimately learned about solutions to their problems and thus went home pleased and at rest.[364]

Ayesha's role in interveneing between them was not a useless and blind justification of women; Ayesha defended them because they were right. She did not refrain from admonishing women who were wrong, who went too far or who were trying to force their way past the boundaries of religion. Justice and equity was the essence of her decision-making process. To be clear, Ayesha did not defend women because they were female. When it was necessary, she criticized women sharply and did not hesitate to warn them, helping them see and correct their faults that she noticed.

After many years passed, and with new conquered territories, believers had come into contact with different societies and ideas. Some women were also affected by the new situation. Particularly, some women did not protect their former sensitivity and began to show different attitudes. Poignantly, Ayesha summarized her grief as follows:

"If the Messenger of God saw the current state of women, he would prohibit them like the women of the children of Israel and ban them from coming to the mosque."[365]

Ayesha's knowledge of Islam was very thorough, her decisions making this point quite notieceable. At the same time, her words were an indication that time can change decisions; the conditions in the time of God's Messenger were perhaps more suitable for women to attend congregational prayer, for example. Indeed, that they attend such was

---

363 Ibn Maja, Nikah 12 (1874); Ahmad ibn Hanbal, Musnad, 6:136 (25087).
364 Bukhari, Libas, 23, (5825).
365 Bukhari, Sifatu's Salat, 79, 98310; Muslim, Salat, 144 (445).

recommended. But the situation in latter days was different than before and perhaps a new decision ought to be given considering the differences.

Ayesha was sensitive regarding the issue of hijab and she admonished women who did not show the necessary concern. Meticulous and critical, she wanted everyone to show the same care on religions issues and often underlined that there should be no sluggishness when it came to following through with religious practices.

One day, the daughter of her brother, Abdurrahman, went to visit her. As soon as she saw the sheer headscarf of Hafsah bint Abdurrahman, she took it and folded it in half. Then she brought Hafsah to her side and warned her:

"Do you not know what God revealed in the chapter *Al-Nur* [Qur'an, chapter 24:31-32]?"

Ayesha asked the people nearby for a thicker scarf. They gave one to her and Ayesha covered her niece's head with it, showing her how to cover, and thus put an end to the matter.[366]

Ayesha explained how they used to cover in the time of the Messenger of God, by relating personal memories to her:

"At the time of God's Messenger, if horsemen rode toward us while we were wearing pilgrim's garments, we covered our faces right away, and when they passed by, we uncovered our faces again."

Pilgrim's garments are worn for the *Hajj* (Pilgrimage), and distinguished scholars, such as Abu Hanifa, have said that a woman could uncover her face while in pilgrim's garments because it is a place of worship and the possibility of evil thoughts at that time is low compared to other times. Yet, Ayesha was very sensitive, explaining that they covered their faces when they saw a stranger coming, even though they were wearing

---

366 Muwatta, Libas, 4, Bayhaqi, Sunan, 2:235; ibn Sa'd Tabaqaqat, 8:72.

pilgrim's garments. Furthermore, she mentioned the difficulties that she encountered while she wore the *hijab* and stated that a fearless struggle was necessary. When she became ill during the Farewell Pilgrimage and had no choice but to go with her brother's place in pilgrim's garments, she had many difficulties, but never lost her sensitivity, neither on that day nor after. She showed people that what she said was what she believed; not fiction but real life.[367] Her life was a kind of lesson, from beginning to end. Ayesha did as much as she could for those who visited her, but when there was a male visitor, she separated herself from them behind a curtain even though she was the mother of believers,[368] as confirmed is in the Qur'an. When she witnessed societal changes, she remembered yearningly the era of the Holy Prophet and told her female Companion about their deep belief and sincere practicing of the commandments of God. She would sigh and say:

"My God, bestow mercy to the immigrant [*muhajir*] female, the Companions of former days! They competed to fulfill the order as soon as God commanded them to draw their veils over their bosoms, wrapping themselves up in their garments."[369]

She heard that some women in the recently conquered provinces walked around unrestrictedly compared to the past and that they acted rather carelessly outside their homes. She started to grieve. One day, when a group of women went to visit her, Ayesha scolded them, saying:

"Are you one of the women who go to public baths? Do not forget that I heard the Messenger of God saying that, 'A woman who takes her clothes off in a place other than her husband's home means to tear the curtain between her and God.'"[370]

---

367 Bukhari, Hayd, 15 (310, 311, 313).
368 Ahmad Ibn Hanbal, Musnad, 6:219 (25883).
369 Bukhari, Tafsir, 31, 94480.
370 Ahmad Ibn Hanbal, Musnad, 6:41, 173 (24186); Tirmidhi, Adab, 43 (28030).

Witnessing that the clothing of the woman who visited her had changed and that the woman had become less covered, Ayesha warned:

"A woman who believes in the Commandments of God in the Qur'an regarding covering the body cannot cover like this. If you are a believer, do not forget that the garments you are wearing are not the garments of believing women."[371]

When someone went to visit her, Ayesha could decipher their intentions from their behavior and attitude. Before they even asked a question, she knew their real purpose, her answers reflecting such. One woman who visited her asked about the opinion of the Prophet regarding henna, and she replied:

"God's Messenger liked its color but not its smell!"[372]

Her dialogue, which he also had with women, not only consisted of details, but she also directed people to a state of mind that God and His messenger would be content with, and advised them to establish peace within their homes. She believed that harmony within the home consisted of peace in this world and the next. She said that both husband and wife should fulfill their responsibilities and expect to make sacrifices. Ayesha showed the proper respect to the ones who were close to the Messenger of God and supplied them with what they needed. Though she tried her hardest to please everyone, she expected the women who visited her to show the same concern as her, expecting other women to behave toward their husbands the way she had behaved toward the Holy Prophet. Once when a woman asked her for advice, Ayesha said:

---

371 Qurtubi, al-Jami, 14:57.
372 Abu Dawud, Tarajjul, 4, (4164), Ahmad ibn Hanbal, Musnad, 6:117 (24905).

"If you had the opportunity of removing your irises to replace them with more beautiful ones in order to please your husband, do it without hesitation."[373]

To Ayesha, family happiness was to be regarded above everything else. And to meet this objective, the wife had an invaluable role. A wife is the source of family contentment, and for this reason, she ought to act more carefully when she is fulfilling her responsibilities toward her husband. To the women who had questions regarding these issues, Ayesha gave longer and more thoughtful answers than they expected. If they asked related questions, she gave longer advice as well. One of them said:

"I have hair on my face. Should I pull it out in order to be attractive to my husband?"

Ayesha answered:

"Just as you wear jewelry and adorn yourself when you visit someone, clean up and make yourself beautiful to your husband. When he orders you, obey him; if he asks you for something, do not neglect his request. Moreover, do not let someone that your husband does not like into your home."[374]

373 Ibn Sa'd Tabaqat'l Kubra, 8:79-71; Dhahabi, Taribu'l Islam, 1: 537.
374 Abdurrazzaq, Musannaf, 3:146 (5104).

Children of the Holy Prophet

————— ❧ —————

THE CHILDREN BORN to Hazrat Khadija included three boys, Qasim, Tahir and Tayyab. According to one tradition, a fourth boy was born to Hazrat Khadijah whose name was Abdullah. However, the general consensus is that Abdullah was another name for Tayyab. All the male children died in their childhood. The Holy Prophet had four daughters, (1)Zainab, (2) Ruqiyya(3) Ummi, Kulthum and Fatimah. All of these children were born before the beginning of the Prophethood of the Holy Prophet. Abul Qasim, the family name of the Holy Prophet, was based on the name of his son Qasim. Ibrahim was born in April, 630 A.D., to Hazrat Mariah Al-Qibitiyyah. The Holy Prophet performed Ibrahim's *Aqiqa* (party thrown on the seventh day after the birth of a child). Two rams were sacrificed. The hair from his head was shaved by Abu Hind. The Holy Prophet distributed silver, equivalent in weight to the weight of the hair removed from Ibrahim's head, to the poor. The Holy Prophet appointed Hazrat Umm-i-Burdah, wife of Hazrat Bra bin Aus, as wet-nurse for his son.

Daughters of the Holy Prophet: Overview

ALL OF THE Prophet's daughters lived a long life, except for Hazrat Fatimah. They all accepted Islam.

Hazrat Zainab

Hazrat Zainab, who was married to Abu al-'As bin Rabi, lost a child due to miscarriage, during her migration to Medina. Later on, a boy, Ali, and a girl, Umamah, were born to her. The boy died at an early age. The girl survived and after the demise of Hazrat Fatimah, she became the wife of Hazrat Ali. Hazrat Zainab passed away in 8 A.H.

Hazrat Ruqayyah and Hazrat Ummi Kulthum

———— ❧ ————

HAZRAT RUQAYYAH AND Hazrat Ummi Kulthum were engaged to Utbah and Utbah respectively, who were the children of Abu Lahaban, uncle of the Holy Prophet. Accordingly, the engagements of Hazrat Ruqayyah and Hazrat Ummi Kulthum were broken before their marriage. After that, Hazrat Ruqayyah and Hazrat Ummi Kulthum, one after the other, became wives of Hazrat Uthman. This is the reason why Hazrat Uthman is called *Dunnuran* (i.e., the one with two lights). Both did not have any progeny. Hazrat Ruqayyah had a boy who was born dead. Her second child, Abdullah, passed away when he was two years old. Hazrat Ummi Kulthum did not have any children.

Hazrat Ruqayyah passed away during the time of the Battle of Badr; Hazrat Ummi Kulthum passed away after the Conquest of Mecca.

Hazrat Fatimah

———— ❦ ————

HAZRAT FATIMAH, WHO was loved by the Holy Prophet the most, was married
to Hazrat Ali after the migration to Medina. Among the daughters of the
Holy Prophet, Fatimah had the closest relationship with Hazrat Ayesha.
They lived together in the same house for a while, until Fatimah married.
Hazrat Ayesha was among those who prepared Fatimah for her wedding.
Though their lives were very simple, their pleasure was immense. In tell-
ing us of the day of Fatimah's wedding, Hazrat Ayesha passed on the
following lessons:

> "The Messenger of God told us to prepare Fatimah since she
> was going to marry Ali. We went to the home immediately and
> brought an amount of soft soil from outside the house, which
> we spread on the ground. We filled two pillow sheets with fiber.
> Then we prepared bowls of dates and grapes, and spring water
> to drink, and placed a stake at one edge of the house for clothes,
> pots and pans to be hung. I have not seen any wedding better
> than Fatimah's!"[375]

Only a wall separated the room that Fatimah lived in with Ali from Ayesha's
room, and that wall had a window. Sometimes, they came together and
talked through this window.[376]

Hazrat Ayesha was Hazrat Fatimah's best friend and shared nearly everything with her. Fatimah talked about her joy, her sadness and her goals

---

375 Ibn Maja, Nikah, 24 (1911).
376 Nadawi, Siratu Sayyidati Ayesha.

she was not able to achieve. One day, when her hands became swollen from grinding wheat into flour, Hazrat Fatimah asked God's Messenger for a maid. She returned without getting getting any servent and Ayesha was the one who she shared her problems with.[377]

Hazrat Fatimah loved Hazrat Ayesha very much. Their love and respect was mutual because for Hazrat Ayesha, Hazrat Fatimah held a unique place. One day, Hazrat Ayesha asked:

"Who was the most beloved at the side of God's Messenger?"

Without thinking, she responded, "Fatimah."[378]

Hazrat Ayesha also said:

"After her father, I have never seen anyone more beautiful than Fatimah." She never looked at Fatimah with malice. She said:

"I did not see anyone, more than Fatima, who looked like the Messenger of God more in terms of the dignity and serenity of her behavior, and the elegance and politeness of her posture, and manner of waking... When she entered the Messenger of God's place, he used to stand up for her, kiss her and make her sit near him. When God's Messenger came to Fatimah's place, she would do the same thing."[379]

The virtue of Hazrat Fatimah was conveyed to the Muslim society through Hazrat Ayesha. During the incident of *Ahl al-Bayt* (household members), taking first Hazrat Fatimah, then Hazrat Ali, Hazrat Hasan and Hazrat Husayn under his wool blanket, the Messenger of God said:

---

377 Bukhari, Khums, 6 (2945).
378 Tirmidhi, Manaqib, 61, 61 (3874); Hakim, Mustadrak, 3:3:171 (4744).
379 Abu Dawud, Adab, 155: (5217).

"These are my *Ahl al-Bayt*."[380]

It is narrated that it was days before the death of God's Messenger when his wives came together and sat in his presence. Then Hazrat Fatimah came and her walking style did not depart from her father's; even her steps were parallel to his. Upon seeing her, the Messenger of God said:

"Welcome, my daughter."

With great respect and concern, he bade her to sit near him. It was as if there had been something missing and her arrival allowed the scene to become complete.

Then the wives witnessed the Messenger of God bend down to Hazrat Fatimah's ear and whisper something to her secretly. The room was filled with a deep silence. Fatima started to cry. Her weeping apparently touched God's Messenger. He went closer to her and again said something in her ear. Shockingly, Hazrat Fatimah, who had been sobbing, began to smile. Hazrat Ayesha could not stand not knowing what made her cry first and smile later, so she went to Hazrat Fatimah and said:

"The Messenger of God preferred to say something only to you, despite the presence of his wives, and you started to cry. Could you please tell me what he said?"

Hazrat Fatimah responded:

"I cannot reveal the secret of God's Messenger."

Hazrat Fatima could not share what the Messenger of God had told her; not even with Ayesha. Yet, Hazrat Ayesha would not give up until she satisfied her curiosity.

---

380 Tirmidhi, Manaqib, 61 (3871); Ahmad ibn Hanbal, Musnad, 6:304 (26639).

After the Messenger of God passed away, Hazrat Ayesha asked Hazrat Fatimah again:

"For the sake of my rights over you, what did the Messenger of God whisper to you that day?"

When Hazrat Fatimah responded by saying "I can tell you now," Hazrat Ayesha became very happy, as if the whole world had been given to her, because she would learn a secret only Hazrat Fatimah knew. And it was about the Messenger of God's feelings for his society.
Hazrat Fatimah said:

"The first time when he whispered in my ear, he told me that although Gabriel usually came once every Ramadan to recite the whole Qur'an, this year he came twice. He said, 'I guess my death is near!' And he advised me to be patient, fear God and not give up piety. When he saw that I had started to cry, he leaned in again and told me the good news that I would be the first one among his family who would be reunited with him. He said, 'O Fatimah. Do you want to be the first lady among believing women or the first lady of this world?' This was the reason for the smile you saw."[381]

Hazrat Fatimah loved the Holy Prophet very much. Once, the Holy Prophet was walking through a street when an evil person threw dirt on the head of the Holy Prophet in the presence of other people. When the Holy Prophet returned home with dirt on his head, Hazrat Fatimah quickly brought water, washed his head and started to cry profusely. The Holy Prophet consoled her and said, "Daughter, do not cry. God Almighty Himself will protect your father and all these agonies will be dispelled."[382]

---

381 Bukhari, Manaqib, 22 (3426).
382 Tarikh Tabri, Vol. 2. P. 80, Press Istiqamah, Cario.

On the day of the pilgrimage, the Holy Prophet received the revelation containing the following famed verse of the Holy Qur'an:

"This day have I perfected your religion for you and completed My favor upon you and have chosen for you Islam as religion" (Qur'an, chapter 5:4).

This verse said, in effect, that the message which the Holy Prophet had brought from God and which by word and deed he had

The Farewell Address of the Holy Prophet at the Occasion of the Last Pilgrimage (Hajjatul Wida'), and His Illness

―――――― ❧ ――――――

IN THE NINTH year of the Hijrah, the Holy Prophet went on a Pilgrimage to Mecca. This was the first Hajj performed by the Holy Prophet. Thus, this event was of great significance as the Holy Prophet himself was practically showing the proper way of performing various rites of the hajj. God Almighty states in the Holy Qur'an:

"And proclaim unto mankind the Pilgrimge. They will come to you on foot, and on every lean camel, coming by every distant track. That they may witness its benefits for them and may mention the name of Allah, during the oppointed days, over the quadrupeds of the class of cattle that He has provided for them. So, eat thereof and feed the distressed and the needy. Then let them accomplish the task of cleansing themselves and fulfilling their vows, and go around the Ancient House" (chapter 22:28-30).

On the day of pilgrimage, the Holy Prophet received the revelation contanining the following famed verse of the Holy Qur'an:

"This day have I perfected your religion for you and completed My favor upon you and have chosen for you Islam as religion" (chapter 5, verse 4).

This verse said in effect that the message which the Holy Prophet had brought from God and which by word and deed he had been exponding all these years, had been completed. Every part of this message was a blessing. The Message now completed embodied the highest blessing which man could receive from God. The Message is epitomized in the name "Al-Islam", which means "submission." Submission was to be the religion of Muslims, the religion of mankind.

The Holy Prophet recited this verse in the valley of Muzdalifah, where the pilgrims had assembeled. Returning from Muzalifah, the Holy Prophet stopped at Mina. It was the eleventh day of the month of Dhul-Hijjah (a month on the Islamic Calender). The Prophet, while sitting on his camel, facing a large gathering of Muslims, delivered an address in a loud voice. It is famed in history as the farewell address of the Holy Prophet. Rabi 'ah ibn Umayyah ibn Khalaf repeated the sermon after the Prophet had delivered it, sentence by sentence.

In the course of the address, the Holy Prophet said:

"O men. Lend me an attentive ear, for I know not whether I will stand before you again in this valley and address you as I address you now. Your lives and your possessions have been made immune by God, to attack one another until the Day of Judgment. God has appointed for everyone a share in the inheritance. None shall now be admitted who are prejudicial to the interests of a rightful heir. A child born in any house will be regarded as the child of the father in that house. Whoever contests the parentage of this child will be liable to punishment under the Law of Islam. Anyone who attributes his birth to someone else's father, or falsely claims someone to be his master, God, his angels and the whole of mankind will curse him.

O men, you have some rights against your wives, but your wives also have some rights against you. Your right against them is that they should live chaste lives and not adopt ways which may bring disgrace to the husband in the sight of his people. If your wives do not live up to these expectations, then you have the right to punish them. You can punish them after due inquiry has been made by a competent authority, and your right to punish has been established. Even so, punishment in such a case must not be severe. But if your wives do not do such things, and their behavior is not such as would bring disgrace to their husband, then your duty is to provide for them food and garments and shelter, according to your own standard of living.

Remember, you must always treat your wives well. God has charged you with the duty of looking after them. Woman is weak and cannot protect her own rights. When you married, God appointed you the trustees of those rights. You brought your wives to your homes under the Law of God. You must not, therefore, insult the trust which God has placed in your hands.

O men, you still have in your possession some prisoners of war. I advise you, therefore, to feed them and to clothe them in the same way and style as you feed and clothe yourselves. If they do anything wrong which you are unable to forgive, then pass them on to someone else. They are part of God's creation. To give them pain or trouble can never be right.

O men, what I say to you, you must hear and remember. All Muslims are as brethren to one another. All of you are equal. All men, whatever nation or tribe they may belong to, and whatever station in life they may hold, are equal."

While he was saying this, the Prophet raised his hands and joined the fingers of one hand with the fingers of the other and said:

"Even as fingers of the two hands are equal, so are human beings equal to one another. No one has any right, any superiority, to claim over another. You are as brothers."

Proceeding, the Hoy Prophet said:

"Do you know what month this is? What territory we are in? What day of the year it is today?"

The Muslims answered the questions in the order the Prophet asked them in. Thus they said the sacred month, the sacred land and the day of the *Hajj*.

Then the Holy Prophet said:

"Even as this month is sacred, this land inviolate, and this day holy, so has God made the lives, property and the honor of every man sacred. To take any man's life or his property, or to attack his honor, is as unjust and wrong as to violate the sacredness of this day, this month and this territory. What I command you today is not meant only for today. It is meant for all times. You are expected to remember it and to act upon it until you leave this world and go to the next to meet your Maker.

In conclusion, he said:

"What I have said to you, you should communicate to the ends of the Earth. Perhaps those who have not heard me may benefit by it more than those who have heard [me]."

The Holy Prophet's address is the epitome of the entire teaching and spirit of Islam. It shows how deep the Holy Prophet's concern for the welfare of man and the peace of the world was; it also shows how deep his positive regard for the rights of women and other weak creatures was. The Holy Prophet knew his end was near. He received hints from God concerning his death.[383]

Hazrat ibn Abbas relates that at the Farewell Pilgrimage, the Holy Prophet said, "O People! What day of the year is today?"

They replied, "It is the venerable day of *Arafa*."

Then he asked, "Do you know what city it is?"

They replied, "It is the sacred city of Mecca!"

Then he asked, "What month is this?"

---

383 Life of Muhammad, 'Hadrat Mirza Bashir uddin Mahmud Ahmad, p. 160-162.

They replied, "It is the sacred month of *Dhulhijjah*."

Then the Holy Prophet said, "Listen! Your bounties, your lives and your honors are as sacred, and their disrespect is as unlawful for you, as the day, this city and this month are revered and sacred for you, and as their disrespect is unlawful for you." He repeated this several times. Then he raised his head up toward the sky and said:

"O Allah! Did I convey Your Message?" He repeated the words many times. Hazrat Ibn Abbas says, and in fact it is backed up clearly in testimony given by the Holy Prophet to Allah the Exalted, that he has conveyed and made the people understand the message in the best possible way. Then the Holy Prophet, while addressing the audience, said, "Those who are here listening to me should convey my message to those who are not here!" He continued, "Do not become infidels after I depart, lest you start slaying each other."

The Holy Prophet's Illness

TWO MONTHS AFTER returning from the Farewell Pilgrimage, the Holy Prophet fell ill. The illness that ultimately led to his demise started while he was in the house of Maimunah. Despite his illness, the Holy Prophet continued to move from one wife's house to another one of his wife's house. When the Holy Prophet became severely ill, he desired to stay in Hazrat Ayesha's house which was close to the mosque. However, the Holy Prophet was shy about asking for permission to do so from the other wives. The Holy Prophet told Hazrat Fatimah to ask his wives about this. She did. All the wives agreed that the Holy Prophet could stay at Hazrat Ayesha's house.

The Holy Prophet's Mosque (*Masjid Nabawi* was adjacent to his residence).

It was the last Monday of the month of Safar. The Holy Prophet went to *Jannatul Baqi* to perform a final duty for his Companion, again making amends for all that had passed with those in their graves.

While he walked back, his head started to ache severely and he became feverish. His temperature was so high that it could be felt outside the turban he wrapped around his head.

At the same time, Ayesha's head began to ache too. To express that they were together even in difficulties, Ayesha turned to the Holy Prophet and said:

"Oh, how bad my headache is!"

She hoped to make the Holy Prophet talk a little and forget his troubles a bit. But she got a response she did not expect:

"How my headache is!"[384]

The Holy Prophet's pain did not seem to cease. He was in this state of his illness for the next eleven days. But he continued to go to the mosque to lead his society in congregational daily prayers.

Even during the last moments of his life, his good manners and sense of justice made him abide by the daily schedule for his wives. Yet all of his wives gave up their turns to Hazrat Ayesha, and because their permission and preference made the Holy Prophet happy, it pleased Hazrat Ayesha even more. It makes sense that Hazrat Ayesha, who had an unparalleled perception and acuity, should witness his final days, to accurately record what she saw and heard.[385]

The Holy Prophet had difficulty standing up, and most of the time he could only "walk" by dragging his feet. He went to Hazrat Ayesha's room with the help of two people. He would stay there until his last breath. He appeared among the people again on Thursday, and despite his pain, he wanted them to write down what he said, to keep them away from wrong steps after his death. He told those close to him:

"Come close to me and let me dictate something. And in this way, you will not fall into heresy after me."

It was a touching scene but many who saw his suffering said:

"Don't you see how the pains of the Holy Prophet have increased and how he suffers? We have the Qur'an and God's book; such is enough for everything."

---

384 Ibn Sa'd, Tabqat, 2:206, 233.
385 Bukhari, Janaiz, 94 (1323).

The Companions were divided in two. Some felt this way (what is stated in the above quote). Others thought they should do as he asked and record what he said. As they continued to discuss such, the Prophet looked uncomfortable, and he turned to them and said:

"Keep away from me!"

He returned to Hazrat Ayesha's room. Despite his high fever and the severity of his pain, he continued to appear in society and continued to perform prayers with people. He went to the mosque for evening prayer and recited the entire chapter of *Al-Mursalat* (chapter 77 of the Holy Qur'an) during the prayer.

Then he returned home again, and the scene frightened Hazrat Ayesha because his illness increased with every minute that passed. He looked as if he did not have the strength to stand up. He turned to Hazrat Ayesha and asked:

"Has the congregational Prayer been performed?"

It had not been. Until that day, they had waited for him, without performing the Prayer before his arrival. Hazrat Ayesha said:

"No, O Messenger of God. They are waiting for you."

He forced himself to stand up and said:

"Prepare water so that I may perform ablution."

What he demanded was done. He raised himself, and with difficulty, performed ablution. As he was leaving for Prayer, he fainted. The Holy Prophet was unable to go to the mosque where he had gone every day. He dragged himself to the mosque and did not return to his house for quite some time. Hazrat Ayesha ran around in desperation. Fortunately, he returned to his house. After a while, he asked again:

"Did the people perform the Prayer?"

Hazrat Ayesha replied:

"No, O Messenger of God. They are waiting for you."

Though it was nice that they had waited for the Prophet of God, he did not think he had the strength to lead them.

One day, the Holy Prophet stood by the window and looked outside at the Muslims getting ready to say the *Fajr* Prayer (Morning Prayer] behind Hazrat Abu Bakr. The People looked at the Holy Prophet's face and waited for him to join them. He smiled at them and indicted to Hazrat Ayesha with his hand. He said:

"Tell Abu Bakr to lead the people in Prayer."

This was understood to be the Prophet allowing his closest Companion to become the leader of his society after he was gone. But Ayesha said:

"O Messenger of God. My father is a tenderhearted person. He cannot hold back his tears when he starts to recite the Qur'an. Why not assign someone other than him?"

Behind her words was her anxiety that no one could fulfill the leadership position of the Holy Prophet. She felt that people would criticize any person who attempted to fill his absence. Ayesha wanted to protect her father from criticism. But the Holy Prophet insisted:

"Tell Abu Bakr to lead people in Prayer!"

Hazrat Ayesha asked again but his answer did not change. Her insistence annoyed the Holy Prophet, and to indicate that her persistence was irrelevant, he said:

"It's as if you are like the women who quarreled about Prophet Joseph. Tell Abu Bakr he should be the *Imam* and lead the people in Prayer."[386]

The Holy Prophet over-ruled her and gestured to Hazrat Abu Bakr to go ahead with leading the prayer. This was the last time Muslims saw their Prophet's face. That day at noon, the Holy Prophet passed away. At the time of his demise, on May 26, 632 A.D. in Medina, Islam reached throughout Arabia.

Hazrat Ayesha relates that she heard the Holy Prophet saying the following during his last illness, until his last breath:

"Allah, forgive me and have mercy on me and grant me nearness to the Companion, the Most High."[387]

Hazrat Ayesha relates that the Holy Prophet passed away when he was sixty-three years old.[388] According to the modern investigation of Dr. Muhammad Shahidullah, a professor at Rajshahi University in Bangladesh, the Holy Prophet passed away on 1st *Rabi'ul Awwal*, 11th *Hijrah*, which corresponds to the 26th of May, 632 A.D.

Hazrat Ayesha understood that leading the people after the death of the Holy Prophet would be difficult, but the Holy Prophet was choosing his successor. It meant her father, Abu Bakr, would manage his duties properly. So, she sent a message to Hazrat Abu Bakr and he led the prayer. But his leadership would not be restricted to only one prayer. After that time, the Holy Prophet could never again attend the mosque, and Abu Bakr would lead the Prayer from then on.[389]

On Sunday, the Holy Prophet was distributing whatever he owned, apparently to leave this world as he had entered it. He gave to such an

---

386 Bukhari, Jama'a, 11 (633), 18, 9646, 6470.
387 Sahih Bukhari Kitabul Mardi, Bab nabi tumanniyal mardil maut.
388 Bukhari, Kitabul Maghazi, Babwafatinnabi.
389 From the Isha Prayer on Thursday until the Fajr prayer on Monday; Abu Bakr led seventeen prayers in total before the Prophet passed away.

extent that Hazrat Ayesha sent their empty oil lamp to a woman and asked for a few drops of oil, in order not to leave the Holy Prophet in the dark.[390]

In their house, no food remained; they gave the Holy Prophet's suit of armor, worn in battle, as collateral to a Jewish neighbor for thirty units of barley.[391]

On Monday, the Holy Prophet moved aside the curtain that opened into the mosque from Hazrat Ayesha's room and looked upon his society. He was pleased with the scene before his eyes: congregation was orderly following its imam and performing their duty of worship. He closed the curtain with pleasure and returned to Hazrat Ayesha's room.[392]

After the Holy Prophet whispered to his daughter, he called his grandsons Hassan and Hussain and kissed them. He then advised them to have good manners. At this time, the other wives went to Hazrat Ayesha's room to witness the final moments of the Holy Prophet. The wives of the Holy Prophet were among those in his presence, giving advice during his last moments. When the Prophet's death approached, the Holy Prophet remembered that he had kept some gold coins with Hazrat Ayesha. He turned to Hazrat Ayesha and said:

"O Ayesha. What did you do with that gold?"

Hazrat Ayesha immediately brought the gold coins that he was referring to.

Taking the pieces in his hand, he counted, "...Five, six, seven. How can Muhammad enter in the presence of God while these gold pieces are with him? Take them and give them as charity!"[393] The Holy Prophet did not want to meet his Lord still having worldly wealth. The Holy Prophet did not leave any Dirham, any goat or any camel as his inheritance. He also did not make a will for anything.

---

390 Ibn Sa'd, Tabaqat, 2:239.
391 Bukhari, Jihad, 88 (2759).
392 Bukhari, Sifatu's Slat, 12 (721).
393 Ahmad ibn Hanbal, Musnad, 6:49 (24268).

His pain grew more severe and he turned to Hazrat Ayesha and said:

"O Ayesha. You should have no doubt that I still feel the suffering of the meal that I ate at Khaybar. I feel as if my veins are being torn today as a result of that poison!"[394]

He covered his face with a piece of black wool cloth. When he felt hot and drowsy, he uncovered his face. Meanwhile, he spoke of Prayer. He repeated the words of Qur'an many times. He told his people to be sensitive and behave humanely toward slaves and servants.[395]

Meanwhile, Hazrat Ayesha sat close to him and recited *Sura An-Nas* and *Al-Falaq* (Qur'an, chapters 113 and114), and stroked his Holy body with her hand in the way she had learned from him.[396] After each recitation, she blew her breath over him and asked God to heal him.

The signs that the Holy Prophet would soon depart this world for the Hereafter were clear. He rested his head on Hazrat Ayesha's bosom and fixed his eyes on the ceiling. Hazrat Abu Bakr's son, Abdurrahman, entered the room with a *miswak* (toothbrush made of wood) in his hand. The Holy Prophet's eyes followed the *miswak*. Our perceptive mother (Ayesha) understood that he liked using the *miswak*; thus, she asked:

"Should I take that for you?"

He nodded. She took it from her brother to give it to the Holy Prophet. But the *miswak* was so hard that Hazrat Ayesha asked:

"Should I soften this for you?"

He nodded again.

---

394 398.Ibn Sa'd, Tabaqat, 2:239.
395 Hakim, Mustadrak, 3:59 (4388); Ahmad ibn Hanbal, Musnad, 6:311 (26699).
396 Bukhari, Maghazi, 78 (4175), Tib 31 (5403).

She softened it and then gave it to the Holy Prophet.[397]

After cleaning his teeth, she held his finger up. His eyes were directed toward the ceiling and his lips were moving. To hear him, Hazrat Ayesha brought her ear close to his mouth. He said:

"Please forgive and embrace me with Your mercy, together with the Prophets, the martyrs and the true believers upon whom You bestowed blessings. Accept me to Your highest abode."[398] Hazrat Ayesha had a gnawing suspiciousn because once when he was healthy, she had heard him say:

"No Prophet's soul is ever captured unless he is shown his place in Paradise. After that point, he either continues to live or is given the option to die or survive."

As soon as she heard that he was asking for the highest abode, Hazrat Ayesha remembered his statement and told herself, "He will not be with us anymore."[399]

This was a time when there were no words. Asking God from the heart was the most vital action for the believer. Hazrat Ayesha implored God while holding the hand of the Holy Prophet. She did not expect it, but just then he pulled his hand away. It was time for him to depart and it was not proper for him to hold onto the world.

When he gave his last breath, his blessed head was on her bosom.[400]

It was Hazrat Ayesha's saddest day. Covering her face with her hands, she sobbed. She tried to stay strong, and placed a pillow under the head of the Holy Prophet. Then she called people to give them the sad news.

For the Companions who had waited for the time when he would return among them, his death was a catastrophe. Medina was filled with

---

397 Bukhari, Khums, 4 (2933).
398 Bukhari, Tafsir, 69 (4310).
399 Bukhari, Maghazi, 79 (4194).
400 Bukhari, Janaiz, 94 (1323).

a mourning atmosphere in one moment. Some, like Hazrat Umar, who considered it impossible to live in a world without the Holy Prophet, did not know what to do. But death was God's order. It had come and taken the Holy Prophet to the other side of the thin curtain that separates this world from the Hereafter.

It was time to perform the final duty for the Holy Prophet. The Companions, who did not know what to do in their suffering, were indecisive about where to bury his pure body. Then Hazrat Ayesha's father, Hazrat Abu Bakr, recalled something in a flash:

"I remembered something that I had heard from the Holy Prophet but had forgotten. The Holy Prophet said, 'No doubt God Almighty takes the soul of a Prophet in the place where he would love to be buried.' So, we must bury him where his bed is."[401]

---

401 Tirmidhi, Janaiz, 33 (1018).

Funeral Prayer and Burial

—— ❧ ——

THE HOLY PROPHET passed away on a Sunday night. His body was kept for two nights and then on Tuesday afternoon he was buried. Hazrat 'Ali and Hazrat Fadl bin 'Abbas bathed the Holy Prophet while Hazrat Usamah bin Zaid and Hazrat Aus bin Khaulah poured the water over the Holy Prophet.[402]

At the time of his demise, the Holy Prophet was wearing a sheet and *Taband* (a cloth worn around the waist) made of a thick coarse cotton cloth. It was customary in those days to remove clothes before giving a bath to a deceased person. Thus, the people had two opinions. Some people were in favor of removing the clothes the Holy Prophet was wearing while others were against doing so.

Hazrat Ayesha relates that at the critical moment of making a decision, God Almighty guided them. Suddenly, everyone felt drowsiness and their heads bowed down while they were standing. Then, they heard a Divine Voice saying, "Give a bath to the Messenger of Allah in his clothes."[403]

So, the Companions were guided through revelation and the Holy Prophet was given a bath without removing the clothes he was wearing at the time of his demise.

The Holy Prophet had given directions regarding his funeral Prayer, before his demise, which were followed. First, Hazrat 'Ali, then Hazrat Abbas, then Ahl-e-Bait, and then the other relatives of the Holy Prophet, offered the funeral Prayer. Everyone offered the funeral Prayer individually. After that, people in groups of ten to twelve entered the room to

---

402 Musnad Abi Hanifah, Kitabul Fadi'l, p. 180.
403 As-Siratun Nabawiyyah Ibn Hisham Jahaz Rasulullah wa Dafinah, vol. 4, p. 313.

offer the funeral Prayer. The first group of people to offer the funeral Prayer consisted of Hazrat Abu Bakr, Hazrat Umar and some *Ansar* and *Muhajirin.*

After all the men had offered the funeral Prayer of the Holy Prophet, first the women and then the children offered the funeral Prayer. There was no Imam for the funeral Prayers. The funeral Prayer continued for a whole day and the Holy Prophet was buried thirty-two hours after he died.[404] He was buried on a Tuesday.[405]

---

404   As-Siratun Nabawiyyah Ibn Hisham, vol. 2. P. 663.
405   Ibn Kathir, vol. 4. P. 517.

Hazrat Ayesha's Dream about Three Moons Falling in Her Room

———— ✿ ————

HAZRAT ABU BAKR consulted the Companions of the Holy Prophet regarding the place where the Holy Prophet should be buried. Some Companions suggested that he be buried in *Jannatul Baqi'* while others suggested that he be buried in the mosque. Hazrat Ayesha mentioned to her father that she had seen in a dream that three moons had fallen into her room. After the death of the Holy Prophet, Hazrat Abu Bakr said that one of the moons was the Holy Prophet and that he was the best of the three.[406]

Touched by the scene, Hazrat Abu Bakr said to Hazrat Ayesha:

"See, this is the first and most auspicious of your moons, O Ayesha."

Hazrat Ayesha left only when she went to Mecca for a pilgrimage, or for short visits; she continued this practice until the end of her life.

Later events showed that the other two moons in Ayesha's dream were Abu Bakr and Umar, who were buried in the same apartment that Hazrat Ayesha lived in, by the side of the Holy Prophet. Based on Hazrat Ayesha's dream, it was decided that the Holy Prophet should be buried in Hazrat Ayesha's room. Accordingly, the body of the Holy Prophet was moved to one side in the room and a grave was dug at the place where his bed was when he passed away. Hazrat Abu 'Ubaidah al-Jarrah was an expert in digging a grave in the style the

---

406 Imam Malik, Al-Muwatta, Burial.

Meccans did such in, and Hazrat Abu Talha was an expert in digging a grave as the people of Medina did. Hazrat Umar sent his messenger to both of them with the intention that whosoever comes first will dig the grave for the Prophet to be buried in. The messenger did not find Hazrat Abu Ubaidah. Thus, Hazrat Talha dug the grave for the body of the Holy Prophet.

The Holy Prophet passed away in the room of Hazrat Ayesha. This room had two doors. One of the doors opened in the courtyard while the other door opened in the *Masjid-e-Nabawi*. After being bathed, the Holy Prophet's body was placed on a cot in Hazrat Ayesha's room. After digging the grave, the cot on which the body of the Holy Prophet was placed on after giving him a bath was kept next to the grave.

Hazrat *Imam* Malik relates that he was informed that the Holy Prophet passed away on a Monday and was buried on a Tuesday. People in many separate groups offered the funeral Prayer of the Holy Prophet. No one led the funeral Prayer. The removal of his clothes to give him a bath was being considered when a heavenly voice told them not to do so. Thus, the Holy Prophet was bathed with his clothes on.[407] Regarding the burial of the Holy Prophet, Hazrat Ayesha's statement had been quoted by Ahmad, *Musnad*, vol. VI, p. 121. At the time of his death, the Holy Prophet said that God may curse Jews and Christians who make the tombs of their prophets a place of worship. Had it not been so the Holy Prophet might have been buried in the open but the danger was that his tomb be converted into a place of worship?"

Hazrat Ayesha relates, "It was one of the favors of Allah bestowed upon me that Allah's Messenger passed away in my house on the day of my turn while he was leaning against my chest. And Allah made my saliva mix with his saliva at the time of his demise. Hazrat Abdur Rahman came to my house with a *Miswak* (bark of a tree usually softened before using; used to clean teeth) in his hand and I noticed that the Holy Prophet was looking toward the *Miswa*. I said to the Holy Prophet, 'hould I get the *Miswak* for you?' He nodded in the affirmative. So, I took the *Miswak*

---

407 Muwatta Imam Malik, Jami Assafat 'Al- Ja' Na; iz Bab Fi Dafanalmayyat.

and asked the Holy Prophet whether I should soften the *Miswak* for him. Again he nodded in affirmative. So, I softened the *Miswak* and gave it to him. He cleaned his teeth with the *Miswak*. There was a water container close to the Holy Prophet. The Holy Prophet dipped his hand in the water, rubbed it on his face and said:

"La ilaha illallahu, inna lil mauti sakaratin" which means, "None is worthy of worship except Allah. Death has its agonies."

Then the Holy Prophet raised his hand up and kept saying this until he passed away. His hand dropped down and he said:

"Firrafiqil a'la" which means, "With the Companion, the Most High."[408]

God had prohibited the re-marriage of the widows of the Prophet. "The Prophet is nearer to the believers than their own selves, and his wives are as mothers" (Qur'an, chapter 33, verse 7).

"And it is not allowed to thee to marry women after that, nor to change them for other wives even though their goodness pleases thee, except any that thy right hand possesses. And Allah is watchful over all things" (Qur'an, chapter 33:53).

The wives of the Holy Prophet had been closely associated with him for a number of years and were in his confidents in a number of the finer points of his Prophethood. The rest of their lives were to be devoted to the spread and implementation of the teachings and preachings of the Apostle. Their duties, fixed by God himself, were as follows:

"O wives of the Prophet! If any of you be guilty of a manifest impropriety, double shall be her chastisements; and with Allah that is easy.

---

408 Sahih Bukhari, Kitabul Maghazi, Bab Maradi-Nabiyyi WA Wafathihi.

But whoever of you is obedient to Allah and his Messenger and does good works, we shall give her her reward twice over; and we have prepared for her an honorable provision. O wives of the Prophet! You are not like any other women if you are righteous. So be not soft in speech, lest he, in whose heart is a disease, should feel tempted; and speak decent words.

And stay in your houses with dignity, and display not your beauty like the displaying of the former days of Ignorance, and observe Prayer, and pay the Zakat, and obey Allah's desire to remove from you all uncleanness, O Members of the Household, and purity be with you completely."

And remember what is rehearsed in your houses; the Sign of Allah is Subtle; he is All-Aware" (Qur'an, chapter 33:31-34).

The Last Will of the Holy Prophet

———— ❦ ————

HAZRAT 'ALI AND Hazrat Anas relate that, "The last words that the Holy Prophet made, at the time when he was breathing his last breath, were, *'Assalata Wa Ma ma malakat Aimanukum* [Take care of Prayer and those who are under your submission].'"[409]

Some historians have stated that the last words the Holy Prophet spoke were:

"*La taj 'al qabri wa thanan* [O my Allah! Do not let my grave become a place of infidelity]."[410]

Hazrat Ayesha relates:

"The Holy Prophet didn't leave any dinar, any Dirham, any goat or any camel as his inheritance; nor did he make a will for anything."[411]

---

409 Sunan Ibn-e-Majah, Kitabul Wasaya, Bab hal Ausa Rasulullah.
410 Musnad Ahamad.
411 Sunan Ibni Majah, Kitabul Wasaya, Bab hal ausa Rasulullah.

Succession to the Holy Prophet

MUSLIM RECORDS STATE that Hazrat Ayesha had narrated that the Holy Prophet had told her the following on his death bed: "Call your father, Abu Bakr, and your brother. I fear that some person, aspiring [for Caliphate], may not say that he is the most deserving, though God and the believers want Abu Bakr to hold this office." [412]

---

412 Muslim: Sahih Kitab us Tafsir.

To Explain Religious Precepts; Hazrat Ayesha, Top of the List

——— ❧ ———

THERE IS NO doubt that all the commandments of the *Shariah* are based on wisdom, but it is not necessary that all the secrets be known to men. God, in His Infinite mercy and Benevolence, has revealed the meaning in the Holy Qur'an of many matters, and likewise, the Holy Prophet explained the prudence behind many of his orders. Those among the Companions who were closest to him knew the esoteric meanings and purposes of the orders. The Holy Prophet himself had indicated the principles and the derivations, and the theologians among the Companions, like Hazrat Umar Hazrat Ali, Hazrat Zaid bin Thabit, Hazrat Ibn Abbas and Hazrat Ayesha, had followed him and investigated and elaborated on things. Hazrat Ayesha is on the top of the list of those who disclosed them (different religious concepts first introduced by the Prophet) and this is seen in the books of *Hadith*.

When the Holy Qur'an is read chronologically, the differences and phraseology noted by Hazrat Ayesha are apparent.

From the point of view of the place of descent of the revelations, the Holy Qur'an can be divided into two parts: one is in the city of Makkah (Mecca) and the other is in the city of Medina. The revelations pertaining to them are different in meaning and composition. The Makkan verses are soul-stirring and appeal to the emotions; they are also eloquent and the sentences are rhythmical; they deal with believers, guidance and good counsels, the Unity of God, the Day of Resurrections and judgments. They are forthright and demand worship and righteousness, contain invitation and preaching and contain no arguments against Jews and Christians. The Medinian verses are succinct, profound and deep, contain law and commandments in legal language and are not very rhythmical. They exhort men to worship and to do good deeds, refute the theories and objections of Jews and Christians and provide for Jihad besides preaching and invitation. The Orientalists take pride in discovering these differences, but 1,400 years ago, Hazrat Ayesha noticed such differences in purpose and phraseology.

The book by Imam Bukhari, *Sahih Bukhari*, records that Hazrat Ayesha stated, "The first *Surah* that was revealed is explicit, making references to Heaven and Hell. When people started accepting Islam, the lawful and unlawful were differentiated. Had the people been asked in the very beginning to give up drinking, they would not have yielded; had they been asked to abstain from adultery and fornication, they would not have listened. The requital of all deeds will be on the Day of Judgment which will be very terrible."

What she intended to say was that slowly and gradually the preaching was extended to cover larger and larger fields. Islam first came to ignorant people. In an eloquent, stirring and effective manner people were told about Heaven and Hell, and were warned to behave. When their souls had been stirred, the commandments, prohibitions and laws were revealed gradually. The language, style and delivery were in keeping with the object and purpose. The language of a book of sermons and good counsels cannot be the same as that of a penal code. Hazrat Ayesha says that both *Surahs* (Qur'an, *Al-Baqarah*, chapter 2, and *Al-Nisa*, chapter 4) were revealed in Medina in the presence of Jews and Christians. Thus, their theories and views had to be refuted. The *Sura Al-Qamar* (chapter 54) was revealed in Makkah (Mecca). Its sentences are short and eloquent, with a view to stir the souls of the people.

The Success of Islam in Medina and Hazrat Ayesha's Point of View

———— ♋ ————

DETERMINING THE SUCCESS of any movement is a historical phenomenon and it is generally assumed that before the 20th century, the world had not reached the stage of development when such questions could even be raised. When authors and scholars find answers to such questions, they consider it a great achievement. But nothing was hidden before that eye which was causing and beholding the events. The success of Islam in the face of bitter and vehement opposition was nothing short of a miracle, but it is not necessary that a miracle should take place in the absence of causes. The collection of different causes at the appropriate time is also a miracle of God. It is not available for very worldly movement; this way, no movement shall ever fail.

Before the advent of Islam, the people of Medina were engaged in warfare. In the tribal feuds, many leaders who very often opposed at every movement of reform, lost their lives. The *Ansar* had so exhausted them that when Islam came, they considered it a blessing and raised no objections to it. The way for success for Islam in Medina had been made smooth by God. Hazrat Ayesha says that the Battle of Badr was an event arranged by God before calling His Apostle to his mission when he came to Medina; the solidarity of its people had been shattered and their leaders had been slain. God had facilitated the entry of its people into the fold of Islam. [413] These reasons for the success of Islam in Medina are related by Hazrat Ayesha.

---

413 Sahih Bukhari, chapter, Alqasama fil Jahiliyya.

326

The Reasons for shortening Prayers during Journeys, Explained by Hazrat Ayesha

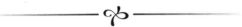

THE PRESCRIBED PRAYERS of four *Rak'ah* are reduced to two *Rak'ah* during journeys. Hazrat Ayesha explained by saying the following: "In Mecca, all the prescribed prayers were of two *Rak'ah*. When the Holy Prophet migrated to Medina, three of the prescribed prayers became four *Rak'ah* while the prayers on journeys were left at two Rak'ah."

Obviously, there is more repose and the prayers could be easily more than two *Rak'ah*. Hazrat Ayesha, "For the morning prayers, there was no addition, for therein longer *Surahs* are recited." The *Shariah* calls for greater devotion in the morning prayers. The emphasis is on the quality and elation of the prayers rather than on the number of prayers said.

The cover of *Ka'ba* was changed on the tenth day of *Muharram* and was disclosed by Hazrat Ayesha.

Even during the days of Ignorance, the tenth of *Muharam* was observed as a fasting day. When the *Ramadan* prayers were prescribed, fasting on the day of *Ashura* no longer remained obligatory. Nobody except Hazrat Ayesha disclosed why fasting was done on the tenth of *Muharram*. She said that this was done as the cover of Ka'ba was changed on that day.

Hazrat Ayesha: 'Why the Holy Prophet Did Not Say Tarawih Prayers Throughout Ramadan'

IBN ABBAS SAYS that no one knew better than Ayesha what prayers the Holy Prophet said during the night.[414] She said that the Holy Prophet did not say more than thirteen *Rak'ah* in the night, whether it was *Ramadan* or not. One day, he said *Tarawih* prayers during *Ramadan* in the night, and in the mosque. Some people joined him. The next day, more people assembled for this prayer. The number increased further on the third day, and on the fourth day, the number increased so much that there was no space in the mosque. The following day, the Prophet did not go to the mosque and the people there were disappointed. The Holy Prophet explained in the morning:

> "I know your feelings in the night but I heard that *Tarawih* may become compulsory for you and you may fail later to observe it." The Companions took care to say it regularly. Those who take the *Hadith* literally consider it *Mustahab* (Praiseworthy), but those who follow the Companions, consider it as *Sunnah* [the practice of the Prophet](*Mowakkada*) calling the explanation.

---

414 Ahmad Musnad, vol. VI, p. 244.

The Reality of Hajj, Explained by Hazrat Ayesha

THE IGNORANT COMMENT that the rites of *Hajj*, like the circumbulation of the *Ka'ba*, staying at certain places and the throwing of stones appear to be meaningless. Hazrat Ayesha says that these rites are calculated to promote remembrance of God. They are not objects of themselves but are places of remembrance of god. The Holy Qur'an says that in the time of Abraham, it was a mode of worship and *Hajj*, which is in memory of Abraham. They retained that mode of worship, which every person with the means to perform such worship must do once in his life time. Those who participate in the *Hajj* actually realize the fervor, the exaltation, the ecstasy and the devotion generated by these rites.[415]

---

415 (Translator's note)The first Hajj was performed by the Prophet Ibrahim; the refferenc of translator is towards to wards him.

Stay in the Valley of Mahsab During Hajj

———— ❦ ————

THE HOLY PROPHET stayed in the Mahsab valley during the pilgrimage and so did the Companions after him. Ibn Umar considered it as part of traditional rites but his view was not shared by Hazrat Ayesha who said, "The Holy Prophet stayed here only for convenience." Ibn Abbas and Abu Rafay agreed with Hazrat Ayesha.

Construction of the Ka'ba and Going Around the Hateem, Explained by Hazrat Ayesha

OUTSIDE THE *KA'BA*, but adjacent to it, is a small space enclosed by short walls. This space is called *Hateem*. Pilgrims go around the *Hateem* during *Tawaf*. Some Companions raised the question that if it is not part of the *Ka'ba*, why do pilgrims go around the *Hateem*? No one except Hazrat Ayesha gave the reason for such. She says she had asked that question to the Holy Prophet who had said that *Hateem* was part of *Ka'ba*. She also asked him, "Why did not the people include it at the time of construction of *Ka'ba*?"

The Holy Prophet replied that the people did not have the means to do such. She further asked, "Why has the door of *Ka'ba* been kept at such a height?" The Holy Prophet replied:

"The door is to control entry inside it."

Ayesha also asked, "Why had not the Holy Prophet himself included the portion inside the *Ka'ba*?"

The Holy Prophet replied:

"O Ayesha f your people were not so near the days of infidelity, I would have demolished the building and raised it anew on the foundations laid by Ibrahim." The people had recently accepted Islam and the fear was that demolition might excite them. The inference is that if there is delay in the execution of any work of

Shariah on the dictates of the situation; it is not a matter of re-proach provided the *Shariah* as it does not require its immediate compliance.

Hazrat Zubair, nephew of Hazrat Ayesha, during the course of his caliph-ate, demolished the building and had it reconstructed on the original foundations, but when Abdul Malik recovered after the assassination of Ibn Zubair, he demolished the building again and had it reconstructed on the previous foundation as he thought that Ibn Zubair had acted on his own volition.

Hijrah

HIJRAH DOES NOT mean merely shifting from one's ancestral place to Medina and Mecca, though one is living comfortably in his place in all security. Ata bin Rabat, a leading Tabaii, had wanted to know from Hazrat Ayesha its real significance and she said, "Now there is no *Hijrah*. It took place when people came running to God and His Apostle in the fear that they might be persecuted to force them away from their new faith. Now God has given supremacy to Islam, and Muslims can fearlessly worship their God anywhere although the merit of *Jihad* and good intentions remains" (Bukhari: Sahih, chapter: hijra).

This explains why Ibn Umar used to say that there was no *Hijrah* after the fall of Mecca as peace and security was prevailing. If a person, however, leaves his birth place to settle down in Mecca to be near God or His Apostle, he will earn merit for his intention.

The Four Rightly Guided
Caliphs and Muawiyya

———— ❦ ————

AFTER THE DEATH of the Holy Prophet, Hazrat Ayesha, who had spent the most time with him and who had carefully observed him in a variety of situations, continued to respond to people's questions or she interfered when something wrong happened. Conveying the message continued, with Hazrat Ayesha as the teacher. She shared the knowledge that she acquired from the Holy Prophet and was reassured that future generations would have healthy information about the religion.

There was a land dispute between some of the Companions; Abu Salam and others could not agree who a piece of land belonged to. Abu Salam shared his troubles with Hazrat Ayesha, probably expecting her support.

But after she listened to him, Hazrat Ayesha told Abu Salam to keep away from that land matter since she had heard from the Holy Prophet that whoever behaves unjustly even for one unit of land will be tormented after death.[416]

On another day, someone went to her and said that a number of people recited the whole Qur'an in one night, in one or two sessions; the person relaying this information wanted to know whether it was proper for people to do the things she told Ayesha about. Ayesha said:

"They recite, but in reality, they do not understand! The Holy Prophet and I used to get up and perform prayer nearly the

---

416 Bukhari, Mazalim 14 (2321).

whole night. He recited *Sura al-Baqarah, al-Imran and An-Nisa* [Qur'an, chapters 2, 3 and 4]. When he came across a threatening expression in the Qur'an, he immediately sought refuge in God from the punishment that the threatening expression warned about. When he recited a verse that included good news, he turned to God and asked for the reward that a given passage said one could obtain.[417]

As before, people continued to bring their new-born children to Hazrat Ayesha's home to ask for prayers and blessings, and Hazrat Ayesha prayed and asked for God's blessing. One day, while Hazrat Ayesha was putting a baby back on his pillow, she noticed an amulet used for fortunetelling, on the pillow. She looked at it carefully and put it aside and asked:

"What is this?"

They said:

"It will protect the baby from an evil spirit."

Hazrat Ayesha became angry. It was a deviation, and such a deviation so early after the death of the Messenger of God meant an open invitation to many mistakes in the future. She threw away the amulet and said:

"There is no doubt that the Messenger of God banned fortune telling, and was very angry with those who did this too."[418]

After the conquest of new lands, people wondered about the permissibility of beverages that they had recently encountered, and so they asked Hazrat Ayesha about such. She approached each issue carefully and

---

417 Ahmad ibn Hanbal, Musnad, 6:92 (24653).
418 Bukhari, Adabu'l: 314 (912).

reminded them of the statements of the Holy Prophet about intoxication, and advised them to avoid drinking beverages of an unknown nature.[419]

During the season of *Hajj*, when all roads led to Mecca, women gathered around Hazrat Ayesha to ask any questions on their minds. It happened so frequently that she would walk with a group of women who gathered around her. She considered their talks as time to convey the message and time to advise them.[420]

When Hazrat Ayesha was in Mina [Mina is the place where pilgrims throw stones, commemorating the occasion that the Prophet Ibrâhîm (Abraham) stoned the Devil that came between him and the command Allah sent him], she witnessed some teenagers laughing together, amongst themselves. Pointing to them, she asked those around her what made them laugh.

They said:

"Someone was tangled up in the tent's rope and fell down, and he was about to break his neck and lose his eye."

She warned them:

"Beware. Do not laugh. I once heard the Messenger of God saying, 'A Muslim is given a [higher spiritual] rank because of the thorn that pierced his foot or any suffering worse than this, and one of his sins is forgiven.'"[421]

Hazrat Ayesha always had the goal of representing justice without considering who addressed her. People knew she was a treasure trove of knowledge, and continued to visit her often to receive the maximum benefit.

---

419 Bukhari, Ashriba, 7 (5278).
420 Ahmad Ibn Hanbal, Musnad, 6:225 (25923).
421 Muslim, Birr, 46 (2572).

The Caliphate of Abu Bakr

⚬❦⚬

WHEN HAZRAT ABU Bakr became the first Caliph (leader of a Muslim community), he was a sensitive and tenderhearted person; he regarded the consent of God above everything else. In the early days of his Caliphate, the widows of the Holy Prophet wanted to send Hazrat Uthman as their envoy, in order to settle the question of inheritance. But in reality, there was no inheritance wealth left by the Holy Prophet. Hazrat Abu Bakr decided to confirm from Hazrat Ayesha whether she had any knowledge of this issue. He asked her because Hazrat Abu Bakr was aware that she was not among the ones demanding the inheritance. But Hazrat Ayesha reminded them that the Prophet had said that he would have no inheritance and that whatever he left, he wanted it to be given to charity. Hazrat Ayesha was shuddered on this issue and she said:

> "Glory be to God! There cannot be an inheritance when the Messenger of God said, 'We Prophets do not leave inheritance and we leave alms."

The other wives and the Caliph then understood: no new judgment was needed on an issue that already was given a judgment. The wives of God's Messenger gave up their request of inheritance and returned to their plain lives.[422]

There are several traditions shedding light on the Holy Prophet's inheritance; such clearly shows that it is stated that the Holy Prophet hardly left anything behind him to be apportioned. The book of Ahadith, complied by

---

422 Bukhari, Khums, 1 (2926, 2927).

Imam Bukhari, is known as *Sahih Bukhari*; it is considered the most authentic source. It states that the Prophet left nothing by way of Dinar or Dirham, cattle or animals, slaves or servants. He had, as custodian of property, a few groves reserved for various purposes. During the Caliphates of the first four Caliphs, their proceeds were spent in the same exact manner as the Prophet himself used to spend such. The yearly allowances of his wives were paid from the income of these groves and during his reign. Hazrat Abu Bakr disbursed the allowances to the widows of the Holy Prophet accordingly.

From then on, Hazrat Ayesha was a significant source of information for Hazrat Caliph Abu Bakr. When immature people tried to confuse or muddle issues, he often consulted Hazrat Ayesha. In those days, Hazrat Abu Bakr had many troubles, large enough to crush mountains into dust. Hazrat Ayesha's knowledge had been invaluable. Nearly two and a half years had passed quickly. There were apostates and false prophets. Hazrat Abu Bakr became tired, but had the serenity of fulfilling the trust of the Holy Prophet.

Hazrat Abu Bakr fell ill but continued to show the same sensitivity during his sickness. He kept his daughter nearby and shared his confidential thoughts. His general demeanor seemed to indicate that his time of life was about to end. Hazrat Abu Bakr had been able to endure the loss of the Holy Prophet for only two years, three months and ten dyes. Hazrat Ayesha, who had witnessed the last days of the Holy Prophet, also took care of her father during his sickness.

Hazrat Abu Bakr was very sensitive during his illness, as he was throughout his life. He called Hazrat Uthman to his side to write a pact. Then he asked Hazrat Ayesha to give his reaming amount of wages to the state's treasury after he died. He said:

> "Umar asked me and I was obliged to take six thousand *drachmas* [currency of that time] from the treasury. All of them are hidden under the wall in such and such place. Please find them and return them to Umar."[423]

---

423 Ibn SA'd, Tabaqat, 3:193.

His words conveyed his perception and intelligence, and indicated whom he chose as his successor as well.

He had something else to tell Hazrat Ayesha, and told her to come closer, as he advised:

"I have spent neither a *drachma* nor a *dinar* of the Muslim people since I have taken on the responsibility of caring for them. On the contrary, I stayed hungry and dressed in the oldest clothes."

Hazrat Abu Bakr decided to give up the burden on his shoulders. He looked at his daughter with compassion. He treated her like a mother of the believers since she was married to the Holy Prophet. He shared the difficult problem that he had held back, and he said:

"My precious daughter. You know that I love you and admire you most among people. Do you remember that I gave land to you? But could you give [it] back to me since I am not fully satisfied with how I allocated it? I want the division of wealth among my children to be aligned with God's Book. In the presence of God, I do not want to be in the position of he who has preferred some of his children over others."

Without hesitation, she answered that she would fulfill his wish at once.[424]

Hazrat Abu Bakr asked his daughter:

"On which day did the Messenger of God die?"

"On Monday," she replied.

By his posture, she understood what he was thinking. He asked:

"What is the day today?"

---

424 Ibn Sa'd, Tabqat, 3:195.

"Monday," came the reply.

He took a deep breath and the following wish poured from his lips:

"I ask and beg of God that there will not be one more night after this."

Then he asked:

"How many shrouds were wrapped around the Messenger of God?"

Hazrat Ayesha replied:

"We shrouded his body with three new white cloths which are called *salhuliyya*. His turban and shirt were not among them."

Indicating to the clothes he wore, Hazrat Abu Bakr said:

"Wash these clothes of mine because there is a *Saffron* [similar to the color yellow] stain in it. Add two more cloths to it and shroud me with them."

The gravity of the situation had become apparent over time. Hazrat Ayesha's father and the Caliph of the Muslim people were his death bed. It is related that she felt confused and had forgotten her own grief because she was so busy due to the requests of various people coming one after the other. By nature, she was very sensitive, but to fulfill her father's last dying request was not easy for her. She was completely aware and sensitive that her father was not just anyone; he was the Caliph and leader of the believers, the trusted successor to the Messenger of God.

She objected:

"But that cloth is very old."

Hazrat Abu Bakr was determined and said:

> "That is okay. Living people have more need for new clothes than dead ones. Either way, the shroud of death will decay."[425]

Hazrat Abu Bakr had another request. He wanted to continue the togetherness with God's Messenger that had started with revelation and lasted twenty-three years. He wanted to be buried near the Messenger of God, away from display and ostentation. He wanted his wife Asma binti Umays to wash his body, and wanted his son Abdurrahman to help her.

Hazrat Ayesha's eyes filled with tears. Hazrat Abu Bakr died in 13 A.H.

She had hoped he was reunited with God's Messenger that night and that he was buried near him. The second noon, which Hazrat Ayesha had dreamt of and which Abu Bakr had interpreted, rose over her room.

Hazrat Ayesha's house hosted the moon of the first Caliph and then the moon of the Holy Prophet.

---

425 Bukhari, Janaiz, 92 (1321).

The Caliphate of Hazrat Umar

꧁

WHEN HAZRAT UMAR succeeded the Caliphate of Hazrat Abu Bakr, Hazrat Ayesha remained an important authority to consult when issues arose. Though he bestowed respect on all widows of the Holy Prophet, Hazrat Ayesha's knowledge made her unique. He addressed her as "the beloved of God's Messenger."

Hazrat Umar first considered the Holy Prophet's widows when he was allocating the wealth gained in territorial expansions, giving each of them ten or twelve thousand Dirhams annually. He gave two thousand more Dirhams than this to Hazrat Ayesha because of her position at the side of God's Messenger.[426] Qazi Abu Yusuf clarified the difference between the widows of the Holy Prophet in terms of wealth given to them; he writes the following in his book *Al-Khiraj*:

> "...That each of them received ten thousand Dirhams annually but according to Hakim's tradition, 'Hazrat Ayesha used to receive twelve thousand Dirhams while the others got ten thousand Dirhams each.'"

Hazrat Umar's Caliphate was distinguished by the excellent administration it had. Hazrat Umar fixed the cash allowances for all Muslims. Hazrat Umar carried a heavy responsibility. He intervened immediately when he saw someone incorrectly deducing religious rulings, and he did not allow religious matters to be discussed randomly. Surely he wanted to avoid mixing the Qur'an and the *Sunna* with other matters. In light of his era,

---

426 Hakim, Mustadrak, 4:9 (6723).

it was a wise decision. In Medina, during the time of Hazrat Umar, when people did not lightly or capriciously discuss religion, Hazrat Ayesha was a leader, issuing *fatwa's* (rulings) when issues were uncertain.

Hazrat Umar was a regular visitor of Hazrat Ayesha; he asked her about anything he had no knowledge about and made decisions based on Hazrat Ayesha's responses. His attitude toward her was the same toward the other widows of the Prophet; he attended to them and gave priority to them always. He asked if they needed anything and preferred for them to benefit first from any opportunities or wealth he gained. When he received some season fruit, he put them in separate baskets and sent them to the wives of the Holy Prophet.[427] When he slaughtered a sacrificial animal, he first remembered them. Hazrat Ayesha said:

"Umar thought of every detail without discriminating, and never neglected to send each of us our share from a sacrificed animal."

When the land of Mesopotamia (modern-day Iraq) was conquered, it was time to divide the gains of war. The leading Companions came together in a gathering to discuss the allocation of such gains. After some brainstorming, Hazrat Umar said:

"In my opinion, their spoils belong to those who worked harder in conquest, and must be shared among them."

Everyone agreed. So, Hazrat Umar asked:

"Then with whom should we start?"

They replied:

"Who may deserve this more than you? Surely you should start with yourself first."

427 Malik, Muwatta, 1:279 (618).

As the Caliph, it probably seemed to the others that he was most deserving because of his status. Yet he had never witnessed the Holy Prophet behave in this way. The Holy Prophet preferred being last when wages were allocated even though he was at the frontline when there was service to be given. Thus, he replied:

"No. I will start with the people of the Holy Prophet's home."[428]

Again, after the same conquest, a small cloth bag full of jewelry was brought to the Caliph. He asked the people around him:

"Do you know the value of this?"

They did not know. Since no one was sure of its value, Hazrat Umar could not allocate it fairly. So he asked:

"Would you allow me to send [this] to the beloved of the Holy Prophet?"

The Holy Prophet's beloved was loved by everyone and without hesitation they replied in the affirmative.

Hazrat Umar used to distribute gifts to these widows in equal measure.

Once with emissaries, Hazrat Umar sent a small cloth bag full of pearls to Hazrat Ayesha after getting permission from others. When it reached her, she opened the bag carefully; when she saw the jewelry, she shuddered and pondered. Most likely, she was contemplating the austere life of the Holy Prophet. She said, "Umar has done me great favors but why does Umar do this to me after the death of God's Messenger?"

With her palms turned upward, she prayed to God Almighty:

---

428   Imam Safi, Musnad, 1:326 (1519).

"O my God. lease do not prolong my life and do not give me even one more chance to receive more favors. lease take my life before I receive such gifts."[429]

Hazrat Umar displayed the same sensitivity when allocating the gains after the conquest of Khaybar. He did not forget the Holy Prophet's wives, giving them the chance to choose between lands or a monthly allowance.[430]

Hazrat Ayesha was shy in front of Hazrat Umar because she had seen that the Holy Prophet behaved differently with Hazrat Umar and because the Holy Prophet said that even the devil was frightened by Hazrat Umar. When knowledge of religion was under consideration, Hazrat Ayesha's status was indispensable for Hazrat Umar. He also continued the tradition of Hazrat Abu Bakr (visiting Hazrat Ayesha or sending an emissary to consult her about problems he faced). It was not the way only for Caliphs; this consideration reflected the general attitude of the Companions and the following generation of Muslim scholars, particularly when an issue related to knowledge of *Hadith*.[431]

One day, Hazrat Umar heard that Amir ibn Umayya had given a roll of cloth to prostitutes who were excluded from society because of their moral corruption; Hazrat Umar became very angry. Umar told Amr ibn Umayya that such charity would not be accepted as charity by God. But Amr ibn Umayya insisted, saying that the Messenger of God said, of prostitution:

"The things that you give to them are considered as alms for you too."

His defense of the action increased Hazrat Umar's anger, and Hazrat Umar said Amr ibn Umayya was slandering the Messenger of God. As

---

429 Hakim Mustadrak, 4:9 (6725); Ahmad Ibn Hanbal, Fadailu's Sahaba, 2:875 (1642).
430 Bukhari, Muzaraa, 7 (2203).
431 Ibn Sa'd, Tabaqat, 2:375.

their quarrel grew, they agreed to go to Hazrat Ayesha for the solution; Amr ibn Umayya said:

"For the sake of God, I want you to tell us: didn't you hear the Messenger of God saying, 'he things that you give to them are considered as alms for you too'"?

Hazrat Ayesha's reply was clear:

"As God is my witness, yes, I heard [that]."

Her response made Hazrat Umar step back in shock because his judgment was notable. He started to question himself and thought, "Who knows how much I missed hearing from God's Messenger while I was busy in my business?"[432]

After ten years of incidents such as the ones above, it was time for the predestined journey of Hazrat Umar. When the Caliph was assassinated, he fell down in his blood. Before he died, he was agitated because he had lacked the courage to tell Hazrat Ayesha that he wanted to be buried near God' Messenger, at his feet.

He called his son Abdullah near him and said:

"Go to the mother of the believers, Ayesha, and be careful not to say the Caliph sent you. From now on, I am not the leader of believers. Say, 'Umar ibn al-Khattab sent me' and then say, 'He is asking permission to be buried near his two former friends.'"

It was a very delicate message. The good manners of the community, addressed by God's Messenger, were beyond comparison. Though his heart was in favor of his request, he did not want to put pressure on Hazrat Ayesha by using his title. He wanted his request to be received as a request of an ordinary person. Abdullah went to Hazrat Ayesha

---

432 Zarkashi, al-Ijaba, 20.

immediately. Hazrat Ayesha had heard the poignant news and was crying because of what happened to Umar. Greeting her first, Abdullah asked for permission to speak and said:

> "Umar sends his greetings to you. He wanted to be buried near his two friends."

Who did not want to be buried near the Messenger of God and a loyal friend? But Hazrat Ayesha knew she must prefer her Muslim brothers and sisters over her own self.

She said she had reserved the place for herself but that she would give preference to Umar and relinquish her own right.

On learning about the answer, Hazrat Umar took a deep breath. The worry he felt before was gone and his eyes were gleaming. It was time to leave. But first he felt a final feeling of anxiety. Perhaps permission for him to be buried where he pleased had been given because of the influence of Caliphate authority. He decided to confirm it once more, and called his son to him and said:

> "O Abdullah. When I die, lay me down over my cedar and take me to Ayesha's door and say, 'Khattab's son Umar asks permission from you.' If she gives her permission again, bury me there. If you realize that she had changed her mind, beware and do not insist. Instead, bury me in the public cemetery like everyone else. I am worried that she felt pressured by the authority of the Caliphate when she gave her permission."

The above several traditions show the thoughtfulness of Hazrat Umar even while he struggled against death. His humbleness and respect for Hazrat Ayesha as mother of believers is depicted by his repeated requests for his burial to be near the Holy Prophet. Hazrat Uma was completely aware that those were the last moments of his life. The painful grief was felt by the city of Medina after the news of his assassination was broken. It was almost as if the city had never experienced disaster until that day.

When Abdullah ibn Umar went to Hazrat Ayesha for the last time, and said his father had asked, Hazrat Ayesha paused for a moment in contemplation. What a lesson in courtesy he had given while leaving this world. Surely, Umar showed greatness, courtesy and delicacy, but it was not unique to him. She had already given her word and she considered it unnecessary to grant permission again. But she repeated herself to be clear and to make the people feel better. And so, Umar began his eternal rest in the place that Hazrat Ayesha had chosen for herself.[433] The third moon fell in the same apartment and rose over her room. As a result, Hazrat Ayesha's dream was completed, in reality.

Hazrat Umar's death and burial was the beginning of a new era for Hazrat Ayesha, for she no longer felt the same comfort when visiting the graves of the Holy Prophet and her father. After the burial of Hazrat Umar, she moved to a place nearby because her room was not large enough for a fourth person.[434]

---

433 Bukhari, Fadailu's Sahaba, 8 (3497).
434 Nadawi, Siratu Sayyidatu Ayesha, 154, 155.

The Caliphate of Hazrat Uthman

───────── ✑ ─────────

THE STATUS AND reverence of Hazrat Ayesha during the two Caliphates prior to Hazrat uthman's continued during the era of Hazrat Uthman's Caliphate. The Caliphate of Hazrat Uthman lasted for twelve years. The first six years of it passed by peacefully. There was safety, serenity and tranquility in these years. Hazrat Ayesha was extremely popular among Muslims and was treated with great reverence in Hejaz, Iraq, Syria, Egypt, everywhere in the Islamic state. Even the outstanding Companions used to consult her to discuss important matters. People from the outlying areas of the expanding borders went to Hazrat Ayesha for the information that would enlighten them. Hazrat Uthman was the leader among them, but his attitude was no different than Hazrat Umar's regarding the wives of the Holy Prophet (SAW), especially Hazrat Ayesha. He tried to fulfill their wishes and make them comfortable when they worshiped and tried to improve their conditions.

Hazrat Ayesha states that the Messenger of God told the following to Uthman, three times:

"O Uthman. hen the day comes, God will make you wear an important shirt by making you leader; if the Hypocrites want to take that shirt off you, be aware and do not take it off!"

In another Tradition, Hazrat Ayesha states that the Prophet advised him that if he were to be the mantle of a Caliphate, he should not put the off.[435]

─────────────

435 Ahmad Musnad, vol. VI. P. 263.

The Holy Prophet (SAW) married two of his daughters to Uthman, and had prayed for him many times.[436]

But the remaining six years of his Caliphate was a period of turmoil. In the seventh year, the signs of trouble were seen and some groups of people started to voice their objections. The door into discord was broken and some people began to think differently of the Caliph. Some began talking offhandedly and tactlessly about him, and as a result, the Caliph became a target.

A Jew by the name of Ibn Saba wanted to defame Islam through the Caliph. Ibn Saba becme a Muslim to promote his own game of undermining the foundations of the Islamic State from within. He started advocating that Hazrat Ali was the rightful heir of the Holy Prophet and took advantage of the growing unrest. He spread a network of intrigue. He went to Kufa, Basra and Egypt, where the garrisons were stationed, and started winning over rebellious people.

Hazrat Ayesha became saddened upon hearing about the internal strife, and warned those who were behind the discord:

"People who curse Uthman are not aware that they will be the target of every kind of curse. Surely god will curse them too. One day, I saw the Messenger of God sitting with his knees touching Uthman. He was receiving a revelation and I was wiping the sweat from his brow. Moreover, God's Messenger married two of his daughters to him. He affectionately called Uthman 'My little Uthman.' Do not forget that the man who was so worthy to God's Messenger was also a valuable servant of God."[437]

Even during the Holy Prophet's sickness, Hazrat Uthman turned to Hazrat Ayesha and said:

"I want some people from my community to come to me."

---

436 Ahmad ibn Hanbal, Musnad, 6:261 (26290).
437 Ahmad ibn Hanbal, Musnad, 6:250 (26173).

Hazrat Ayesha asked:

"O Messenger of God. Should I call Abu Bakr?"

He stayed silent. Hazrat Ayesha asked again:

"Should I call Umar?"

The Holy Prophet's silence continued. It was clear that there was someone he wanted to see, but he would not speak. Hazrat Ayesha asked a third time:

"Should I call Uthman?"

A smile appeared on his Holy face immediately and he said yes.

Hazrat Uthman was called to the presence of God's Messenger and they talked at great length. God's Messenger apparently reminded him of the significance of the responsibility that would be on his shoulders when discord appeared. The Holy Prophet advised Hazrat Uthman to deal with the discord with patience. It would be heard years later, after everything had come to pass, that he said:

"The Messenger of God promised me so I should bare it by being patient!"[438] Muslim historians have quoted various traditions, sometimes stating that Hazrat Ayesha was surely the one who had best understood the position of Hazrat Uthman at the side of God's Messenger. The territories controlled by Muslims expanded from the Byzantine Empire to Africa, and Abdullah ibn Saba gathered and provoked people and invited them to rebel. They chose Egypt as their home. The turmoil spread to other areas and caused sincere people to become indecisive. The leading Companion did not raise any objections and the younger and the

---

438 Tirmidhi, Manaqib, 19 (3711).

more dashing ones, like Abdullah bin Zubair Marwan bin Hakam and Muhammad bin Abi Hudhafah Saeed bin al-A', considered the Caliphate much too elevated for them. Abdullah bin Zubair was the maternal grandson of Hazrat Abu Bakr and a nephew of the Holy Prophet. Muhammad bin Abi Bakr was the younger son of Hazrat Abu Bakr and a step brother of Hazrat Ayesha. After the death of Hazrat Abu Bakr, his mother Hazrat Asma married Hazrat Ali and he was raised by Hazrat Ali. Muhammad bin Abi Bakr, being Hazrat Ayesha's brother, was very close to Hazrat Uthman (adopted son of Uthman). When he came of age in the Caliphate of Hazrat Uthman, he aspired for high office but as Hazrat Uthman did not oblige him to do so, he grew angry and left for Egypt.[439] Muhammad bin Abi Bakr and Muhammad bin Abi Hudhafah took a leading part in the rebellion against Hazrat Uthman. Hazrat Ayesha tried to dissuade her step brother but he was adamant about the rebellion. Hazrat Ayesha's own brother, Muhammad ibn Abu Bakr, was among those rebelling; she told him that he was on the wrong path, but he would not listen. She explained to the rebels that, "God curses the one who curses Uthman." Hazrat Ayesha explained the honorable place of Hazrat Uthman in the sight of God's Messenger. Then she said that those who said off-hand or tactless things about him would be cursed.[440]

---

439 The Cambridge History of Islam, ed. P. M. Holt, Ann K. S. Lambton and Bernard Lewis, Cambridge, 1970.
440 Bukhari, Adabu'l Mufrad, 1:288 (828).

Rebels in Medina

————— ❧ —————

FROM EGYPT, A contingent of about a thousand people were sent to Medina with instructions to assassinate Hazrat Uthman and overthrow the government there. Understanding the matter correctly, Hazrat Uthman assigned Hazrat Ali to send them back. Ali went and indicated clearly that the rebels were wrong. Hazrat Uthman was forced to surrender and they did not let any water reach him. Even an attempt by Hazrat Umm Habiba failed that day; she was about to be killed for bringing water to the Hazrat Uthman and was only able to escape death by running through the large crowd that had gathered.[441]

Hazrat Ayesha went to Mecca to perform the pilgrimage. She did this even though people told her it was better to stay in Medina in peace. After performing *Hajj*, she started her journey back to Medina. Then, the sad news was conveyed to her that the third Caliph of God's Messenger had been martyred. Her first response was directed to those who had criticized Hazrat Uthman:

"The reason for this was your criticizing all that the Caliphate had done!"

Their criticism of Hazrat Uthman, who had tried to bring some of the leaders who had caused discord to his own side, had gone too far. Hazrat Uthman had wanted to decrease the tensions of his society by bringing opponents to his side and assigning them with notable duties. But

---

441 Tabri, Tarikh, 2:672.

people did not understand his attempts for peace. They had not kept themselves away from saying openly that the Caliph was doing wrong.

When Hazrat Ayesha met Talha and Zubayr, she said to them:

"They had escaped from the poisonous atmosphere of Medina to the peaceful city of Mecca. The people who filled the streets were far from righteousness or justice, and what they might do was not clear."

Hazrat Ayesha then recited a part of the chapter *Al-Hujurat*, chapter 49 of the Holy Qur'an:

"And if two parties of believers fight each other, make peace between them. Then if after that, one of them transgresses against the other, fight the party that transgresses until it returns to the command of Allah. Then if it returns, make peace between them with equity, and act justly. Verily, Allah loves the just. Surely all believers are brothers. So, make peace between your brothers, and fear Allah, that mercy may be shown to you (Qur'an, chapter 49:10-11).

She then added:

"People need to hold fast to these verses at this moment."[442]

The turmoil resulted in the murdering of the Caliph Hazrat Uthman. They had shed blood which was forbidden to be shed, in the city where bloodshed was forbidden, and tried to take wealth that was forbidden to them during the Holy months. Hazrat Ayesha said that even if the rebels were numerous enough to fill the whole world, she did not consider all of them to equal even one finger of Hazrat Uthman, because of the malice of their actions.[443]

---

442 Malik Muwatta, Siyar, 1002; Hakim, Mustadrak, 1:168 (2664).
443 Tabarani, Musnadu'sh Shamiyyin, 2:75.

The trouble of yesterday stayed in the past and it was time to take a new step. Being able to control the streets depended on the designation of a new Caliph. Hazrat Ayesha's candidate for Caliphate was Hazrat Ali and she made this clear to whoever went to her. Building up the Muslim state after the time of Hazrat Uthman was significant in its own right, and careful plans needed to be made. But the environment of the day was an obstacle for sound thinking; the purity of the Messenger of God's time disappeared more every passing day; everthing had become muddled.

The Caliphate of Hazrat Ali

HAZRAT ALI'S CALIPHATE lasted for four years. The obvious choices for the Caliphate were Talha, a son in-law of the first Caliph Zubair, ibn Awwam, a cousin of the Holy Prophet, and Sa'd bin Abi Waqas and Hazrat Ali. Sa'd had gone into seclusion and was not interested in being a Caliph. The people of Basra supported Talha while the people of Kufa favored Zubair. But the Egyptians and the bulk of the insurgents headed by Malik Ushtur. Yasir and Muhammad bin Abi Bakr favored Hazrat Ali. Those who had not aligned themselves with any party favored Abdullah son of Hazrat Umar. After three days of hectic discussions, Hazrat Ali was selected as the Caliph by common consent of the people of Medina.

To stop turmoil and reestablish safety, Hazrat Ali started by replacing the provincial governors who had been involved in the discord *(fitnah)*.

Opposition in Hijaz; in Syria, its overnor Amir Muawiyya was dreaming of independence, and in Egypt Muhammad bin Abi Hudaifa declared independence. The murder of Hazrat Uthman in the precincts of the Haram in a prohibited month appalled everyone. Even those who were opposed to Hazrat Uthman were horrible. Before the tragedy, Malik Ushtur consulted Hazrat Ayesha and she had told him that he had no right to kill the *Imam.* The enemies spread the rumor that she was also involved in the conspiracy. Some people gave credence to it as Muhammad bin Abi Bakr happened to be her brother, though she had tried to dissuade him from his plans. She openly said, "By God, I never desired that Uthman should be disgraced. If I desired it, may God disgrace me similarly. I never wished that he should be slain. If I ever wished it, may God get me slain in like manner. After this, no one should delude you. The deeds of the Companions of the Prophet were never ridiculed till the birth of the sect which reproached Uthman; they said what should not have been said, they recited what should not have been recited and they prayed what should not have been prayed. Their own acts and behaviors were not even a shadow of the ompanions."[444]

Hazrat Ayesha received the news of Hazrat Uthman's assassination from the insurgents, when she was her way back to from Makkah. As she proceeded, she was met by Talha and Zubair who said that they left Medina with their belongings when people were confounded and perplexed. They could neither recognize what was right, reject what was evil protect themselves. Hazrat Ayesha said that they should discuss to bring this matter to justice. She recited a couplet:

"Had the leaders of my people listened to me, I would have taken them out of this turmoil and danger."

She retraced her steps to Makkah and people began to flock around her. She said, "There is no community which turns away from the Quranic commandments."

She recited a couplet:

'Had the leaders of my people listened to me I would have taken them out of this turmoil anmnd danger.'

She recited the following verses from the Qur'an:

"And if two parties of believers fight each other, make peace between them. Then if after that, one of them transgresses against the other, fight the party that transgresses, until it returns to the command of Allah. Then if it returns, make peace between them with equity, and act justly. Verily, Allah loves the just." (Chapter 49 vers 10-11).[A82].

---

444 Bukhari: Juzul Khaliq Afa'al ul Ibad, p. 76 (1: Name of the book, "Hazrat Ayesha Siddiqa," compiled by A. Saiyid Sulaiman Nadvi, p. 22, published by Illamic Bood service).

The Need for Reform

THE CONFLICT HAD broken out. Talha, Zubair and Hazrat Ayesha raised their voices for reforms; these Companions wanted to set things right. Tallha was one of the foremost Muslims, the victor of many battles at the time of the Holy Prophet. And Zubair had received the title of "friend of the Holy Prophet." Both of them were apart of the electoral body set up by Hazrat Umar to choose his successor. The invitation for reform was accepted by a large number of people. An army that would punish ibn Saba and his rebellious supporters was established by constructing a headquarters in Abtah. Two wealthy people, Ibn Aa'mia and Ibn Manabba, contributed several hundred thousand Dirhams and a great number of camels. Hazrat Ayesha wanted to proceed to Medina which had become the strong hold of insurgents and followers of Ibn Saba. But in a meeting held at her place, it was decided that they should proceed to Basra because it was thought that the people who murdered Hazrat Uthman were from Basra. Their intention was to avenge Hazrat Uthman and reform the system that had fallen apart.

The caravan they used was joined by a large number of people of the Omayyed clan who were leaving Medina to find shelter in Makkah. They were not interested in reform, the created hurdles for Hazrat Ali[A82]. The caravan assumed the shape of an army of three thousand men.

Hazrat Ayesha and the other wives of the Holy Prophet were together. But they stayed behind when the crowd went to Basra, and with tears, wished them a safe journey.

When Hazrat Ali came to know about it, he started with his army for Basra. Abu Musa Aash'Aasth'ari, the governor of Kufa, advised people not to participate with either camp, for it was going to lead to internecine warfare. Speakers of both sides were trying to lean people toward their points of view. Hazrat Ayesha advised them to be determined in the way of God and to support justice. In one of her speeches, she said:

"People used to criticize Uthman and speak ill of his officers. They used to come and consult me. When we made inquiries, we found Uthman innocent, and to be a righteous person, and we found the critics to be sinners, traitors and liars. When their number increased, they forcibly and without any reason entered the house of Uthman and shed his blood and looted his property, which they had no right to plunder. Beware! You have to do a job which you cannot legitimately refuse and it is to capture the assassins and to comply with the Words of God."

Hazrat Ayesha recited the following verses from the Holy Quran:

"Hast thou not seen those who have been given their portion of the Book [the Torah]? They are called to the Book of Allah, that it may judge between them, but a party of them turns away in aversion [of them]" (Qur'an, chapter 3:24).

She delivered a long speech. The following is the conclusion of that long speech: "I have become a target of people's questioning as to why I have come out with a force. My objective is not to search out or to look for turmoil, but to quench it. I pray to God to shower blessings on the Apostle Muhammad and to appoint his successor as he appointed successors of Prophets."[445]

The public listened to the speech with rapt attention and many of them who were previously in an opposing camp joined hers. Questions and cross questioning started, and as the situation began to take an ugly turn, Hazrat Ayesha withdrew with her men. The commander of the

---

445 Ahmad bin Abi Tahir Balaghat-un-Nisa.

governor's forces, Hakeem, led an assault but he was speared to death by a person when he uttered something foul against Hazrat Ayesha. Thrusts and counter thrusts ensued but a truce was reached on the agreement that an envoy should be sent to Medina to find out from the people whether Talha and Zubair had pledged their fealty to Hazrat Ali willingly or under duress.

They had multiple options. In the first case, they will hand over Basra to them and in the other case they would themselves leave the city[A 82]. The envoy reached Medina and he asked, at a gathering, if Talha and Zubair had willingly pledged their fealty or if they were forced to do so. Everyone kept quiet. Usamah bin Zayd, the adopted son of the Holy Prophet, rose and said that they had not willingly pledged their fealty. Several Companions including Abu Ayub confirmed Usamah bin Zayd's statement. Hazrat Ali wrote a letter to the governor of Basra. It said that even if Talha and Zubair were compelled to pledge fealty, it was done to smother internal differences and for the unity of the community. The opponents showed the letter of Hazrat Ali. The differences could not be reconciled and discussions ensued. Basra's forces were routed and Basra was captured. The salaries of the soldiers were distributed from the Basra. Treasure and information was sent to Kufa, Damascus, Medina, etc. Muhammad ibn Abu Bakr and Muhammad ibn Talha, who asked Hazrat Ayesha how to act in situations where Muslims fought their Muslim brothers, reminded them of the sad story of the two sons of Adam. hough Cain intended to kill, Abel promised not to raise a hand against him. Hazrat Ayesha Said:

"O my dear son! If you are able to do what the most auspicious son of Adam did, do it!"[446]

The Battle of Camel happened on the 26th *Rabi-ul-Awal* (month of March), 36 A.H.

---

446 Ibn Abi Shayba, Musannaf, 7:544 (37823).

The Battle of the Camel, and Hypocrite Abdullah ibn Saba

———— ♋ ————

HAZRAT ALI HAD started from Medina with a force of 700 men. Seven thousand men joined him in Kufa. By the time he reached Basra, his army was comprised of twenty thousand men. Hazrat Ayesha had thirty thousand men behind her. The two forces confronted each other on a plain. Nobody wanted to fight but everyone was convinced that his or her point of view alone was correct and was not prepared to compromise. Zubair cried, "What a tragedy that Muslims who had acquired the strength of a rock are going to be smashed by colliding with one another." Some chieftains of Kufa tribes contacted their tribes living in Basra in mosques, but they refused to forsake Hazrat Ayesha. A chieftain contacted Hazrat Ali to settle the matter. Hazrat Ali did not want to fight and he agreed not to fight. He then contacted Hazrat Ayesha and spoke to her: "Is it wise to shed the blood of five thousand for punishing five hundred men?" She agreed to settle the matter. Once more, they felt the rightness of the decision not to fight. They planned to rest during the night and return to Medina after the first light of dawn appeared.

But the Hypocrite Jew, Abdullah ibn Saba, and his friends, who killed Hazrat Uthman and enjoyed creating discord, were not pleased with peace. They thought that if a settlement was reached, they would not be safe. During the night, they concocted wretched plans to make the two groups fight each other. Those who attacked Hazrat Ayesha and her people pretended to be Hazrat Ali's soldiers, while others who assaulted Hazrat Ali and his army used Hazrat Ayesha's name. Hazrat Ali was restraining his men but nobody was listening as everyone thought that the other party had committed a breach of trust. Confusion prevailed throughout the night. In the morning, Qazi K'ab of Basra advised Hazrat Ayesha to mount her camel and ride to the field. This way, people might listen to her. Hazrat Ali met Talha and Zubair and reminded them of a prophecy of the Holy Prophet, namely that they would one day fight with Ali without justification.

"You, O Zubair! Do you remember the day you saw me entering the presence of God's Messenger and he smiled at my arrival? And the Messenger of God asked you, 'Do you love him?' And you replied, 'Yes.'" He continued: "But one day, you will behave unjustly with Ali against him on the opposite side."

After that, both Tallha and Zubair left the field. Zubair made his way for Medina in regret, but he was waylaid in a valley by a Sabait (follower of Ibn Saba) who beheaded him while he was saying his prayers.[447] Tallha was seen by Marwan Amvi who shot him with a poisoned arrow. Tallha died because of injuries he received from Amvi's poisoned arrow. Marwan Amvi thought that Tallha had disgraced the Omayyed clan by running away from the battle field. Thus, Hazrat Ayesha's two generals were murdered, one for initially opposing Hazrat Ali and the other for supporting him by leaving the field.

In the absence of Hazrat Ayesha's generals, her army started to disintegrate. She was made the target of attack. The cradle on the camel's back she was occupying had been pierced by innumerable arrows, but her gallant supporters made an impenetrable ring around her. They were laying down their lives but were not yielding ground. Hazrat Ali's commanders decided that until Hazrat Ayesha's camel was brought down, the battle would go on.

Seventy soldiers lost their lives shielding Ayesha's camel. An enemy soldier managed to reach it when he cut off one of its legs, causing it to fall down. With its fall, the battle ended. Then Hazrat Ali called Hazrat Ayesha's brother, to ascertain if she had been wounded. Hazrat Ali had

---

447 Tabri, Tarikh, 3:55.

prepared a safe place for her and invited her there through her brother Muhammad. Both were sad. Hazrat Ali assured Hazrat Ayesha that she could go into safety to Makkah and that no one would be able to harm her. She was initially taken to the house of one of her supporters in Basra and later to Makkah along with her brother Abi Bakr and forty respectable female leaders of Basra to accompany her so she would not feel alone. Hazrat Ali and the Muslims in general accompanied the convoy for some distance. Hazrat Ali's son Hassan accompanied them for many miles. At the time of their departure, Hazrat Ayesha announced that she had no ill feelings against Ali.[448] Despite the sorrow they had experienced, both sides were careful to be just. On the day when Hazrat Ayesha was leaving, she said to those around her:

"O my sons. Unfortunately we hurt each other, experienced upsetting incidents and became very tired. After this moment, no one should look at each other with malice or fight about what happened or about the wrong statements others made. Surely, there is no problem between Ali and I that is greater than any normal matter between a woman and her brother-in-law. Although I experienced some troubles, he is the most auspicious man for whom I wish goodness and well-being."[449] She remained for some months in Makkah and then settled down permanently in Medina. She used to regret that the method she had adopted for bringing about reform was improper. Ibn Sa'd records that she used to say, "I wish I were a tree. I wish I were a stone. I wish I had been exterminated." Hazrat Ayesha was grave, knowing that Hazrat Ali had a special place at the side of the Holy Prophet. Ayesha would treat Ali as she always had, and thus destroyed the hopes of those who wanted to exaggerate the incident. Hazrat Ali was touched because the speaker had been taught by the Holy Prophet. But

---

448 Tabari History.
449 Tabari Tarikh, 3:60-61. Muhammad bin Abi Bakr was the younger son of Abu Bakr and a step brother of Ayesha. After the death of Abu Bakr, Abi Bakr's mother Asma married Ali. In light of this, Hazrat Ali is the brother-in-law of Hadrat Ayesha.

he was hurt too because many of his relatives were killed in order to assure peace. Responding to the statement that had mollified the injuries, Hazrat Ali said:

"She is telling the truth and I swear to God, how beautiful she expressed it." Hazrat Ali turned to those who were nearby and said:

"There is only this small distance between her and me. Surely, she is the most benevolent wife of God's Messenger, both in this world and the hereafter."[450]

She used to recite the Quranic verses, "O wives of the Prophet, stay at home and do not appear in public" (Al-Ahzab, Qur'an, chapter 33:32). When asked by someone, she had said that amongst females, Fatima was dearest to the Prophet and among males, Ali was dearest to him. Ali was staunch in prayers and fasting (Tirmidhi:Manaqib). She said that Ali was amongst the Ahle-Bait (people of the house).

However, the gates of discord had been broken in their era. There is no doubt that they did not judge their world by past events; they continued their relations on the grounds that they should live. From this perspective, we see that Hazrat Ali came to Hazrat Ayesha on every matter he had not been able to solve, while Hazrat Ayesha consulted Hazrat Ali when she was indecisive on an issue.

When she heard about the assassination of Hazrat Ali in Kufa, she said, "O God! Have mercy on Ali. When anything pleased him, he used to say, 'God and His Apostle are true.' The people of Iraq made insinuations against him and exaggerated everything."[451]

---

450 Tabari, Tarikh, 3:61.
451 Ahmad: Musnad, vol. VI., p. 86, 87.

The Caliphate of Amir Muawiya

THE PERIOD OF Hazrat Ali's Caliphate lasted for four years. It ended with his assassination. After that, Muawiya ibn Abi Sufyan became the undisputed ruler for the Islamic world for two decades. He was the second Caliph from the *Umayyad* clan, the first being Hazrat Uthman ibn Affan, who was third among *Khulafae Rashideen* (Rightly Guided Caliphs).

Hazrat Ayesha saw eighteen years of Muawiya's reign. She led a secluded life because she was plunged into a silent contemplation, and she lived entirely focused on the Hereafter. She spent time worshipping and pursuing knowledge. But she responded to all people who asked her for her advice. Hazrat Ayesha was like a safe harbor for those who were uncomfortable in grief. She tried to pacify them no matter who went to her for help.

Amir Muawiya wrote a letter to her, asking for some advice. She responded, "I had heard the Prophet of Allah saying that whosoever seeks the good pleasure of God without caring for the goodwill of people, God will protect him from the ill-will of the people. But those who seek the goodwill of people, displease God. God will entrust him to the people."[452] This was a concise and succinct assessment of the life of Amir Muawiyah.

The above narration of Hazrat Ayesha had been added by *Imam Tirmidhi* in his collection. It was worded as follows:

"May God's peace be upon you. To put it briefly, I heard the Messenger of God say, 'Whoever is after the consent of God, despite people's opposition, God Almighty will protect him against

---

452 Tirmizi: Jamii. Chapter: Piety.

the troubles caused by people. Whoever is only after the consent of people without taking God's wrath into consideration, God Almighty will manifest His wrath and leave that person to his people and to their anger.' Peace be upon you too" (Tirmidhi, Zuhd, 64, 2414).

Muawiyya wanted to appoint his son Yazid as his successor. Marwan, governor of Medina, suggested the name in a public gathering. Abdul Rahman, brother of Hazrat Ayesha, opposed the idea of Yazid as successor. Marwan wanted to arrest him but he took refuge in Ayesha's house. Marwan asked, "Is this the person about whom the Quranic verse was revealed? That is, the person who said to his parents, 'Fie on you both; do you threaten me, that I shall be brought forth again, when generations have passed away before me?' And they both cry unto Allah for help and say to him, 'Woe unto thee! Believe, for the promise of Allah is true.' But he says, 'This is nothing but the fables of the ancients'" (chapter 46:18). Hazrat Ayesha answered behind the curtain that no verse was revealed about her except the verse which absolved her of the scandal. She was not happy with the proposal to have Yazid as successor.

Imam Hassan, the grandson of the Holy Prophet, died in 49 A.H. during the reign of Ami Muawiyah. His great wish had been to be buried near the Holy Prophet. One day, he gave the following directions to his brother:

"If I die, you go to her [Hazrat Ayesha] and ask for her permission to bury me near the Messenger of God. If she allows it, bury me there in her house. But perhaps people will not consent to what you ask for. If they reject the idea and as a result sedition may appear, do not insist. In that case, take me to the Muslim cemetery [Jannat-tul-Baqi] and entrust me there."

When Husayn attempted to comply with his brother's final wish, he met a severe reaction from Medina's governor Marwan ibn al-Hakam, even though Hazrat Ayesha agreed to his request. People were gathered around Husayn and the governor and his men, and it seemed a riot was about to break out. Then the leader, Abu Hurayra, spoke up and reminded them of Hassan's own words about sedition, and so they decided to bury him in *Jannatul Baqi*. Hasan would lie next to his mother Hazrat Fatimah from that day on.[453]

Like the previous Caliph Muawiyya's, men visited Ayesha [A82] and brought clothing, silver and other beautiful things. When Hazrat saw them, she started to cry. She murmured something in a low voice that the envoys were not able to hear, but the people nearby heard what she said. What she said is the following:

"The Messenger of God never touched any of this, nor owned anything like it." Hazrat Ayesha turned around and asked them to give all of the gifts to needy people.

Hazrat Ayesha did not abstain to criticize Muawiyya, despite his generous gifts and his respect toward her. She criticized the murders of Hujr ibn'Adiy and his seven friends who, like Hazrat Ali, were killed after various developments; she also criticized the dividing into groups after the Camel incident. In a letter she gave Abdurrahman ibn Harith to give Hazrat Ayesha, she requested the following from Amir Muawiyya.

"If your promise has value and we are able to change the progress of affairs, we want to prevent the assassination of Hujr. This is a hard test for us."

But her efforts were not enough to save Hujr and his friends. She was shaken by the news of their martyrdom while Abdurrahman was on his way to Muawiyya. It was already too late.[454]

---

453 Ibn Abdilbarr, Istiab, 1:392, Suyuti, Tarikhu'l Hulfa, 1:170; Ibnu'l Athir, al-Kamil Fi'.
454 Tabari, History, Vol. Vii., p. 145.

In another narration, it is stated that when Amir Muawiyya went to visit her, Hazrat Ayesha was upset because she had been late to request the acquittal of Hujr, and she talked about him with gratitude.

When Hazrat Ayesha came into the presence of Muawiyya, she said:

"Where is the gentleness and good temper of Abu Sufyan? Where are you?"[455]

Hazrat Ayesha tried to explain the difference between Muawiyya and his father.

Later, Amir Muawiyya went to Mecca to perform Pilgrimage. He visited Hazrat Ayesha; she always was the one to speak frankly. Then he immediately brought the conversation around to Hujr and asked:

"O Muawiyya. Didn't you fear God when you killed Hujr and his friends? Why didn't you have mercy on Hujr? Why did you withhold it from him?"[456]

Amir Muawiyya was embarrassed and said:

"I did not kill Hujr and his friends."

It did not subdue Hazrat Ayesha. He was Caliph and this murder happened on soil under his control. Truthfully, Muawiyya felt his responsibility and was depressed because of its burden. He said:

"We cannot judge this matter here in this world. Please leave the matter between them and me until the day we will reunite with our God!"

---

455 Tabari History, Vol. Vii. P. 116.

456 Tabari History Vol. Vii. P. 135 (Hujr ibn 'Adiy was among the Companions and his seven friends who were among the protectors of Hadrat Ali).

Muawiyya bin Abu Sufyan was a Companion of the Holy Prophet and on several occasions the Holy Prophet used his services to ascribe to the Qur'an. In this capacity, he is respected by all Muslims. It is his role as a historical figure where differences among Muslims, concerning their attitude toward him, arise. While his accomplishments are noteworthy, he is also known as the Emir who condoned the cursing of Hazrat Ali bin Abu Talib [A82] in public, a practice abandoned fifty years later by the Caliph Omar bin Abdel Aziz. Most regrettably, Muawiyya imposed his tyrant son Yazid on Islamic history. Muawiyya and the Holy Prophet were brothers-in-laws after the Holy Prophet married Muawiyyah's sister Ramla bin Abu Sufyan. Muawiyya, the Holy Prophet and Hazrat Ali shared the same great-great-grandfather Abdu Manaf bin Qusay, who had four sons: Hashim, Muttalib, Nawfal and Abdu Shams. Hashim was the great grandfather of Hazrat Ali and the Holy Prophet Muhammad. Umayyah bin Abdu Shams was the great grandfather of Muawiyya.

Death of Hazrat Ayesha.

———— ⌘ ————

HAZRAT AYESHA FELL ill during *Ramadan* in 58 A.H. She was not yet sixty-seven years old at the time. Her illness lasted for only a few days. When people went to ask about her health, she would say she was well. Ibn Abass spoke to her once: "From eternity your name has been Mother of Believers. You were the most favorite wife of the Holy Prophet. You are shortly going to leave us. Because of you, God revealed the verse of *Tayammum*. Many verses of the Qur'an refer to you and are recited daily in every mosque."

Hazrat Ayesha replied, "Spare me of this eulogy. I wish I had been extinct."[457] At the time of her death, she wanted to be buried in the common graveyard, near other wives of the Holy Prophet. She died in the night of the seventeenth of *Ramadan* in 58 A.H. Her bier was accompanied by many people. The acting governor of Medina, Abu Huraira, led the funeral Prayers. Her death plunged the whole of Medina into gloom because still another light of the Prophet's family had been extinguished.

Muslim Women Owe a Debt of Gratitude to Hazrat Ayesha

The greatest favors that Hazrat Ayesha has done for women is demonstrating that a Muslim lady, living in *Purdah*, can actively participate in literacy, religious, social and political activities, and by exhortation, counsel and guidance can work for the betterment of the community. Her life is a living example of how Islam improved women's lives from lives of inferioty.

---

457 Hakim: Mastadarak; Bukhari: Sahih.

The women among the Companions used to reach the Holy Prophet through Hazrat Ayesha and she would put in a word for them. Uthman bin Maz'aun used to live like an ascetic. His wife approached Hazrat Ayesha and informed her that her husband kept fast every day and spent the whole night in prayers. Hazrat Ayesha mentioned it to the Holy Prophet who called on Uthman and said to him, "Islam does not advocate monasticism. Could you not follow my pattern? I fear God much greater than you do and take care to fulfill His commands. Yet I fulfill the duty I owe to my wives."[458]

Hala used to spend whole nights in prayers. Hazrat Ayesha mentioned this to the Holy Prophet when she went to meet her. The Holy Prophet advised her, "Do only as much as you can bare to do."[459]

A woman was punished for theft. She became penitent but even so women did not like to meet her. Hazrat Ayesha would visit her and would convey her requests to the Holy Prophet. Hazrat Ayesha used to get angry if anyone considered women as low and inferior. In deciding juristic points concerning women, she used to keep their convenience in view and would cite the Quranic verses and *Hadith* to support her opinion. Her views are followed in most Islamic countries. Ibn Zubair held the view that women should cut their hair up to a breadth of four fingers as a concluding rite of *Hajj*, but Hazrat Ayesha pronounced that it would be quite adequate for them to cut off a bit of hair from any side of their head.

Before Islam, women had no rights in inheritance. Islam gave this right to them. Many details regarding such are mentioned in the Qur'an, but occasions arise when inferences have to be drawn from the Qur'an and *Hadith*. One such situation is when there is no son of the deceased alive; only daughters, grandsons and grand daughters are living. Abdullah bin Masud held the view that in such a case the grand daughters would have no share, but Hazrat Ayesha thought otherwise.

---

458 Ahmad: Musnad, ol. VI. P. 226.
459 Ahmad: Musnad, ol. VI. P. 264.

If a man has declared divorce once or twice, he has to deal with the expenditure of his wife during the waiting period, but if he had declared it three times, opinions differ. That is, people differ on the following question: does the person declaring divorce three times need to maintain the divorce during the stipulated period that intervenes before re-marriage? Some thought that the only reason for her staying in her husband's house was the possibility that they may reconcile their differences and again enter into wed-lock. But this applied to cases where up to two declarations have been made. After the third declaration, the divorce is complete and they cannot remarry without an intervening marriage with another person. The main reason seems to be that it has to be ascertained; if the divorcee is pregnant, the responsibility to maintain the woman rests with the former husband. If anybody forces a person to divorce his wife, threatening imprisonment or death, according to Hazrat Ayesha, the divorce is not valid. Except for Abu Hanifa, all other leading doctors of law have accepted her views. But if not for this, it would have been difficult for respectable women to escape the greed and tyranny of unscrupulous rulers.

In the days of Ignorance, neither the number of divorces the periods for return to wedlock were regulated. It was not unusual for men to divorce their wives and to take them back before the end of the period of return and to do it repeatedly for some ulterior gain. Such a case came up before Hazrat Ayesha and she referred it to the Holy Prophet whereupon the following revelation came: "Such divorces may be pronounced twice; then, either retain them in full of manners or send them away with kindness. And it is not lawful for you that you take anything of what you have given them [your wives] unless both fear that they cannot observe the limits prescribed by Allah" (Qur 'an, chapter 2:30).

Asma bint Abu Bakr's Family

—— ❧ ——

ASMA BINT ABU Bakr was Hazrat Abu Bakr's daughter. Her mother was Qutaylah bint Abd-Uzza and she was the sister of Abdullah ibn Abu Bakr. Her half-sisters were Ayesha and Umm Kulthum bint Abu Bakr, and her half-bothers were Abdul-Rahman ibn Abu Bakr and Muhammad ibn Abu Bakr. She also had a stepmother from the *Kinana* tribe named Umm Ruman bint Amir, and a stepbrother named al-Tufail ibn Harith al-Azdi.[460]

---

460 Muhammad, ibn Saad, Tabaqat, vol. 8. Translated by Bewley. A. (1995). The Women of Medina, p.193. London: Ta-Ha Publishers (Bewley/Saad, p. 178).

Biography

<u>Early Life: 595-619 A.H.:</u>

Asma's parents were divorced in the *Jahiliyya*, i. e. before Islam.[461] She remained in her father's house.

Asma was one of the first to accept Islam, being listed fifteenth on Ibn Ishaq's list of, "Those who accepted Islam at the invitation of Abu Bakr."

---

461 Al-Tabari, vol. 39, p. 172.

Marriage of Hazrat Asma (Ra)

Hazrat Asma was the elder sister of Hazrat Ayesha and was ten years older than Ayesha.

She was married to Hazrat Zubayr some months before the *Hijrah* (Migration) to Medina. She was pregnant at the time of *Hijrah*. At the advent of the *Hijrah* to Medina, she was 27 years old; she was 25 years old at her wedding. If Hazrat Abu Bakr's eldest daughter lived with her father for 25 or 26 years as an unmarried woman, why would Abu bakr marry his younger daughter at the tender age of nine?

Bibliography

1. Holy Qur'an, edited by Malik Ghulam Farid, published in 1981, The London Mosque.

2. The Life & Character of the Seal of Prophets, Hazrat Mirza Bashir Ahmad, vol. 11.

(May Peace and Blessings of Allah be upon him). (Sirat Khatamun-Nabiyyin Urdu). Hazrat Mirza Bashir Ahmad, vol. 11, Qadian, India, 1920. (English rendering) Islam International Publication, Ltd. Islamabad, U.K, published 2013.

3. Saheeh Bukhari by Imam Bukhari.

4. Saheeh Muslim by Imam Muslim.

5. Jamia'ah Tirmidhi by Imam Tirmidhi.

6. Sunan Abi Dawood by Imam Abu Dawood.

7. Sunan Ibn Majah by Imam Ibn Majah.

8. Musnad by Ahmad bin Hanbal.

9. Sunan Nasai by Imam Ahmad Ibn Shoaib.

10. Tehzib-ul-Tehzib by Ibn Hajar. Al-asqala'ni, Dar Ihya al-turath al-Islami, 15th century, vol. 10, p. 50.

11. Tabqat by Ibn Sa'd.

12. Al-Kamal fee Asma ur-Rijal by Wali-Uddin Al-Khateeb.

13. Al-Bidayah-wan-Nihayah by Ibn Kathir, vol. 8, p. 372, Dar Al-Fikr al-Arabi, Al-Jizah, 1933.

14. Tarikh Tabri by Tabri Mohammad bin Jareer.

15. Al-Seerat-un-Nabawiyyah by Ibn Kathir.

16. Seerat-un-Nabi by Shibli Numani.

17. Seeratu's Sayyidati Ayesha Siddiqa (Urdu) by Sayed Sulayman Nadvi, March 10th 1945. Publisher: Mushtaq Book Corner, Al-Kareem Market, Urdu Bazar, Lahore, Pakistan. And Hazrat Ayesha Siddiqa, English Edition, 2010, published by Abdul Naeem, Islamic Book Service New Delhi-110002, India.

18. Fatih Messiah by Hazrat Mirza Ghulam Ahmad, vol. 9, Qadian India, 1895.

19. English booklet, Prophet of Islam by Maulana Muhammad Ali, 1924.

20. Holy Prophet of Islam, Hazrat Muhammad Mustafa (May peace and blessings of Allah be upon him), by Dr. Karimullah Zirvi, K. Z. Publications, 14-21 Saddle River Road, Fair Lawn N. J., 07410, USA, published in September 2009.

21. The Excellent Exemplar-Muhammad, Chaudhary Muhammad Zafrullah Khan, alislam.org.

22. Aisha, The Wife the Companion, the Scholar by Resit Haylamaz, published by Tughra Books, 345 Clifton Ave, Clifton, NJ, 07011, U.S.A., printed by Ayhan Matba, Istanbul, Turkey.

23. Tarib wa Tahthib Kitab al-Bidayah wan-Nihayah by ibn Kathir, published by Dar al-Wathan Publications, Riyadh Kingdom of Saudi Arabia, 1422 Anno hegira (2002), compiled by Dr. Muhammad ibn Shamil as-Sulami, ISBN: 978-19-0.

24. Muthhar Aaili Zindgi by Amtul-Rafiq Zaffer, published by Lajna Ima'illah, Lahore Pakistan, 1995.

25. Mishkat al-Masabih, edition with Urdu translation published in Lahore, 1986, vol. 3. P. 300-301.

Web Resources

* wwwalislam.org

*http://en.wikipedia.org/wiki/Abu_Bakr

*http://aaiil.org/text/acus/islam/aishahage.shtml

*http://www.hindustantimes.com/columnsothers/hazrat-aisha-was-19-not-9/article1-408894.aspx

*http://www.wattpad.com/3302758-hazrat-ayesha%27s-age-at-the-time-of-her-marriage

*https://search.yahoo.com/yhs/search?hspart=mozilla&hsimp=yhs-002&ei=utf-8&fr=ytff1-yff30&p=Islam-The%20Right%20Path&type=

*http://www.muslim.org/

*http://ahmadiyya.org/WordPress/2008/10/19/life-of-muhammad-asad/

*https://realdeen.wordpress.com/2006/07/30/real-age-of-hazrat-aisha/

*http://www.paklinks.com/gs/religion-and-philosophy/132602-age-of-hazrat-ayesha-at-the-time-of-marriage-2.html *http://www.hasaan.com/2012/04/hazrat-aishas-real-age-at-marriage-time.html

*https://truthhazratayesha.wordpress.com/wp-login.php

*http://www.sunniforum.com/forum/archive/index.php/t-84431.html

*http://jerusalem.com/articles/islam/muhammads_night_journey_to_jerusalem-a6295

*http://en.wikipedia.org/wiki/Mut%E2%80%98im_ibn_%E2%80%98Adi

*https://www.youtube.com/watch?v=IkW09UIHTkk

*http://www.ilaam.net/articles/ayesha.html.

*http://en.wikipedia.org/wiki/MuawiyahI

*http://en.wikipedia.org/wiki/Asm%C4%81%27_bint_Abi_Bakr

*http://en.wikipedia.org/w/index.php?search=Total+children+of+Hazrat+Abu+Bakr+saddiq&titl.*http://en.wikipedia.org/w/index.php?search=Total+children+of+Hazrat+Abu+Bakr+saddiq&title

* http://en.wikipedia.org/wiki/Abd_Allah_ibn_al-Zubayr

*http://en.wikipedia.org/wiki/Uthman

Index